MICROPROCESSORS for MANAGEMENT

CAD, CAM, and ROBOTICS

MICROPROCESSORS for MANAGEMENT

CAD, CAM, and ROBOTICS

DIMITRIS N. CHORAFAS

PBI
a petrocelli book
new york / princeton

Designed by Diane L. Backes
Typesetting by Backes Graphics

Printed in the United States of America
1 2 3 4 5 6 7 8 9 10

Library of Congress Cataloging in Publication Data

Chorafas, Dimitris N.
Microprocessors for management, CAD, CAM, and robotics.

Includes index.
1. Microprocessors. I. Title.
QA76.5.C48 1982 001.64 82-13311
ISBN 0-89433-183-3 AACR2

CONTENTS

Part Three
Broadening the Applications Horizon

Preface

ALTHOUGH WE know what we have already achieved in computer technology, we must also admit that presently we are unaware of the nature of future systems. This manuscript presents some of the latest technological advancements, though they are not the ultimate of what can be done with the power of the microprocessor.

The driving force behind the development and use of electronics is competition. Being a successful contender in today's industrial arena is no easy task. On one hand, a company must possess the basic ability to manufacture products which the user wants at a cost attractive to the potential buyer. On the other hand, it must offer products of indisputably superior quality.

As products change and benefits they offer the user evolve, management must possess foresight and skill in terms of design, manufacturing and marketing strategy. However, the ability to analyze current sales trends and determine which products will be most in demand in the future should be matched by technical abilities.

We live in a fast-moving technological and marketing world, and security often lies in rapid innovation. The development of the planar transistor integrated circuit at Fairchild occurred when that organization was only two years old. The birth of the microprocessor at Intel also occurred only two years after that company was founded.

The growth of microelectronics has affected areas of society such as business systems, education, home appliances, autos, telecommunications, and home computers. If a company lacks a valid computers and communications system of adequate capacity and up-to-date technology, it cannot function as an efficient enterprise.

This book is designed as a learning experience for busy managers faced with decisions related to the use of microprocessors in their company's product line or manufacturing capability. It is not written for the specialist as its goal is to demistify the most often-used concepts of microprocessors and show how they can be put to work to meet corporate goals.

Part One begins with a technology update. The purpose of the first chapter is to introduce the reader to horizons opening in many professions, such as new physics and semiconductor realities. Chapter 2 follows with an introduction to application perspectives by microprocessor technology.

In order to assure a reasonable familiarization with microprocessors, the next two chapters are respectively dedicated to device architecture and product incentives which have followed technological development. Part One closes with an information policy: Unless we have a coherent, well-established view of our goals, we are not going to profit from this "brave new world."

Part Two deals with design, manufacturing and interfacing requirements for microprocessors. The first chapter focuses on the wafer from design process to prevailing marketing strategy. The next chapter underscores the need for quality assurance and brings to the reader's attention difficulties involved with VLSI testing.

The printed circuit board and the development of microcomputers from microprocessors is the subject of Chapter 8. The following chapter describes how boards can be interfaced. Chapter 10 is devoted to firmware, microcode design and to resulting tradeoffs.

Special attention is given to software because it, not hardware, will be the challenge of the 1980s. The Japanese have realized this point: Their first five-year plan (1970–1974) was devoted to designing the plug-compatible mainframe. The result is the M Series CPU compatible to IBM. The second five-year plan (1975–1979) focused on semiconductors, and in the last year of this plan the Japanese conquered 42% of the American market for 16 KB chips. The third five-year plan (1980–1984) is stressing software. The goal is to excell in black art from system analysis to online coding, testing and documenting.

The aim of Part Three is to broaden the reader's applications knowledge to help him make decisions with respect to products propelled by the microprocessor. Whereas Parts One and Two are introductory and general for all professions, here I had to make a decision of orientation, and it is: CAD, CAM, and Robotics.

Computer Aided Design (CAD) is treated in two chapters that aim to explain to engineers and managers the process of supporting design activities by computer. Emphasis is on practical applications: the integration of CAD with Computer Aided Manufacturing (CAM); display methods; software support; and the effects this methodology can have on productivity. After all, able men are still a company's most valuable resource.

Chapter 13 presents Robotics as an innovation to manufacturing practices. Productivity and competitiveness are the key subjects. The reader is shown the present state of technology, and what can reasonably be expected from the results of early applications. However, to get the most out of microprocessor-propelled machinery, a company should definitely tune its manufacturing capability, which is the theme of Chapter 14.

Finally, special attention is given to the need of controlling the process. Quality monitoring should be a top priority. Examples are given on how to accomplish this, mainly taken from the computer industry. A data processor has much in common with a robotics factory, and our experience to date on layered approaches, converting production resources, and removing functional defects is much greater with the former than with the latter. We should always learn from experience.

Typical readers of this book will be managers of technical departments in industries, design engineers, production managers, sales engineers, and other management and professional personnel. Their common characteristic is involvement in making decisions about where and when to use microprocessor devices.

The material is projected and presented for management personnel and presumes no previous background or specialized knowledge of digital computer devices. However, interest in learning about this fast-developing and promising field in terms of business opportunity will facilitate the assimilation of technical information.

Let me close by expressing my thanks to everyone who contributed to this book: to my colleagues for their advice, to organizations I visited in my research for their insight, and to Eva-Maria Binder for the drawings, typing, and index.

Valmer and Vitenau
1982

Dimitris N. Chorafas

PART ONE

The Challenge of Continuing Development

1 New Horizons

INTRODUCTION

THE DOMAIN of science has been subdivided since the beginning of this century into a large number of narrow specialties. Twenty years ago, no one would have thought of rapid unification. Yet, the most remarkable characteristic of present-day science and technology is the tendency toward unification of different disciplines. We have finally come to realize that some of the most diverse scientific endeavors are based on essentially the same problem and principles.

Physics has made great strides toward a unified theory that may eventually relate cosmology, the science of the ultimately large, to particle physics, the science of the ultimately small. However, basic scientific discovery seldom comes easily; energy, persistence, intelligence and open-mindedness are required. These are the high marks of the trade in any profession.

Experiments lead to theories, and theories suggest cause-and-effect relationships which are valid until replaced by newer theories. Research into so-far unknown properties calls for more efficient experiments and more powerful machines to conduct them, while each type of machine is likely to produce as a spin-off its own unique discoveries.

The major advances of science are, almost by definition, those that are not foreseen, and this is just as true of the great forward leaps technology has accomplished, a case in point being semiconductors. Technological knowhow has its roots in scientific discovery but, as Figure 1–1 illustrates, there is a significant lead time between establishment of the physical principle and its technological application. Revolutionary discoveries in physics are interspersed by years of steady, often slow, progress toward practical applications.

Another important observation is the accelerated pace of discovery and development. Statistics show that half the engineers and scientists who ever lived are alive and working today. Even more importantly, we

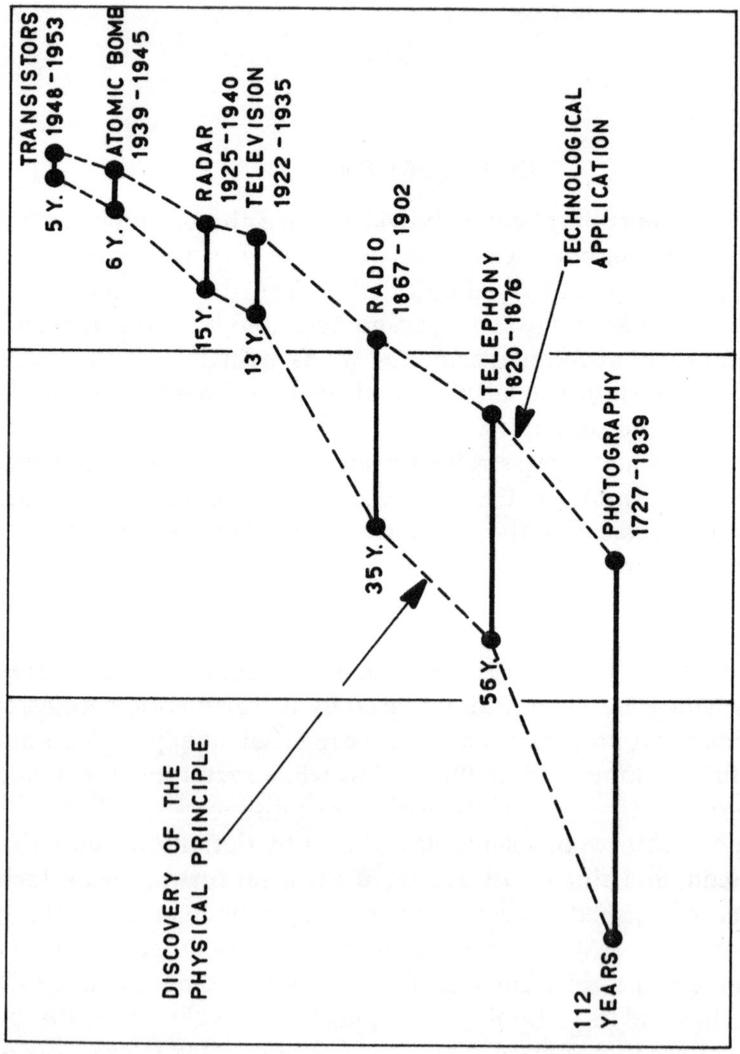

FIGURE 1-1 Two noteworthy trends: The discovery of physical principles and accelerated technological applications.

are now about to enter an era in which, through microprocessors, humanity will be able to take part in a great technological adventure.

The products and processes technology has brought—such as new physical sciences and microelectronics—can radically change how we see our world. Work in advanced science can also accelerate time scales, bring new technological breakthroughs, and alter our values. This is the message to the reader from this first chapter.

When we think creatively, we need the broadest possible set of facts so we can sift them back and forth to see what will work. If we lack such a broad set of facts, we cannot eliminate ones that are not worth serious consideration, whereas a lack of facts may severely limit our visibility. Hence, in this and the following few chapters we will basically talk about facts. Afterward, we will speculate on how to use them to plan our future.

These are basic reasons why prior to speaking of microprocessors and their properties, we will be well advised to look at the frontiers of knowledge; from there will come the new media to enhance the power of the human mind. Scientific and technical progress is inevitable. A civilization that ceases to inquire about the physical universe gives up its future.

THE NEW PHYSICS

Not long ago, a Nobel prize was awarded in recognition of a theory which shows that unification of certain fundamental forces in the physical sciences may be underway. As modelled by some of the best minds of our time, such achievements promise to match the unification theory James Clerk Maxwell demonstrated in the early 19th century between electricity and magnetism. Noticing what was then an inconsistency between equations for magnetism and those for electricity, Maxwell put his insight to work on these equations. Maxwell thereby enabled electricity and magnetism to be treated as different aspects of electromagnetic force, and paved the way for the invention of the telephone, radio, television and, in general, of electronics.

Aided by achievements in nuclear physics of the last 15 years, scientists today are on the threshold of new major breakthroughs. A new chapter is beginning in particle physics which rests on two conceptual developments of the late 1960s and early-to-mid-1970s:

1. Growing evidence that virtually hundreds of types of subatomic particles are composed of three basic units: *quarks*, *gluons*, and *leptons*. These seem to be the ultimate building blocks of matter.

2. The fact that scientists now think in terms of three basic forces: *gravity*, *electromagnetism*, and the so-called *strong-and-weak* force.

The "strong" coupling bonds atomic nuclei together. The "weak" force, a billion times weaker than the strong, is found in many radioactive decay processes. With the "electroweak" theory only partially tested, physicists are already attempting a further unification combining electroweak and strong forces. In fact, the real scientific interest for weak coupling is the switching it makes with the strong force.

David Politzer developed the theory of strong and weak forces in 1973 and it is unlike any that physicists had previously known. A coupling force is weak when objects are in close proximity, and becomes stronger as they are pulled apart. Experiments have fairly well proven the accuracy of the quark-force hypothesis which has paved the way to the larger theory of "quantum chromodynamics," or QCD, which predicts the behavior of quarks and their forces.

Quarks come in different varieties. One way in which they differ is in a property that determines how different quarks will combine, and which is analogous to electrical charge. But what's a quark? Politzer's theory was an answer to a challenge which arose in the late 1960s. At that time, an accomplishment similar to that of Maxwell's was achieved by Steven Weinberg and Abdus Salam. They succeeded in providing a unified mathematical description of electromagnetic and weak forces.

Like all good theories, the blueprint developed by Salam and Weinberg made precise quantitative predictions about subatomic matter. Experiments were needed to test the theory, the most decisive being confirmation of the prediction that, at high energies, certain specific particles not seen before will be created. Two of these particles are tentatively called "W" and "Z".

As is well known, scientific experiments depend upon machines. The more advanced these experiments, the more powerful must be the required machines, and this is as true of cyclotrons as of microprocessors. In subsequent chapters, when we speak of the power of the microprocessor, we will generalize this postulate by saying, "Intelligent machines are the lens of the mind's eye."

In this sense, microprocessor-based equipment is ideal for efficient and effective support to everyday tasks, from office chores and related professional activities to household duties. If available some forty years ago, microprocessors might have been a physicist's dream; back in 1930, Otto Fritsch, one of the fathers of the atom bomb, bought bits of equipment at Woolworth. However, that time is long past.

In 1911, the Dutch physicist Kammerlingh Onners discovered that at close to absolute zero° C some metals lose all resistance to electrical current and become superconductors. Seventy years later, commercial applications of this discovery are being developed in computer circuitry, fusion reactors, and other fields. From the machinery physicists are using to unearth laws of the universe will come admittedly rare revolutionary discoveries which will replace existing natural laws and eventually offer humanity a new escalation in the standard of living.

UNLOCKING NATURE'S SECRETS

The 1920s, 1930s, and early 1940s were influenced by the conceptual revolution of quantum physics and the theory of relativity. With the mammoth (for its time) nuclear program of the 1940s and other scientific endeavors including missile technology, postwar physics faced new challenges. At one end were space probes and high-magnification telescopes to stretch humanity's horizon to the farthest recesses of the universe, at the other end, particle accelerators became a vital tool in the search to identify the tiniest indivisible constituents of matter.

In this race to gain new knowledge there was, and continues to be, no foreseeable end. The world's largest telescope, a 21-mile-wide structure that cost $78 million, opened in 1980 in New Mexico, while the Voyager spacecraft reached Saturn at a cost of about $340 million. In 1981, CERN, the international laboratory for particle physics, will be completing a $120 million project to smash antimatter into matter, and is already seeking a budget to build a $550 million machine to smash electrons into positrons, while Brookhaven is building $275 million equipment to accelerate protons.

The range of equipment necessary to serve the new physics widens. Proton machines are needed to study quarks and gluons; electropositron systems are required to test the electroweak theory; and other equipment is needed to satisfy humanity's curiosity about the universe. Significant discoveries will almost certainly arise from these scientific investments.

Spectacular economic impact is unlikely to emerge until the next century, but the wisdom of financing research in the new physics has become a major topic about this expensive but rewarding cost item.

Just as microprocessors promise to change most aspects of our everyday lives, the discovery of new elementary particles promise to change the world of physics. Only fifteen years ago, experimental work with high energy accelerators transformed the physicists' view of matter being composed of a few elementary particles—electrons, protons, and neutrons —to the realization that matter contains literally hundreds of different particles, none more elementary than another. Furthermore, the behavior of these particles seemed to be governed by the distinct forces which we mentioned.

One major achievement was the demonstration that the heavier of those newly-discovered particles (as well as the proton and neutron) is a compound structure, a combination of still more elementary components than earlier experimentation revealed. It is these components which were named *quarks*. The prevailing hypothesis is that they are similar in some respects to lighter-weight particles, such as electrons.

Quarks are structureless and point-like. Pairs or triplets of quarks are bound by *gluons*; such conglomerates make up most particles. All particles are influenced by the strong nuclear force that binds the nuclei of atoms. Protons and neutrons are the commonest quark-gluon combinations. An effect predicted by this theory is that the proton is slightly radioactive and, therefore, all matter is ultimately unstable and will decay.

The structureless reference is very critical. Prior to the abovementioned theory, protons, neutrons, and similar particles were thought to have an inner structure. Now, physicists postulate they are composed of quarks; this finding is a stroke of ingenuity. The detectors that surround target areas of particle accelerators show no direct traces of such particles. Only when accelerators smash protons or electrons do they sometimes produce the kinds of debris expected if the quark concept is true.

Another fundamental physical principle involves strong and weak forces. Particles not subject to the strong force are indivisible. Electrons are the most familiar of these particles, which are called *leptons*.

Quarks are also thought to exist in both matter and antimatter form: antimatter is like ordinary matter except that certain properties are reversed. A positron is the positively charged antimatter form of the electron. As we know from experience, matter and antimatter annihilate one another when they meet, transforming their mass into radiant energy. Conversely, pairs of matter-antimatter particles can form out of pure energy. These processes of creation and transformation produce the distinctive patterns of debris which physicists look for in accelerator experiments.

Three approaches are being followed to achieve the enormously powerful collisions necessary for the creation of new particles. One approach involves the use of superconductive magnets as the power within machines capable of smashing protons into one another. The other two approaches involve smashing matter into antimatter, for when they collide they release far more energy than collisions between ordinary matter. Scientists would also like to smash electrons into positrons; such collisions would probably result in a shower of new particles, including the "W" and "Z" we have mentioned.

What advanced physical sciences are now seeking, especially in electron-positron collisions, are patterns in which debris shoots out in jets. Physicists speak of six types of quarks, each paired with an antiquark: (1) "up," (2) "down," (3) "strange," (4) "charmed," (5) "bottom," or "beauty," and (6) "top" or "truth". As any truth, the latter is not yet experimentally confirmed.

Events involving gluons should produce two oppositely-directed jets that become increasingly thin as collision energy increases. Double-jet events observed during the past five years support QCD predictions; not only electromagnetism but also strong/weak forces derive from common origins on the quark scale. Eventually, gravitation and QCD might be contained in a Grand Unification Theory that would encompass every domain from elementary particles to the entire universe.

Incidentally, quantum chromodynamics is a theory we will be well-advised to watch. Starting with the hypothesis that quarks bond with gluons, QCD is based on postulates analogous to quantum electrodynamics which describes the interaction of particles through electromagnetic force. Interestingly, lacking names for the many new properties found in subatomic matter, physicists have assigned colors to the various types of quark charges, hence the term *chromodynamics*.

Will these developments lead to new processes and products similar to the inventions that followed Maxwell's electromagnetic unification theory? It is difficult to be certain at this stage, but as Dr. Robert Noyce (one of the inventors of the integrated circuit) stated, "As an act of faith, I would say yes!" Microprocessors are not the ultimate product of science and technology, but they are the best presently available. Many developments are yet to come.

RESEARCH ON CONDUCTIVITY

We have underscored the fact that there is lead time, often significant, between a physical discovery and its technological implementation. After three decades of familiarity with basic principles characteristic of semiconductor materials, we are now able to appreciate the impact of the small, low-power amplifier that replaced the large, power-hungry vacuum tube. The discovery came at the right time given parallel advances in computer technology and in communications.

In 1839, Becquerel discovered that voltage could be generated by shining a light on a liquid that conducts electricity. Protons in the light cause electrons to be emitted in the liquid; this is the photoelectric effect. In 1905, Einstein explained this phenomenon, using Planck's new quantum theory, and by the 1930s his explanation became a means for describing the behavior of electrons.

Physicists have been working with this knowledge for years; the first significant event of R&D on conductivity was in the early 1940s. At that time, Marvin Kelly, director of research for Bell Laboratories, witnessed a demonstration using silicon, a then little-understood "semiconductor". This demonstration was given by a researcher named Russell Ohl who displayed a small black rectangular block of silicon with two metal contacts. When light illuminated a narrow region near the middle of this piece of silicon, a photoelectromotive force (emf) of about 0.5 V was produced.

This was the embryonic stage of the p-n junction transistor. Six years later, research on capabilities presented by semiconductor materials was given a boost by Bell Laboratories' interest in the future use of semiconductors in circuit devices and the possibility of a solid-state amplifier. The research team was headed by William Shockley, a theoretical physicist, Stanley Morgan, a circuit expert, John Bardeen, Gibney, and Walter Brattain.

Their mission was to investigate semiconductor properties of materials with conductivity between that of an insulator and a conductor. (A barrier exists on resistance to the flow of electrons, though the strength of the barrier can be varied by manipulating an electric field. Thus, an electric field applied to a semiconductor can be used as a valve to regulate the flow of a current.)

The researchers soon realized that despite work done before and during World War II, physicists were still far from understanding the semiconductor process: Copper oxide and other semiconductors on which the early work had been performed are very complicated solids. Silicon and germanium are simpler solids; so, the researchers decided to investigate these first. Specifically, they performed fundamental research on problems concerning the effect of impurities.

Progress was slow in the beginning, but in November of 1947 Brattain and Gibney overcame the blocking action of surface electrons with a strong electric field and an electrolyte in contact with the semiconductor. Within a month, a breadboard transistor was created. Bardeen and Brattain soon after invented the point-contact transistor which included a plate of n-type germanium and two gold contacts. Shockley contributed work that led to the junction transistor with no point contacts, just a tiny rod of germanium with a p-type layer sandwiched between two n-type layers.

The junction transistor was produced in 1948, though three years of effort were required to make it work. Ironically, when it was made public in June, 1948, it attracted little interest. Engineers familiar with vacuum tubes were not eager to switch, and at that time the public was not interested in the nuts and bolts of electronics.

Price was also an inhibiting factor. In 1953, a single transistor sold for $21; twenty-five years later, with integrated circuits, it cost one-thousandth of that original price. The trend continued though other products—such as magnetic cores—showed no price improvements, and this was their downfall (Figure 1-2).

In 1954, the production of transistors reached one million; by 1957, thirty million were being produced yearly, and the price was falling. By 1978, there were 10^{12} semiconductor "bits and gates" manufactured, and perhaps 10^{18} by 1984. To survive the semiconductor industry needs to increase its business by a significant margin every year, and given falling prices this means a yearly growth in physical units of forty percent to fifty percent.

THE MIGHTY MICROPROCESSOR

We previously made reference to "bits and gates". Bits and gates are units of measurement, given that between switching circuitry and storage devices a certain relationship exists in regard to quantitative needs. A gate uses many bits and is the basic concept of the integrated circuit. Robert Noyce, of whom we spoke in the preceding section, and Jack Kilby independently invented the integrated circuit.

The development of integrated circuits called for expertise in etching and diffusion. Etching makes feasible a circuit pattern on a wafer of sili-

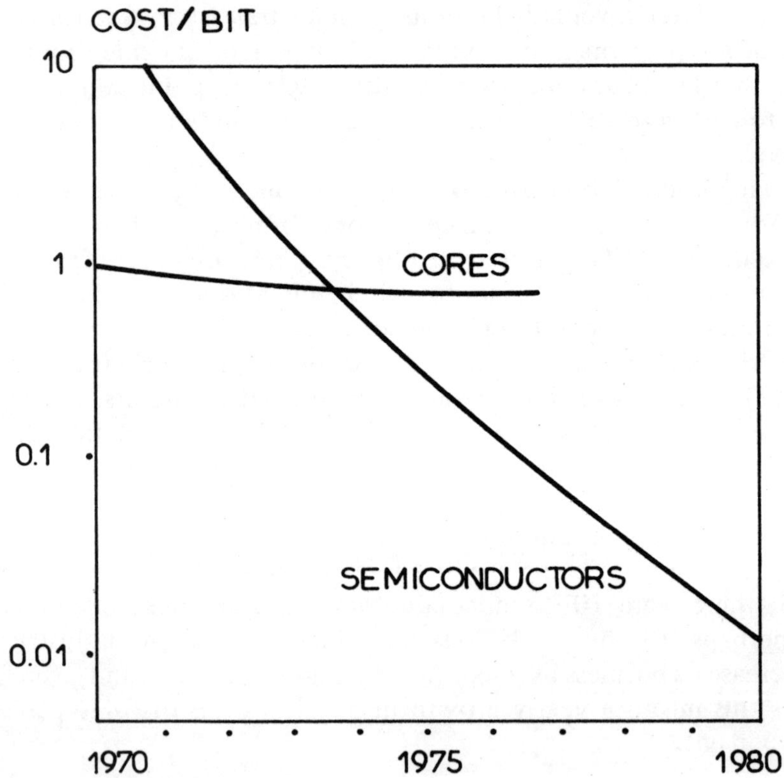

FIGURE 1–2 A decade of cost reductions in the semiconductor business.

con; diffusion fires "impurities" into silicon to produce positively- and negatively-charged regions. The goal is to make a surface which eliminates the need for wires connecting one circuit to another by depositing a thin layer of connective material. Intel's fortune was built on this invention of Dr. Noyce, its cofounder.

As with every invention, key developments were required to ensure progress. By the mid-1950s, engineers had learned how to define the surface configuration of transistors by means of photolithography: Etching was a developing discipline. The principle of solid-state diffusion for introducing impurities that create "p" and "n" (positive and negative) regions was also known. Therefore, it is of no surprise that batch processing of many transistors on a thin wafer sliced from a large crystal of germanium or silicon began to displace the earlier technique of handling individual transistors.

The concept of the integrated circuit (IC) was born several years after the invention of the transistor as a way to further exploit the characteristics of semiconductors. The body resistance of the semiconductor and the capacitance of junctions between positive and negative regions could thereby be combined to form a complete circuit of resistors, capacitors and amplifiers. From this simple concept evolved the ability to pack increasingly larger numbers of components on a chip (Figure 1-3).

Noyce's and Kilby's research fit into a technology which regarded the miniaturization of components as of increasing importance. Communications, computers and weapons systems were and will continue to be built with thousands of parts. A pressing need is to make objects smaller in order to save space, to simplify the interconnective wiring of components, and to increase reliability.

At Texas Instruments, Kilby's IC cost about $25,000 and more when it was conceived, and another $75,000 to show the concept would work. The first integrated circuits were demonstrated in September, 1958. A patent application was filed in February, 1959, and the invention was made public. Once again, the reaction was skeptical; few people realized at that time the importance of this breakthrough.

The integrated circuit, as conceived and developed in 1959, separates and interconnects transistors and other circuit elements electrically rather than physically. The elements are interconnected by a conducting film of evaporated metal that is photoengraved to leave an appropriate pattern of connections. An insulating layer separates the underlying semiconductor from the metal film except where contacts are desired.

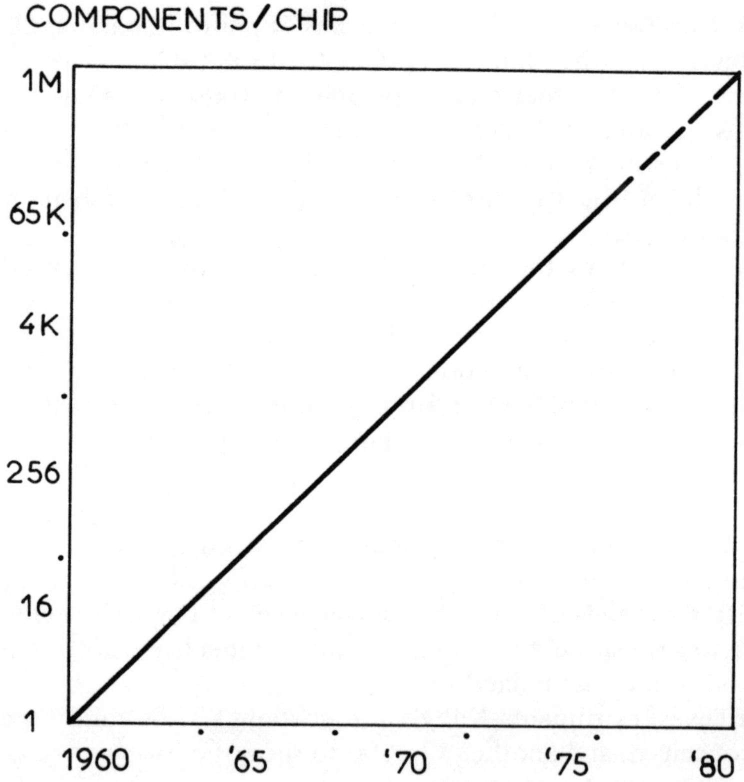

FIGURE 1–3 A twenty-year trend in greater density of components per chip.

As technology reduced costs, improved reliability and made many more processes feasible, the pace of events accelerated. In the mid-1950s, semiconductors replaced vacuum tubes as the main logical elements in electronic circuits. In the early 1960s, manufacturing technology made small-scale integration (SSI) possible to emplace twenty (elementary) logical functions in one circuit. SSI was a stepping stone to greater achievements; the process to higher and higher integration had begun. SSI brought R&D and manufacturing engineering closer together. It is not enough to develop a product; just as important is producing specialized production machinery.

Similarly, applications perspectives must be broadened. This is helped by integrated circuits which not only answer market demands for computers, communications, and weapons systems, but also feed a much larger market. This latter market requires very large numbers of active circuits in contrast to systems which provide analogue amplification (such as radios). So, the cheaper and more reliable a component, the futher one can improve and expand a system.

As scientific advancements altered design concepts, a major shift toward digital systems has propelled advances in microelectronics. Analogue equipment cannot handle large numbers of microcircuits, whereas a digital system requires them. A pocket calculator contains 100 times as many transistors as a radio or television receiver: The emphasis is on processing power. As Figure 1–4 demonstrates, the 1970s produced explosive growth in the number of types of microprocessors.

As with integrated circuits, Intel and Texas Instruments coinvented the microprocessor from the basic idea to put extra functions on a single chip. In the summer of 1969, a Japanese firm asked Intel to design integrated circuits for a new family of calculators. Intel's Ted Hoff studied their design, a rather complicated arrangement with many logical functions distributed on the calculator, and was impressed by how much could be centralized on a memory chip.

Hoff's solution was presented to the Japanese as a way to meet their cost budget and to make their system more elegant, but little occurred until the next spring when Frederico Faggin joined Intel. While Hoff designed the computer architecture, Dr. Faggin developed the circuits. At that time, calculators typically required ten chips; the Hoff-Faggin solution required three. (Meanwhile, in late 1969, Texas Instruments also developed a single-chip processor and patented the chip.)

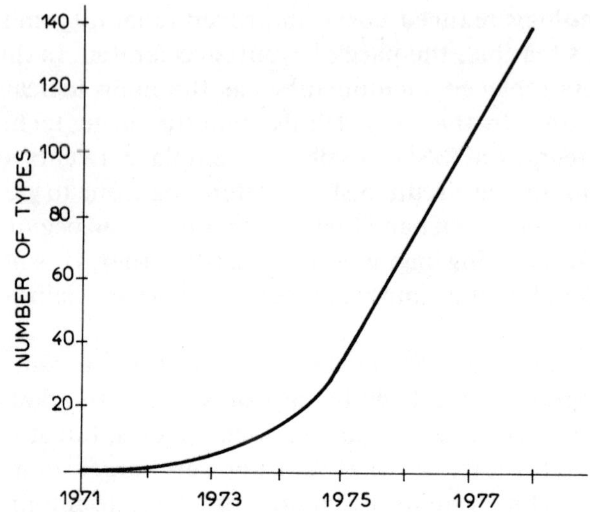

FIGURE 1–4 The explosive growth of the number of types of microprocessors in the 1970s.

The microprocessor simplified computer circuitry, cut production costs, and opened a new horizon for progress. The men who engineered the great advances in semiconductors, like those in the new physics, are not working in ivory towers. They are practical scientists applying themselves to reasonable problems. They are also risk-takers willing to make mistakes and to recognize and learn from them. This is how the avenue of progress is paved.

2 Applying Microprocessor Technology

INTRODUCTION

WE QUITE often fail to appreciate technological advancement. Since the introduction of the planar transistor in 1959, the number of elements in integrated circuits has nearly doubled every year (Figure 2-1) to the point that an integrated circuit on a quarter-inch-square chip can embrace more electronic elements than could the most complex piece of electronic equipment twenty years ago. Today's microcomputer, costing less than $500, has more computing capacity than the first generation of large electronic computers. It computes far more rapidly than any of the latter machines, has a much larger memory, is far more reliable, and consumes much less power. Furthermore, due to the ever-increasing degree of integration, the microprocessor-based computer occupies 1/30,000 the volume and costs 1/10,000 as much as its large-scale predecessor.

At the time of this writing in mid-1982, it is an educated guess that the now-emerging 32-bit desktop microcomputers will be included in many offices, factories, and computer centers. Hewlett-Packard has introduced the most impressive microprocessor to date, a chip with 450,000 transistors, and scientists and technologists expect to develop chips with a much higher density which will exceed the power of present mainframes. Furthermore, the coming use of 32-bit microprocessors in telecommunications is so promising that Bell Laboratories is actively working on this product. It seems only yesterday that handheld calculators replaced bulky electromechanical devices found in every office. These handheld calculators and the technology they represented led the way to new developments in the 1970s (Figure 2-2). In the 1980s, the same challenge will be led by computers. With large-scale integration, computers will be on chips, personal desktop computers will be more powerful, terminals will be smaller and more "intelligent", and local networks will

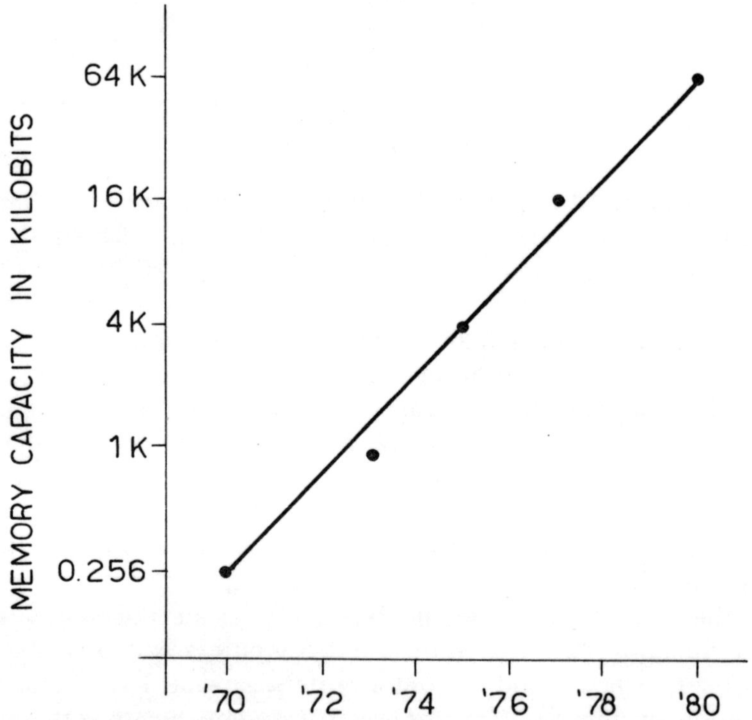

FIGURE 2–1 The integrated circuit memory degree of integration is doubling every year.

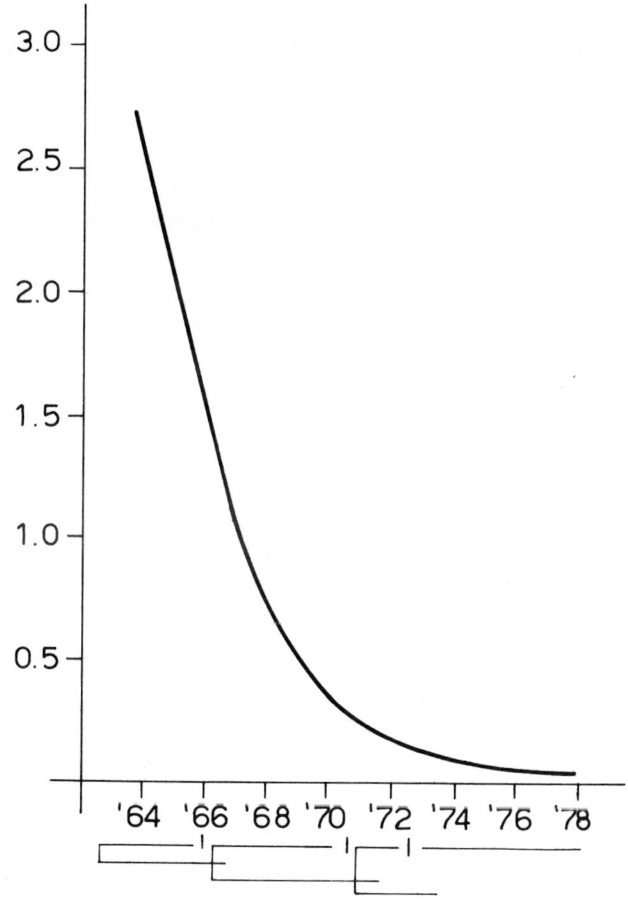

FIGURE 2-2 Fifteen years of price trends of personal calculators.

make it feasible to integrate office and factory functions into computers-and-communications-based systems.

As each new product requires more microelectronic devices, experience is gained in their use and larger quantities are produced to satisfy market demands, leading to further cost reductions. In turn, this process opens new markets for the devices, leading to increased production, further developmental research, and even lower costs due to mass effects and less expensive production methods.

All products of technology are sensitive to the economics of scale. There is a basic law with semiconductors resulting from the large, fixed capital investments which are needed in the design and in the manufacturing side: All other matters being equal, each time the production doubles, the price can be sharply reduced.

Yet, an often-overlooked fact about technology is that it needs the proper understructure to support rapidly-expanding activities so that growth is not detrimentally affected. Different marketing strategies are necessary to deal with SSI computers than with the 32-bit *micromainframe* (we will return to the latter in Chapter 4.)

A MOUNTING CHALLENGE

Let's look briefly at recent technological evolution. In the late 1960s, TTL (Transistor Transistor Logic) came into being; small-scale integration was giving way to medium-scale integration (MSI). In the early 1970s, one kilobit (KB) chips regrouped on chip electronic components were capable of reasonably complex logical functions (Figure 2-3), with each chip in a box. Shortly thereafter, multi-layer manufacturing processes (such as six-layer printed circuits) permitted some 800 elementary logical functions to be located on one board.

In the mid-1970s, CML (Current Mode Logic) replaced TTL, which had reached its limits; presently, CML allows for increasing integration and reliability of components. By the late 1970s, CML technology permitted up to 8,000 logical functions on a board. In proportion to functions-per-board in the early 1970s, the ratio is 10 to 1; to the early 1960s, 400 to 1.

Figure 2-4 refers to active elements per chip. The active element group (AEG) represents electronic circuits at their simplest level. The number of AEGs in a product provides a measure of its total electronic content. It is important to notice that the cost of AEGs has dramatically

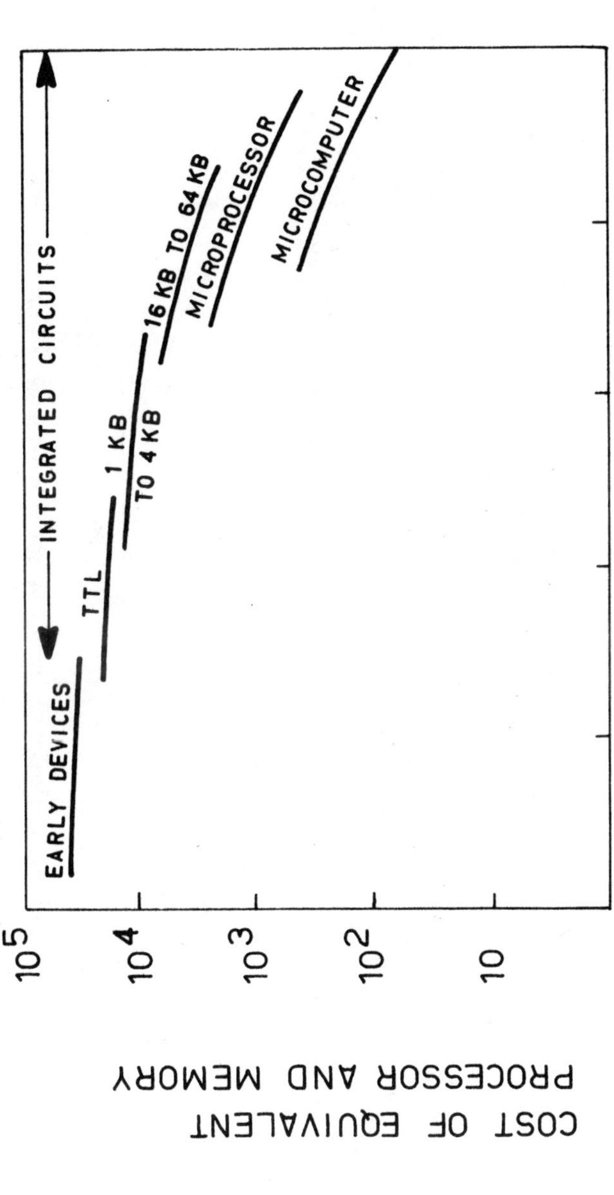

FIGURE 2–3 A chronological evolution from the semiconductor devices of the early 1960s to the present day costs for processor and memory.

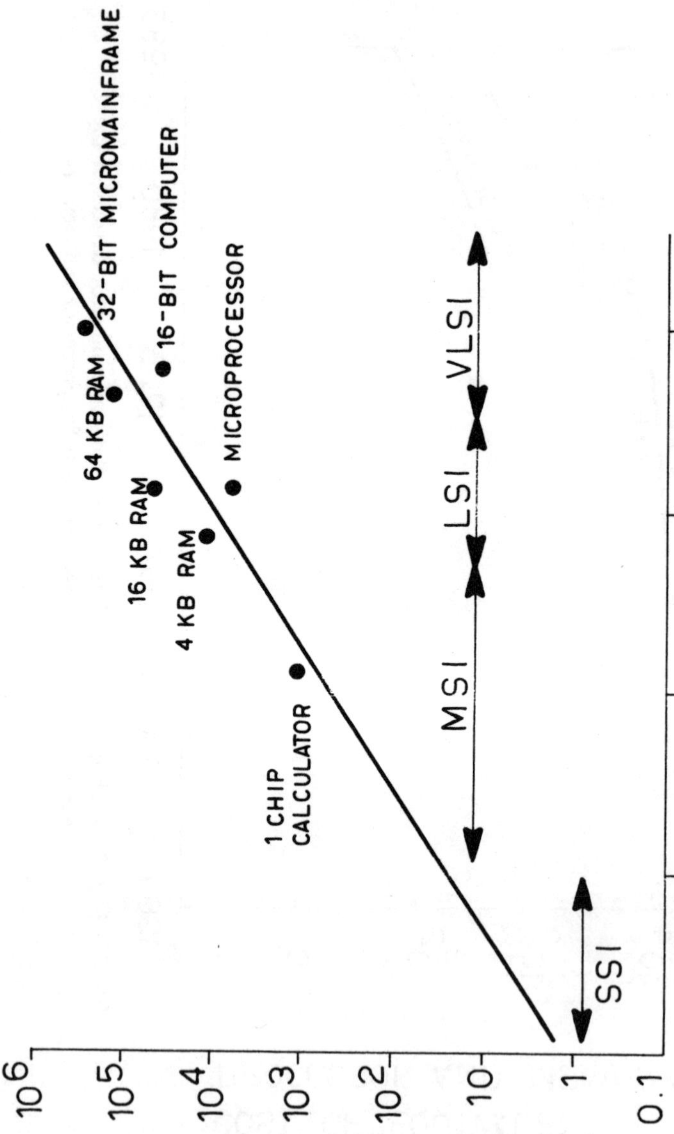

FIGURE 2–4 Active elements per chip: A line of developments from SSI to the 32-bit "micromainframe."

decreased from about $7.00 in 1960 to one-tenth of a cent today; by 1990, the cost may be one-hundredth of a cent.

Statistics dramatize the impact of AEGs. In 1970, the average home had about a hundred AEGs; the average is more than a thousand today. It is predicted that in several years most homes will have 4,000 AEGs, an electronic circuit equivalent to the most popular general purpose computer of the 1950s, the IBM 650. By the end of this decade, the average household may have almost 500,000 AEGs.

The technological developments which made possible such evolution are impressive and have been utilized in a variety of fields as business, industry and housewares. In addition, tremendous competition encouraged by thirty percent-per-year reductions in semiconductor prices force innovation in practically every field of business activity. Only about a decade ago, the number of digital semiconductors used in consumer, automotive and non-computer applications was almost trivial, and it is impressive how designers have implemented cost/effective applications which we now experience.

While we reap these benefits, however, we often fail to appreciate the fantastic amount of manpower required by research on semiconductor-based processes and products. Expertise, money, and time are at a premium. By 1981, for instance, IBM is estimated to have invested an impressive *10 man-centuries* of effort into R&D for a new computer generation based on Josephson technology, and the product is still several years from completion.

At the Yorktown Heights Laboratories, what started with two researchers in 1967 now involves 150 scientists and engineers in their largest project. The R&D cost so far is about $100 million for salaries, instruments, computer power and other expenses, and there are still many technological problems to overcome.

The goal of this R&D is a computer in the 60 to 100 MIPS (million instructions per second) range which is ten to twelve times that of the recently announced 3081 computer, the largest in the current IBM line. Critical to this new generation is the cramming of about 1,000 gates on a chip about a quarter-inch square, and linking such chips in a small experimental version of the machine. It is expected this will occur within the next two years, though the full version and its commercial implementation may not occur until the late 1980s.

Even such "supercomputers" might only be forerunners, as scientists think that technology will be capable of producing in the 1990s computers with twenty-five to fifty times the power of the 3081. (The first such machines will probably be built to handle special scientific tasks, but eventually will be available for general business applications.) These supercomputers would represent the emergence of an entirely new line of machines, and the same may occur in the "nanocomputer" and "picocomputer" generations. Just as importantly, more functions will be supported for common use at the nano level than by present-day microcomputers. By 1990, we can expect the power equivalent to an IBM 3033 on a single chip, with such chips incorporated into "intelligent" equipment such as terminals (the cost of which is expected to level off at about $1,500 to $2,000 apiece), factory robots and many other electronic-based items.

Quite evidently, this distribution of computerization will have great implications. The sociological impact is more evident if we say that the cost of microprocessor-based terminals, for example, will be no more than two percent of the monthly salary of their owners. At the same time, average programmer salaries may go beyond $100,000 by 1990. Due to such high salaries relative to equipment cost, the pressure to automate the manual task of programming will be intense. So, the end user will have languages to help him write his own applications program (AP) and to develop professional inventories of structured solid-state applications for processing paper, databasing, and all types of communication capabilities.

CREATING OPPORTUNITY

The 30-year history of the computer industry contains many significant milestones: von Neumann's machine, the magnetic drum and disc, the magnetic core memory, the removable disc, video terminals, the digital modem, ROM (read only memory) and RAM (random access memory), solid-state memory, and the microprocessor. The growth of the microelectronics industry illustrates the extent to which investment in research can create new opportunities.

This industry also includes concepts which proved infeasible, such as holographic memories, fluid logic, the digital microfilm chip, and ternary logic. What separated successful developments (which reaped millions of dollars for those who invested in them at an early stage) from those that exhibited equal initial brilliance but failed to be of practical value? Was it luck, soothsaying, expert timing, superior science, astute engineering, ingenious promotion, devotion, dedication, or simply hard work? Many possible breakthroughs failed because early experiments were not consistent, initial experimental results were too optimistically interpreted, or costs of production units were too great. In addition, many other promising projects went astray due to timetable problems, unclear goals, and lack of financial assistance.

To be successful in technological R&D, one needs persistence and confidence in one's work in spite of adversity, or even because of it. At Texas Instruments, prior to inventing the integrated circuit, Kilby made himself understand TI's cost structure and found it to be quite different to structures with which he was familiar. TI's business was silicon rather than germanium; silicon requires a large overhead of expensive equipment, and Kilby realized that whatever he devised had to have a large silicon content. Silicon was the item TI could utilize competitively.

This is just one instance in which financial goals dominate a potential breakthrough. Kilby had to consider not only whether he could make various types of components–resistors, capacitors, transistors–with silicon, but also at what price. He strove to succeed in those dual objectives; sensitivity to fundamental problems along with confidence and persistence are any inventor's top qualities.

In many cases of R&D on integrated circuits, efforts failed because development consumed so much time that newer and better techniques overtook the projects. Occasionally, early announcements of success are more promotional than technically factual, estimates may be erroneous, or costs may be too high. Yet, in other cases, wrong estimates have actually helped make fortunes.

When the Japanese contracted to develop the 4-bit microprocessor, some in Intel thought that granting exclusive rights to the Japanese did not matter. They argued that the microcomputer market might eventually reach 20,000 units a year and that Intel might sell only 2,000–too small a chip market to consider. In the mid-1950s, when IBM introduced the 650 computer (which became the bestseller of its time), an unofficial estimate foresaw a yearly market of no more than fifty machines. Usually, misjudging market potential leads to stillborn devices as projects are understaffed, underfinanced, and receive a minimum of management attention.

In other cases, laboratory engineers create devices and then leave it to users to find practical applications for those devices. Faced with expending unknown amounts of time and effort in which to utilize the devices, users may (rightly) choose obvious applications, and this process restricts any new product's chances to be successful.

Therefore, the challenge is to either substitute old for new devices with better performance ratios, or to create more cost/effective systems from existing tools. Unfortunately, engineering expertise and applications expertise seldom reside in one individual or one company. So, what can we learn to help us evaluate new advancements?

First, we should not underestimate the power and momentum of entrenched technology and of investments. The major computer companies have well-established methods involving hardware design, software practices, and applications libraries. These are protected by massive investments in products, factories, production equipment, marketing networks, and training. A breakthrough may be technically sound and promising, but is unlikely to succeed if it requires a significant change in the status quo of above-mentioned methodologies.

Second, in general, the more fundamental a development, the greater its chances of being successful. Among the most basic and widely-used units of modern technology are semiconductors and magnetic storage. Also, though technology is quite far from the fundamental limits imposed by the laws of physics, further miniaturization is less likely to be limited by physical properties than by the laws of economics.

TAKING ADVANTAGE OF TECHNOLOGY

Society requires most engineers and physicists to be reliable practitioners of established rules, with eyes open to technological development. Trends are foreseeable, and the major technological trends for this decade will be increased circuit and memory density, lower cost per instruction, reduced cost per byte of storage, slowly decreasing communications costs, more bandwidths for communications, and assisted programming environments.

During the last ten years, circuit costs for large data processing systems have been dramatically reduced, and this trend is expected to continue. However, this welcome trend has not been without challenges to established values and concepts of "yesterday"; new products have practically eliminated those already established, and companies have been shaken by these occurrences.

Figure 2-5 describes the life-cycle of a memory chip from the one KB to the present 64 KB. The pattern is repeated: Introduction of the initial product is concurrent with a constant cost/effectiveness ratio. As more competitors bid for market shares, effectiveness decreases, but a

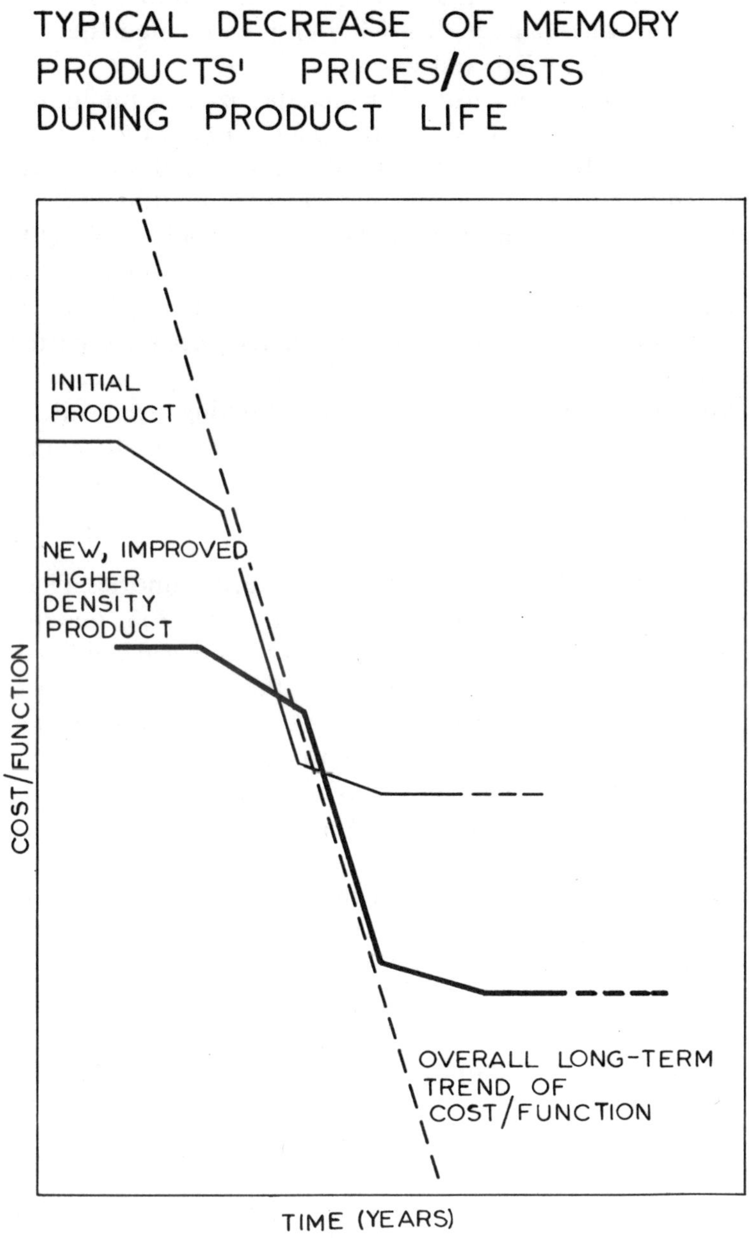

FIGURE 2–5 **Life cycle of a memory chip as a function of time and cost/effectiveness.**

dramatic change occurs when a new product is introduced with greater functionality. In this manner, the 4 KB chip eliminated the 1 KB, the 16 KB eliminated the 4 KB, and so on.

Sharp reductions obviously influence the size and functions of processing units. With the 360/Model 65 system, one MIPS cost approximately $4 million. IBM's 168/AP cost about $1.5 million per MIPS; the 3033 reduced that to $750 million, and the 3081 continued the trend.

Switching speed is another fundamental consideration. IBM's top-of-the-line computer, the 3081, has a cycle time of twenty-six billionths of a second and offers internal performance about twice that of the 3033 processor. Its two processors operate in a paired design for performance and availability.

Figure 2-6 shows the growth curve in switching speed which characterized computing devices for thirty years. Contributing to computation speeds is the dense circuit packaging: Some 750,000 logic circuits are contained within four feet, increasing computer speed by shortening the distance electrical signals must travel.

Similar developments characterize high-speed memories. The average main memory size has increased significantly; in 1965, one-megabyte memories were "big"; by 1981, the size grew to between eight and twelve megabytes. The density of recording and the transfer rate of distinct access (disc) storage have both changed significantly during the 1970s. High-density recording and very large central memories can revolutionize computing: In complex application environments they have less disruptive effects on systems resources such as programs, transactions, databases, and networks.

Each new application requires a greater amount of microelectronic devices, and the experience gained from developing such applications leads to further technological development and further cost reductions. In turn, wider markets are created for the devices (the more so as semiconductor electronics represents a small fraction of an equipment's total cost). Even in electronic machinery, less than ten percent of the monetary value is in integrated circuits; a $10,000 minicomputer contains less than $1,000 worth of integrated circuits; a $300 television set contains less than $30 worth.

Despite such low costs, semiconductors have great importance to most of the world's $100 billion electronics industry which in some way depends on integrated circuits. The substitution of microelectronics de-

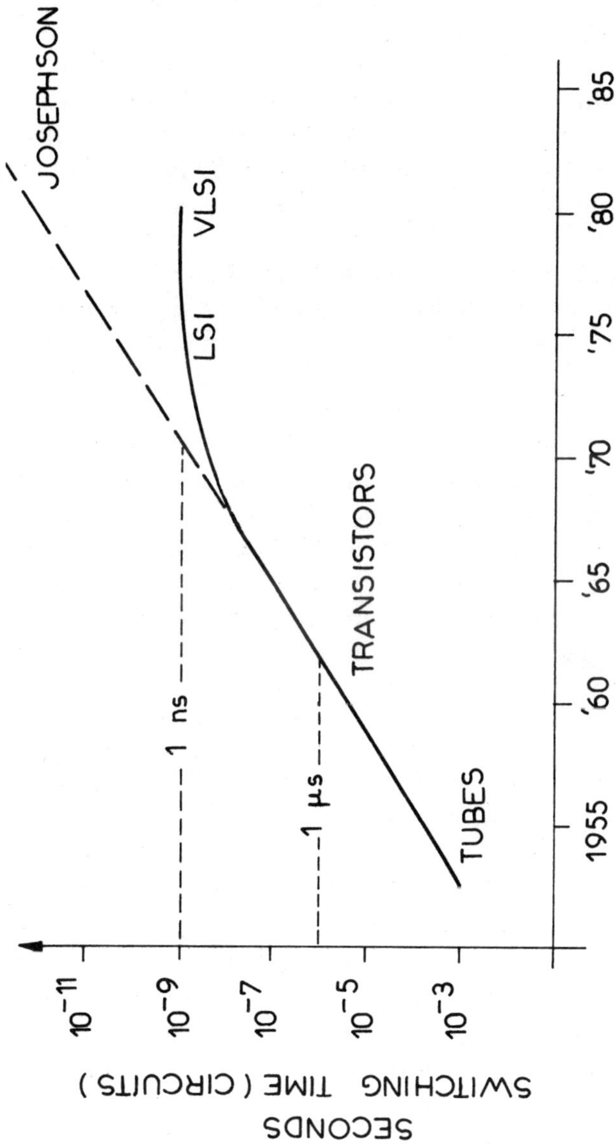

FIGURE 2-6 Growth curve in switching speed. The improvement is of the order of 1,000 in ten years.

vices for discrete components reduces costs not only because the devices are cheaper but for a variety of other reasons.

First, an integrated circuit contains many interconnections that were previously required, and this saves labor and materials. Second, interconnections of the integrated circuit are much more reliable than solder joints or connectors, the result being savings in maintenance which is the sore point of electronics systems. Third, since integrated circuits are much smaller and consume much less power than components they replace, they make savings possible in support structures such as cabinets, racks, power transformers and cooling fans. Fourth, less intermediate testing is needed in the course of production because the correct functioning of the integrated circuits has been ensured. Finally, the end user needs to provide less floor space, less operating power, and less air conditioning for the new equipment.

Automobiles, washers, microwave ovens, sewing machines, and even lawn sprinkling systems may include microprocessors. As an industrial strategy for profits and survival, the use of microprocessors is generally valid whether motives are defensive or aggressive, and whether or not a basic product line appears to be threatened by competition with a technical advantage. It is still relatively simple to improve products or invent new ones by using standard microprocessors. This is why small firms have successfully invaded existing markets with innovative approaches, though this may be changing.

A ROLE FOR MICROELECTRONICS

As the complexity of microelectronics increases—Intel's 32-bit micromainframe chip is a good example—so does the sophistication of necessary skills, techniques, and basic physical resources. Furthermore, where microelectronics are to be applied to an established product and the resulting combination is a rather radical departure from past practices (such as with the sewing machine), the project needs the strong commitment of management and calls for a certain isolation from the rest of the firm during the period of development.

Such a policy protects new ideas from negative thinking within the firm and helps prevent premature disclosure. Two key people should be present in each development team. One should have considerable knowledge about the product or process in which the microelectronic applications are being made, and must have expertise in several technical disciplines along with an understanding of electronic and microprocessor technology. The other person is the software designer upon whom depends much of the long-term success of the product in regard to efficiency, versatility, and reliability of supporting software or firmware.

One strategy practised with good results by several companies is to invest most of a product's sophistication in the micromemory rather than in mechanical components. By making minimal demands on such components, later design changes can be effected rapidly and at relatively low cost.

In terms of implementation, the most difficult design consideration involves interfaces between the microelectronic and mechanical parts of the product. Many firms have found that training their personnel in electronics is more effective than bringing in microelectronics experts and familiarizing them with the needs of the product and its user.

Among companies with established product lines, a common marketing strategy is to introduce the microelectronic version of a product at a cost above more conventional products. As microelectronics allows new features to be incorporated, this is a logical strategy: The greater profit margins normally found in higher-priced items help repay development costs and finance improvements and replacements that will be necessary when competitors move in.

Another advantage in top-of-the-line strategy is that the price level of higher-priced products avoids locking the company into the design too early by limiting demand while production capacity is being built, and while problems in the product are being ironed out. One more advantage is that microprocessors have an impact on product planning and life cycles; their advent shortens the lives of other products, thus enabling a more rapid payback of development and tooling costs. Higher turnovers bring higher profits.

Valuable lessons can be learned from experiences companies have had with advanced technology. In the early-to-mid-1970s, electronic watches were the "miracle product" which made several fortunes and caused numerous losses; growth companies suddenly failed when the Japanese reduced the quartz assembly price from $6.00 apiece to $.50 by reducing the polishing on it and fixing it to the casing with a special cement rather than with springs.

Cost-cutting is a double-edged sword; there is both risk and opportunity in the fact that the most striking characteristic of the microelectronics industry has been a persistent and rapid decline in the cost of a given electronic product. For example, the cost of what became the hand-held calculator declined by a factor of 100 in the past decade.

The rapid decline in cost is partly accounted for by a learning curve: the more experience an industry acquires, the more efficient and competitive it becomes. A list of surviving firms typically includes those who know how to use technology and whose managers are adept at cutting costs.

Most industries reduce costs (in constant dollars) by twenty percent to thirty percent each time their output doubles. This holds true of microelectronics, but it is not enough in itself. Data for the semiconductor industry shows that integrated circuit costs have declined an average of twenty-eight percent with each doubling of the industry's capacity, but a more impressive cost reduction came to those companies that knew how to fully utilize advanced technology.

Indeed, the cost of electronic units has been declining even more rapidly than the cost of integrated circuits since the complexity of the latter has been increasing as prices decreased. If we assume a transistor represents one circuit function equatable to a logic gate or one memory bit in an integrated circuit, then the annual use of transistors has doubled eleven times in the last seventeen years, providing the circuit producer with a feasible method to absorb sharp cost reductions and still make a profit.

In conclusion, advantages obtained through an efficient use of microprocessor technology are: economy through specialization; the avoidance of large complex subsystems; simpler programming; less development time; a firm basis for separation of programming from database management and communications capabilities; shared data through better specialized interfaces; the ability to develop and share different processors; flexibility to serve both remote and central locations; higher reliability and security; and easier changeover. However, there are also prerequisites to these benefits, as we will see in the following chapter.

3 Device Architecture

INTRODUCTION

DURING THE past two decades, the development of microelectronic circuits has made high-quality transistors progressively cheaper and more abundent while providing a limited selection of resistors and capacitors. As a result, circuit configurations have evolved that exploit strengths of the technology and avoid its limitations. This chapter describes the evolution of digital logic circuits which employ bipolar semiconductor devices, and further describes how transistors are adopted for almost all functions involving switching and circuitry.

Microcircuits evolved over the years. In the mid-1950s, with transistor resistor logic (TRL), attention was focused on including resistors in electronic items since they were the cheapest suitable devices; in the early 1960s, with diode transistor logic (DTL), performance was improved by substituting semiconductor diodes for many resistors; and by the late 1960s, resistor transistor logic (RTL) became the first microelectronic technology. At this time, a transistor was supplied for each input and only a few small-value resistors were required.

In the 1970s, transistor transistor logic (TTL) became the common form of bipolar microelectronic technology. The techniques learned in making gates for digital logic have also been applied to the development of other microelectronic devices. Circuits that process analogue signals, indispensable in equipment such as telephones and radios, were now made in microelectronic form.

By the late 1970s, industry realized it is more productive to handle analogue signals by converting them into digital form for processing, and when necessary reconverting them to analogue form. So, microelectronic applications broadened well beyond the designers' original goals. For the 1980s, originality will lie in the way we combine previously unrelated areas of knowledge and simplify as far as possible problems which we encounter.

LOOKING AT MICROCIRCUITS

An electronic device is composed of active circuit elements such as transistors in combination with other passive components such as resistors, capacitors, and inductors. An active element can change its state in response to an external signal; resistors, capacitors and inductors have no such capability.

The industrial practice has been to manufacture components separately and then assemble a device by connecting the components with metallic conductors. The advent of microelectronic circuits has not, for the most part, changed the nature of the basic functional units; the major difference is that all these elements and their interconnections are now fabricated on a single substrate in a continuous stream of operations.

The underlying structure of a silicon circuit is typically a silicon crystal, alternatives being sapphire and GaAs (gallium arsenide). These materials are used for their physical and electrical characteristics. Since the primary material of microelectronic circuits is silicon, the development of microelectronics has depended in large measure on the invention of techniques for making the various functional units *on* or *in* a crystal of this material. (Design and manufacturing methods have been developed for fabricating most standard devices.)

New designs require new manufacturing methods; the designs of earlier and bulkier technologies have not merely been adopted and miniaturized. The change in scale has brought a change in resources available to the designer, followed by alternatives in how those resources are deployed. The foremost development in design is that a growing number of functions have been relegated to transistors as they are most easily fabricated in silicon and offer the best performance. Silicon is far from being an ideal material for every function, and it offers only modest values of resistance and capacitance. Practical microelectronic inductors of silicon cannot be formed at all. Yet, silicon is without equal for the fabrication of transistors, and the abundance of these active components in microelectronic devices more than compensates for shortcomings of the passive elements. It is no wonder that electronics designers have placed emphasis on transistor logic and have worked hard to increase the density of bits and gates on a chip.

Integrated circuits developed during the last two decades in terms of density on a chip. In the late 1960s and early 1970s, we had the one KB and four KB chips; the mid-1970s, saw the four and sixteen KB chips;

and in the late 1970s, the sixteen and sixty-four KB chips. The early 1980s will see about 128 KB per chip; in the mid-to-late 1980s we will most likely have 512 KB per chip, and sometime in the early 1990s one megabit (2^{20} bits) and possibly two MB per chip.

We can foresee implanting 50,000 logical circuits per chip in the 1980s, and in the following decade 250,000 to 500,000 circuits per chip. Such values on a chip will exceed the total number of gates on currently available computers.

LARGE-SCALE INTEGRATION

The property which makes transistors indispensable in microelectronics is the capacity for gain, or amplification. This can be better understood by considering both passive and active circuit elements as black boxes examined only through an input/output method: A signal applied to the input of a black box that contains a resistor, capacitor, or inductor can be transformed in many ways; invariably, the signal power is reduced. However, a black box that contains a transistor can transform a low-power signal into a high-power one.

The two basic types of transistors, bipolar and Mosfet (Metal Oxyde Semiconductor/Field Effect Transistor), compose the two large families of microelectronic circuits. Bipolar devices were the first to be developed, and a great variety of bipolar devices have evolved. However, the greatest density of circuit elements per chip may eventually be achieved with Mosfet technology, though this would not make bipolar circuits obsolete.

Figure 3-1 outlines the evolution of MOS technology (both current and projected over a 15-year period. Figure 3-2 compares bipolar and MOS technologies to other memory devices in terms of access time and cost of storage (in cents per bit).

In general, integrated circuit technology with more than 1,000 gates is large-scale integration (LSI), whereas sixty-four KB or more is very large-scale integration (VLSI). LSI and VLSI have rapidly influenced microcomputer and minicomputer designs, more so than midi and maxi (mainframe) designs due to specialized functions performed with the latter.

VLSI has a greater impact on the lower rather than higher end of the minicomputer spectrum, but design rules may change this. Microcomputers are overtaking minicomputers in market shares and are being significantly implemented in both general and special situations. Such developments are the vanguard of significant changes which will arrive within

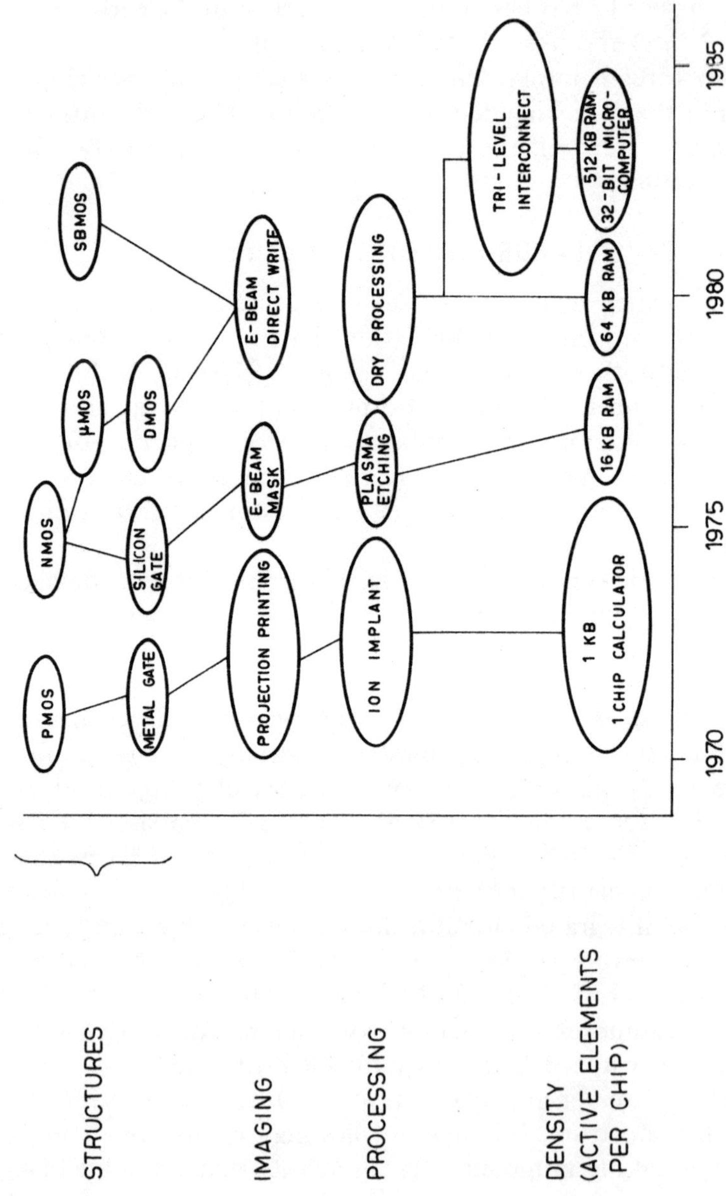

FIGURE 3–1 Evolution of MOS technology, current and projected, over a fifteen-year period.

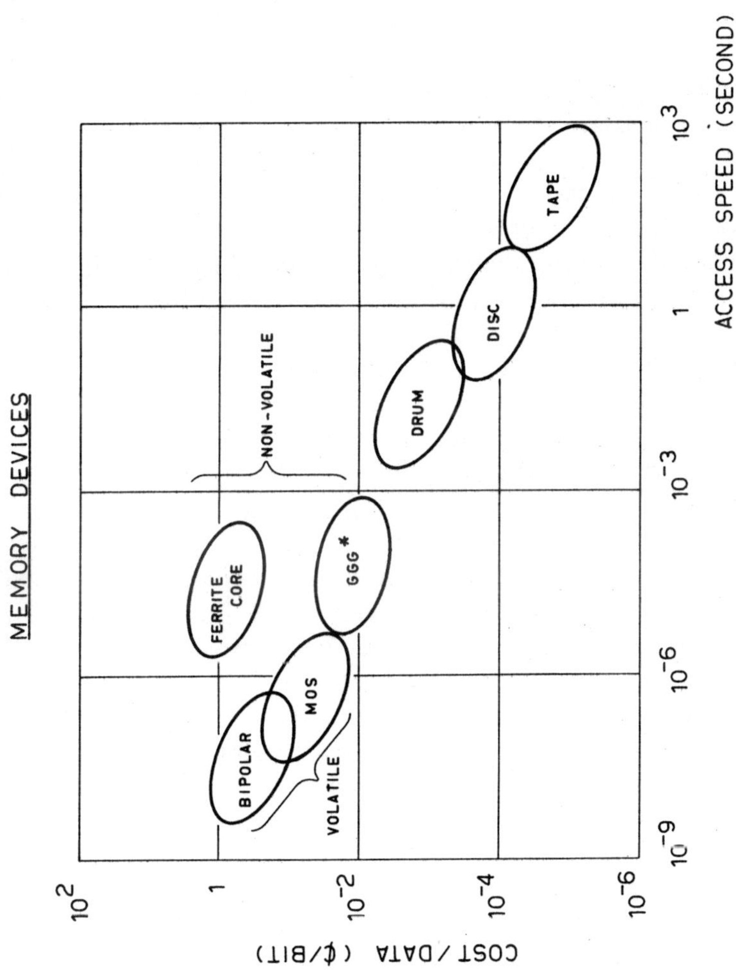

* GALLIUM COMPOUNDS

FIGURE 3–2 A comparison of bipolar and MOS technologies to other computer memory media in terms of access time and cost of storage.

ten years in maxicomputer design with one and two MB density per chip; this will achieve a truly distributed memory and will provide hybrid analog and digital solutions on a chip.

Though design is making great strides, lasting effects will be obtained by changes in the understructures. Packaging technology is one example. The number of pins on a package is increasing rapidly; in several years there will be 100-pin packages, going through the intermediate steps of 48- and 64-pin packages. In addition, packaging is drastically reduced every two to five years. Power supply and frame costs must also be reduced as they may otherwise impede development when, in a few years, they cost more than the computers.

The answer lies in *micropackaging*, an assembly technique which permits the direct interconnection of integrated circuits and so allows manufacturing automation from the initial silicon wafer (which carries the chips) to the final assembly on a board, without the need for standard caging. As technical innovations continue in areas such as LSI and microprocessor technologies and LSI packaging methods, computers offering better price/performance will be possible.

Figure 3-3 demonstrates the use of LSI chip technology in mounting circuit boards.

One approach to gain the best technological economies and capabilities is to build very simple and, therefore, very small circuits for the reason that more will function correctly due to their simplicity. This sounds reasonable, but it is not necessarily the best approach.

Small circuits are inexpensive; simple logic is available for as little as $.10 apiece. The costs of testing, packaging and assembling the completed circuits into an electronic system, however, must also be considered; indeed, in many complex systems, minimum cost is achieved with more expensive, larger circuits costing closer to $10.00 apiece than to $.10. If cheaper, less powerful circuits were to be used, many more would be needed to construct the system, and testing and assembly costs would tend to accumulate. We will discuss these concepts in chapter 6.

MICROPROCESSOR-SUPPORTED FUNCTIONS

Some basic considerations in chip design are changing radically; this obliges us to be conscious of whether our ideas can be logically integrated with available technology. If we study functions evolving in all components, we can see transformations perhaps more dynamic than that which

FIGURE 3-3 **Using LSI chip technology: from component chip to mounted circuit board.**

led to the first integrated circuits: Complex functions develop within a single unit while technological processes are being refined.

The basic requirements for any logic family are flexibility, speed, availability of complex functions, high-noise immunity, lack of internally generated noise, a wide operating temperature range, low power dissipation and low cost. Functional requirements related to the new generation of microprocessors will make possible the implementation of new functions from arithmetic and logic to databasing, programming and maintenance, and will alleviate the rising cost of operating a computer system.

Exactly what is implied by the term "microprocessor"? Typically, a microprocessor is a device on a chip 250-mills-square. A "processor" represents logic gates, registers, and an arithmetic and logical unit. Microprocessor circuitry can act as a computer by adding memory either to the same chip or externally.

This integration of functions logically follows the technological evolution from single components to integrated circuits (Figure 3-4). As we progressed from small-scale integration to medium- and large-scale integration, the development of the microprocessor was inevitable.

Witten aptly suggests that a microprocessor is a device that follows a plan—provided it can be specified precisely as a sequence of steps. The state of the art microprocessor can do any information handling task expressed in an algorithmic (hence, procedural) way. By the end of this decade, this will probably give way to heuristic approaches incorporated first in intelligent machines and then on a chip.

A complete microprocessor design usually involves four components:

1. a CPU (central processing unit),
2. Memory,
3. Interfaces to the Peripherals, and
4. Channel(s).

The microprocessor can be seen as a black box (Figure 3-5) with three major sets of functions: Data, addresses, and control (reset, interrupt/request, and read/write). If we look at the internal structure, we see that the data, address and control circuits are served by busses, the arithmetic and logical unit (ALU) is the core, ROM (read only memory) and RAM (random access memory) are the microprocessor's equally basic units, and the peripheral interface connects the device to the external world (Figure 3-6).

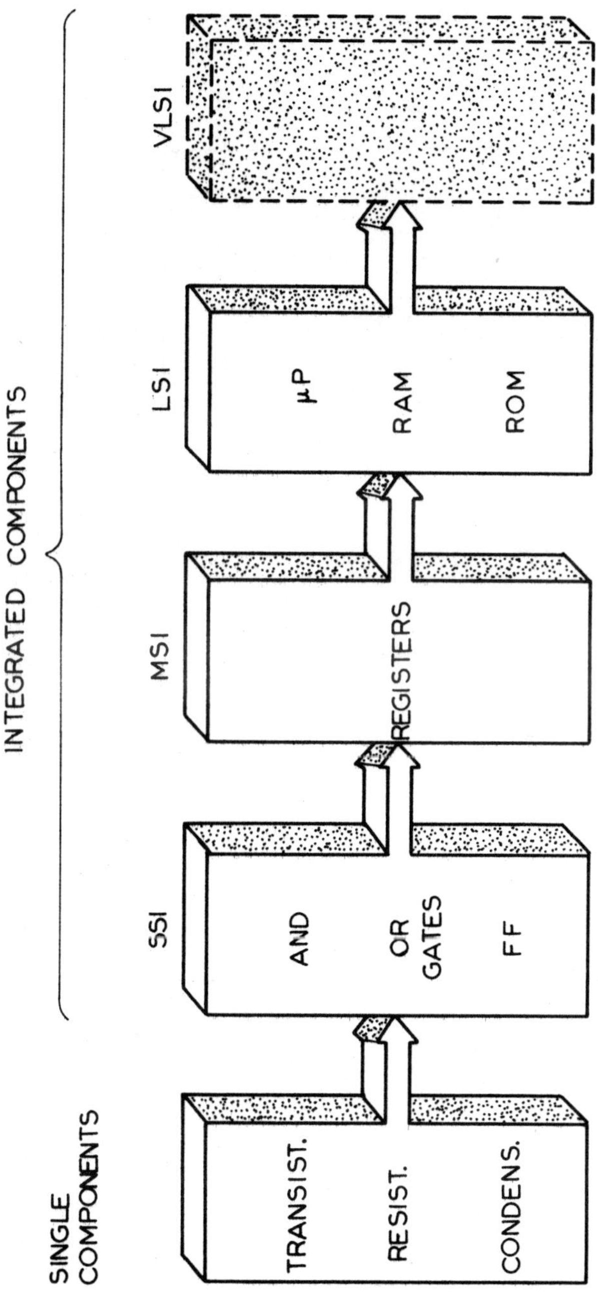

FIGURE 3–4 A step-by-step technological evolution from single components to integrated circuits.

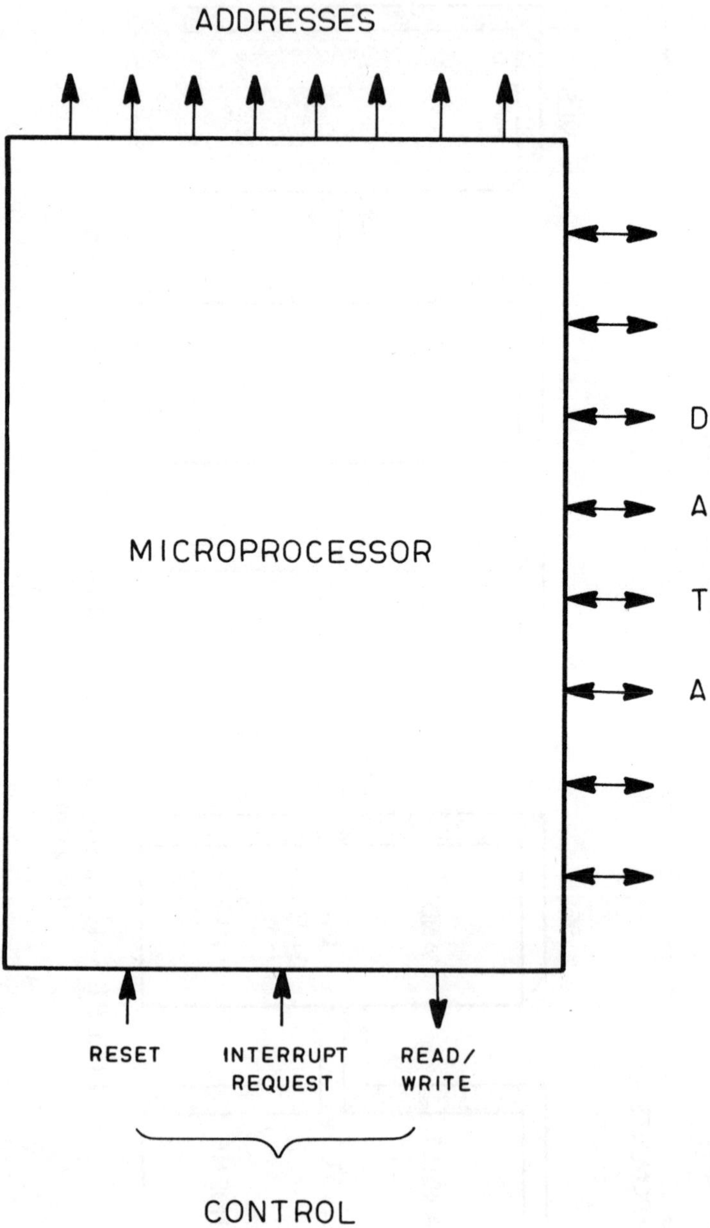

FIGURE 3–5 The microprocessor as a black box with data, address and control circuits to connect to the external world.

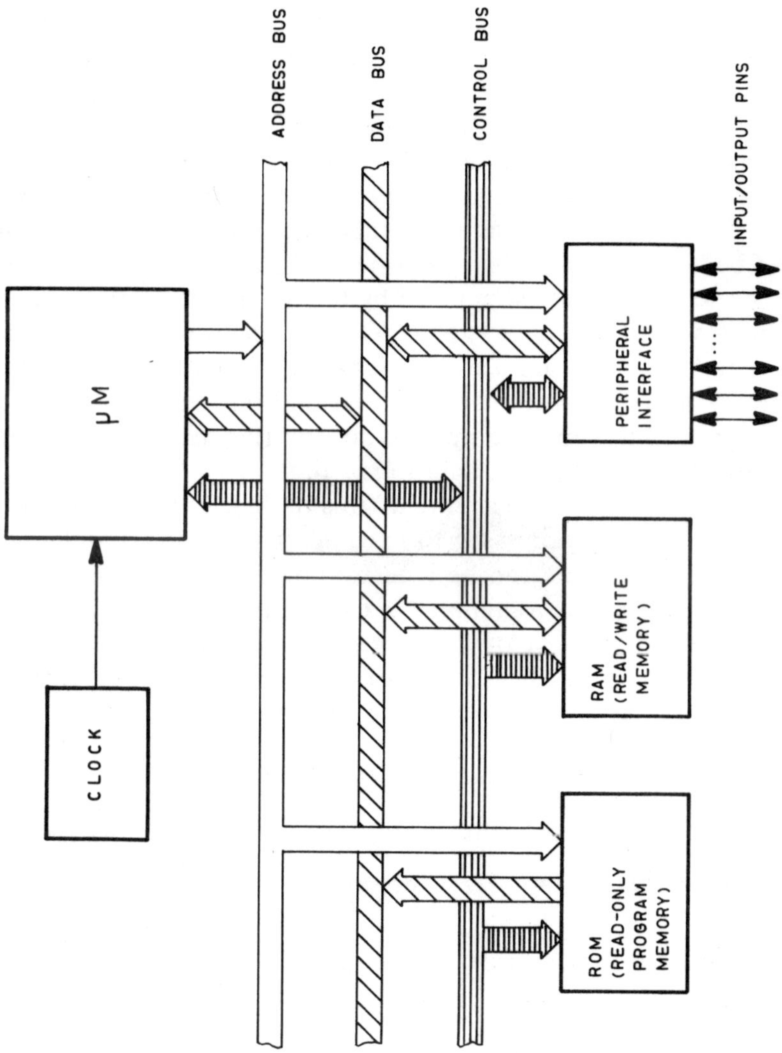

FIGURE 3–6 A basic system structure, including a microprocessor; clock; data, address and control busses; ROM, RAM and peripheral interface.

The CPU capability increases with the complexity and sophistication of the system. In the 1950s, functions of the CPU were largely limited to the arithmetic and logical unit. Today, the CPU of a computer is multifunctional; the supported faculties include interrupts, priority handling, special registers, vertical and horizontal microcode, specialized arithmetic and logical operations. Eventually, CPUs will include multiple ALU units probably with a voting capability based on the results of processing, with out-voting and replacement in case of error.

Let's however properly underline that the CPU is no more the central component of the system. It is just one of the subsystems like the memory, the interfaces, and the channels. Still another subsystem is *software*, which can be looked at as *deferred hardware design*.

The more faculties are supported by microcomputers, the more the latter grow toward full-scale systems, which explains why an increasing number of manufacturers are searching for ways to connect several microcomputers to make powerful and flexible multiprocessors. This is the usual manner in which microcomputers are entering minicomputer territory, sometimes offering better solutions.

A *microcode* capability is part of this design. This term refers to the code required by a processor to execute instructions it is designed to handle. The microcode can be read by only memory (firmware) or random access memory (programmable capability). Basic design characteristics consider the object of the process, the handling faculties, and functional characteristics. The object of a process calls for a consideration of:

- the type of data (binary; octal; decimal; or other)
- bits per word (four, eight, twelve, sixteen, or thirty-two)
- data resources (external registers, internal registers, main memory)
- the data memory size (one KB, four KB, sixteen KB, sixty-four KB, or more than sixty-four KBs, and
- the program memory size (*idem*).

As we will see in the next section when we talk of bits per word, the amount of central memory directly addressable by a computer is determined by the number of bits allocated to the address fields of its instructions and the size of its address bus. For instance, sixteen bits allow the ability to address up to 65,536 words. Memory access speeds are comparable to conventional devices with access times of 500 nanoseconds, but even faster memories are available for use with the faster microprocessors.

Handling faculties typically involve sort, transmission of data blocks, data search, add/subtract, multiply/divide, logical operations, number of I/O (input, output) ports, data transmission speed, branching (including number of conditions), number of interrupts, the existence of priority, and response time. Functional characteristics are basically oriented to the function the product is to perform:

- One-chip microcomputers with a 4-bit word are usually categorized for consumer electronics.
- 8-bit, one-chip microcomputers are better suited to configuring systems.
- Communications requirements are served by 16 and 32 BPW microcomputers.

As the new product lines unfold in the mid-1980s 8 BPW processors will characterize the *handheld* computers; 16 and 32 BPW processors the *personal/professional* computers; and 32 BPW the minicomputers—moving from there to the mainframes. Understandably, all three characteristics require high performance and reliability. Speed and performance are mainly dependent on the state of technology, but the matter of choice is always present; for a given application, a user will choose a slower implementation if it performs similarly at a lower cost. However, differences in cost and performance are not always due to speed. Such differences may also have their origin in the package type, the functional temperature range, and the number of interfaces. Most computer systems have both external and internal interfaces. External interfaces which define systems boundaries are often standardized by manufacturers, such as the IBM channel interface and the DEC unit bus. Internal interfaces are essentially hidden. In either case, the boundaries of a microprocessor-based system are very sensitive to the interfaces. Also, as component interfaces are more visible and often must be more uniformly designed, the microprocessor-based system bus is a key standardization link allowing a wide mix of components, designs, and final use.

This section has been written with the understanding that users are familiar with the criteria of boundaries and capabilities.

BITS PER WORD

During the last decade, design changes have been significant with reference to chip density and the number of bits per word (BPW) supported by microprocessors. Some specialists foresee the performance of computers increasing by thirty percent each year, or maintaining the same level of performance while prices decrease thirty percent each year. An increase in performance is closely linked to the bits per word. In the early-to-mid-1970s, the 4-bit microprocessor was the rule; today, most users want 8-bit or 16-bit microprocessors, and demand for 32-bit words is increasing.

Equipment designers usually specify that a processor's performance should be at least equivalent to TTL-based minicomputers. The architectural design should be such that requirements external to VLSI are minimized, while only those VLSI processing technologies presently being used in low-cost mass-production should be considered. Customized circuitry is usually not cost/effective.

The introduction of 16-bit and 32-bit microprocessors is altering applications perspectives and is generating a reevaluation of what is necessary for calculation and memory support in order to perform a given function.

Chronologically, in 1972 the 4-bit microprocessor (Intel 4040) was introduced; in 1977, the 8-bit; in 1980, the 16-bit; and in 1981, the 32-bit microprocessor. Together with the change in BPW, microprocessors gained a significant increase in MIPS (millions of instructions per second). Both changes made feasible a larger database, a higher communications bandwidth (buses), and, therefore, new applications. The number of bits relates to the power of the processor: The fewer bits in a word, the more steps the processor must perform to obtain a given result. So, the number of bits in a processor's working registers (the registers it uses to perform arithmetic and logic functions) is an important consideration.

To date, the five common types of microprocessors are 4-bit, 8-bit, 12-bit, 16-bit and bit-slice (2-bit and 4-bit; see following section).

The 4-bit types are mainly used for small controllers and calculators. Such designs are mainly equipped for decimal arithmetic functions and for handling 4-bit BCD (Binary Coded Decimal) numbers, one digit at a time. As a result, they are very limited in processing power and speed, and still require a moderate amount of support.

The 8-bit types have been for some time the most popular microprocessors. These are used in both computers and communications. Most characters used in communications applications fit an 8-bit format, while calculator-based microprocessors equipped with an 8-bit structure can handle a sizable number of program instructions.

The 12-bit types are not particularly in favor; though they provide more arithmetic resolution than 8-bit processors, their design is based on a one-instruction per 12-bit word format. Since the instruction word must also include address information, the instruction set and addressing capability of this processor is somewhat limited compared to typical 8-bit devices and is, therefore, less powerful. Its competitive advantage is that equipment which it supports is able to draw from the large software library developed for PDP-8.

The 16-bit microprocessors are the favored design and will eventually overtake 8-bit functions both in computers and communications. While this type may be replaced by 32-bit designs, its staying power will be largely decided by applications required in microprogramming, such as using bits of memory to replace integrated circuit logic gates.

Figure 3-7 gives a present-day market share perspective of the microprocessor types we have discussed.

BITS AND GATES

It is difficult to determine precisely how many bits are required to replace one gate; with 4-bit functions, four bits are required, but more generally eight to sixteen bits are necessary. If we assume that eight bits replace a gate, then a four KB ROM can replace 512 integrated circuit gates. There are economic advantages to such a replacement, and we should note its effects on the economics of the industry and on system architecture.

The economics of such replacements are that bits and gates become a unit of measurement of the semiconductor industry's output and, therefore, of its ability to survive. In 1978, an estimated 10^{12} bits and gates were manufactured; an estimated 10^{18} are expected in 1984. This difference of six orders of magnitude is expected to occur within only six years.

As for the architectural aspect, the trend toward 16- and 32-BPW chips increases addressable memory, and this certainly favors more complex architectures. Another reason for higher BPW designs is that program portability is made easier if word formats do not change in the process. Minicomputers and other machines will be accordingly restructured by these changes.

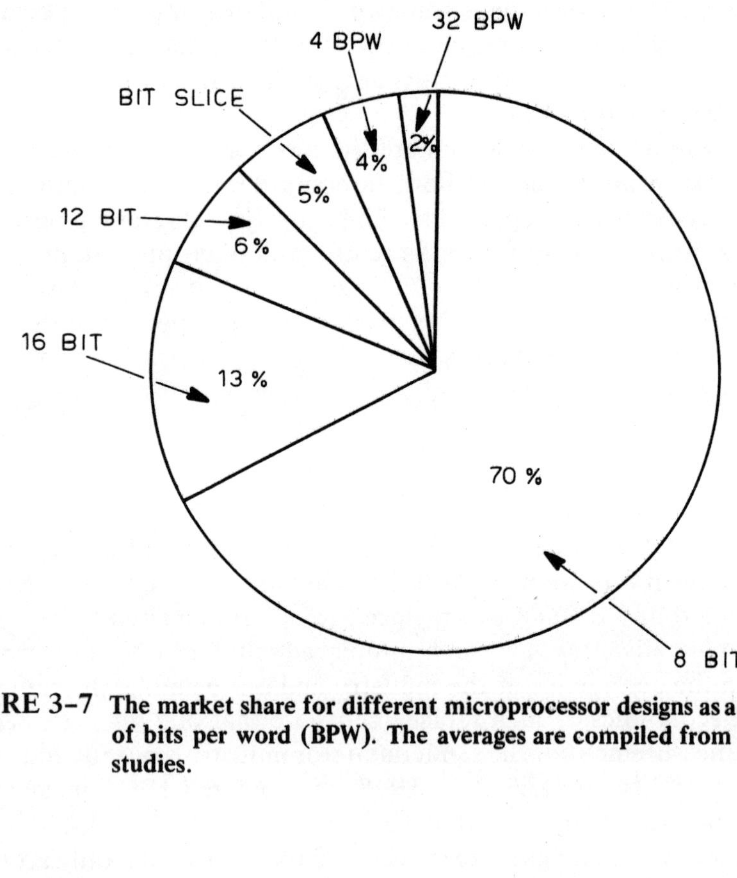

FIGURE 3–7 The market share for different microprocessor designs as a function of bits per word (BPW). The averages are compiled from different studies.

Under present-day conditions, some 32-bit designs are based on 3-chip aggregates. This is more of a mainframe-type process rather than a microcontroller process, and it reflects the fact that up to now the basic requirements in the computer industry have been for 8-bit, 12-bit and 16-bit levels. Not to be underestimated is the software impact in this process; high-end micro-CPUs migrate to 32-bit achitectures because programs are becoming more and more sophisticated.

So, in regard to design, 32-bit processors incorporate much more memory, which is good for high data rates and complex Cobol programs. This is one way in which the semiconductor industry directly creates the tools for implementing the information revolution and, at the same time, sets a competitive pace.

Another example of a valid and potentially far-reaching semiconductor tool are *bit-slice* microprocessors. These are usually microprogrammed devices, equipped to execute *microinstructions* which are primitive operations. More complex and powerful instructions are executed by equivalent combinations of microinstructions which can be combined to form microprograms (the latter are stored in a cache memory associated with the microprocessor). The machine operates by retrieving *macroinstructions* from the system's central memory, determining the type of macroinstruction retrieved, and executing the appropriate microprogram routines that perform the functions specified by the macroinstructions.

Sets of bit-slice microprocessors can be arranged to form an aggregate whose word size is any integral multiple of the bit-slice size (4-bit, 8-bit, 16-bit, etc.). These aggregates can be tailored with changes in their microprograms, and so they can be programmed with instruction sets appropriate to their intended application, including the case of being programmed to emulate other processors.

Bit-slices can be variously arranged; for example, a 4-bit-wide device can be expanded in word length by combining five such devices to make a 20-bit processor. Such designs are highly flexible, but also involve a higher cost and are, therefore, used only with those applications which make the design cost/effective.

With a bit-slice machine, we can create our own instruction sets. This allows us to emulate other products using existing software, to achieve higher speeds, to create a special instruction set coding for tailor-made tasks, to answer variable word-length requirements, and to assure flexibility in a changing environment.

An example is the use of bit-slicing in a diagnostic process unit to replace a 12-bit processor. Though it was necessary to emulate a 12-bit processor with 4-bit chips, an astute integration of functions produced two instead of the original three boards. Furthermore, the new design allowed an extension of diagnostic functions toward the input/output controller of the computer system.

Generally, bit-slice microprocessors are a special class of devices that may not even contain complete CPUs. The term implies that a microprocessor represents a "slice" of a CPU which can be combined with additional "slices" and appropriate supporting circuitry to construct a complete microprocessor CPU of a given word length. Bit-slice microprocessors are often fast, bipolar, and designed for high performance, and a bit-slicing machine is one in which microprocessors have a flexible rather than a fixed word size.

4 Product Incentives

INTRODUCTION

We have been talking about device architecture and how to apply microprocessor technology to a wide array of products. Now we shall discuss product incentives. Mircoprocessor technology presents new business opportunities, and alters the traditional manufacturer's role. The old technological pioneers are absorbed by larger concerns while new venture capital breeds next year's rising competitors.

Figure 4-1 shows how new products profited semiconductor manufacturers from 1969 to 1978. With such profits came risks; Intel and National Semiconductor are now the only major semiconductor firms which have not significantly diversified or which have been acquired by larger firms. The United Technologies and Schlumberger purchases of Mostek and Fairchild added to the list of firms with outside ownership.

The significance of this is that virtually all semiconductor entrepreneurs who produce integrated circuits have had to sell to other companies to finance their firm's growth. Table 4-1 outlines by income bracket and affiliation the 20 top semiconductor manufacturers in the United States.

Another aspect of the semiconductor industry involves the time-lag (mentioned in Chapter 1) between a discovery and the development of a marketable product. Whether this lag is long or short, at some stage it becomes clear that a plan of action is necessary for the product or process under development if it is to be a commercial success.

Like technological breakthroughs, marketing successes do not occur by chance or as a matter of course after a certain amount of effort. Such successes require forethought, proper planning, and the ability to select priorities. They call for objectives both wisely designed and shrewdly implemented.

Managerial expertise and competence are prime requirements. In the pursuit of a dynamic course, an organization is faced with new and

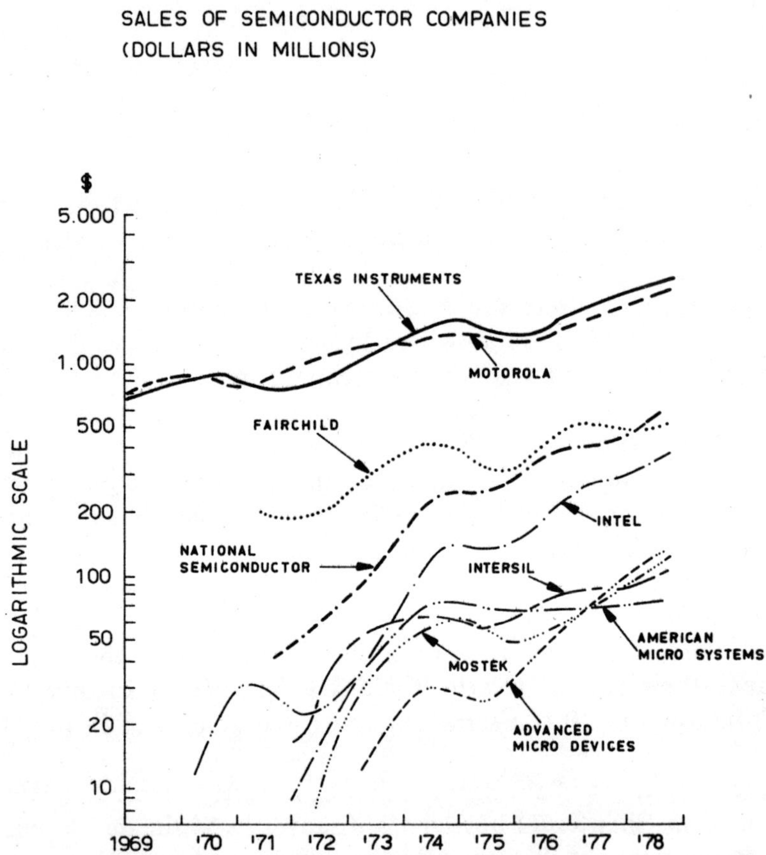

FIGURE 4–1 A 10-year period (1969–1978) of developing business for the major semiconductor manufacturers.

TABLE 4–1

The 20 Top American Semiconductor Firms*

1. From One–Half to One Billion Dollars	*Division of*
Texas Instruments	=
Motorola	=
Intel	=
2. From $250 Million to One–half Billion	
National Semiconductor	=
Fairchild	Schlumberger
Signetics	N.V. Philips
3. From $100 Million to $250 Million	
Advanced Micro Devices	Siemens
Mostek	United Technologies
RCA	=
Harris	=
American Microsystems	Robert Bosch
4. From $50 Million to $100 Million	
Rockwell	=
General Instruments	=
Intersil	Northern Telecom
Synertek	Honeywell
5. Up to $50 Million	
Analog Devices	Standard Oil
Monolithic Memories	Northern Telecom
Siliconix	Lucas Industries
Solid State Scientific	Adolf Schindling
Zilog	Exxon

*Only semiconductor businesses are listed.

compelling problems, and communications, computer and semiconductor companies are no exception. To be successful, they must continue to demonstrate an ability to bring order to their products, operate within a framework of planned activities, abide by timetables, and impose corrective action where needed. Planning is a way to orderly behavior, and the correct implementation of a plan is more important than the plan itself.

TRENDS OF TECHNOLOGY

For companies working on the fringes of technology, successful product development must somehow lead the major technological trends. In the computer field, these are:

- increased circuit and memory density
- reduced cost per byte of storage
- a control over communications costs
- increased communications bandwidth
- lower cost per instruction
- computer-assisted programming environments.

Chapters 1 to 3 have shown that during the last ten years circuit costs for large data processing systems have been dramatically reduced, and that this trend will continue for several more years with large-scale integration costing a few cents per circuit. Sharp cost reductions will influence the size and function of high-speed memories as the average memory size for very large-scale integration grows even further, and such reductions will lead to new system architectures—a set of building blocks that can plug into one another in virtually unlimited permutations to suit the system builder and end user.

Figure 4-2 follows up on this reference. The 1981 IBM report to stockholders singled out four products to document technology's forward steps:

1. A hand-sized logic module in the new 3081 processor containing 45,000 circuits, equal to the total logic circuitry of an intermediate-sized System/370 Model 148 computer.

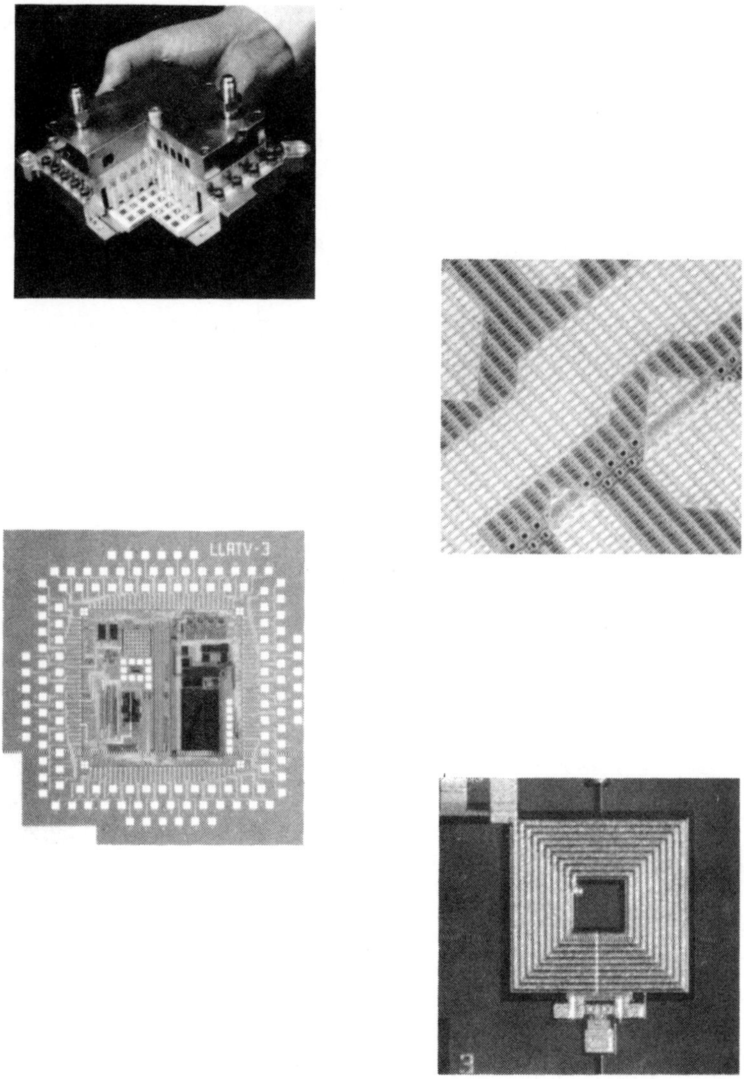

FIGURE 4–2 **Four examples of forward steps in technology: (a) a hand-sized logic module; (b) a dense silicon chip for a commercial product; (c) an experimental silicon chip containing 4,000 logic switches; and (d) a spiral input coil with an experimental superconducting magnetic sensor.**

2. A silicon chip for new models of the 3683 supermarket terminal, representing the densest solid-state memory reported for a commercial product. This quarter-inch chip can store 72,000 bits of information.

3. An experimental silicon chip, one-sixth-inch square, containing 4,000 logic switches in the black rectangular area which is considerably denser than circuitry in present computers. Experiments have shown that such a chip can contain 10,000 logic switches, or 250,000 bits of memory.

4. A spiral input coil which is an experimental superconducting magnetic sensor. The operating characteristics of such research devices are approaching limits of fundamental laws of physics. The sensors can potentially measure changes as small as one-millionth of one-millionth the intensity of the earth's magnetic field, with applications areas in electronics, geophysics, and biomedicine.

We have been speaking of memory developments. In the mid-1960s, one megabyte memories were the "big" ones. Fifteen years later, the size grew to between eight and twelve megabytes, and in May, 1981, Fujitsu announced a new Facom computer with 128 MBytes of central memory. Still, during this time, the price in dollars per MIPS of raw processing power has been highly reduced, while the MIPS capacity of each processor has significantly increased. For example, with IBM's System/360 Model 65, one MIPS cost approximately $4 million; the 370/168 SP cost about $1.5 million per MIPS; the 3033 shrank that to $750,000, and this cost decreases still further with new announcements.

This decadc will hold interesting trends in this regard. Gone is the time of Grosch's Law which, in 1960, stated that for large-scale systems cost increases at the square root of performance. Incidentally, Grosch's Law was not established on the basis of what it costs to produce machines but rather on how pricing was performed by computer manufacturers. It was not based on technology; it was a pricing strategy "law."

Due emphasis has to be given to the fact that from the mid-1970s onwards, pricing changes have been dramatic. When technology allowed us to put an entire microprocessor on a chip, within only ten years (1967-1977) basic processor prices shrank to about ten percent of their previous level. Vast improvements in price and performance became commonplace.

Since 1950, the cost per bit of storing information has dropped a thousandfold. During this same time, the price of 100,000 calculations shrank from $1.56 to one cent. Also, during the last few years, the cost of computer memory decreased by forty percent per year, and that of logic by twenty-five percent.

Along with this shrinking of prices, a second phenomenon arose which we can call "superpower." A good example is the special-purpose computer with a sustained speed of a billion floating-point operations per second, possible for 1986. Power and memory size are not the only goals. Users are increasingly focusing on quality, reliability, maintainability, security, and the ability to meet these requirements at an affordable cost and on schedule. Computer manufacturers must ask questions such as: What are the new customer demands, policies, and expectations? How can emerging requirements be met? Do cost tradeoffs reflect true economics in reliability and maintainability?

Maintainability has become a major preoccupation. With online systems we cannot afford downtime, while maintenance costs must be reduced and diagnostics automated. However, how is testability best assured during design, production, and operation? How are new maintainability specifications applied to computers and communications systems? What are affordable costs?

To steadily reduce cost figures and thus survive within a highly competitive environment, the trend has been to mass produce even what were thought to be specialized circuits. One example is the *gate array*, in the form of a partially completed wafer, which awaits the customer's logic requirements. This allows the user to design only the last two masks of layers to complete the fabrication of his wafer, which permits the equipment maker to reduce costs and decrease design time. Gate arrays can also be more cost/effective than a full custom chip, especially if the need is for only several thousand units.

Cost reduction is not necessarily relegated to the cost of components, but also to associate subjects like printed circuit boards, connectors, cabling, power supplies, and the box. These are the elements which help reduce costs and increase capabilities.

It is possible to buy logic chips and arrange them on circuit boards, but this requires testing and debugging after the boards have been stuffed along with the cost of the boards and labor. Thus, the impetus is for items such as gate arrays. As we put more and more of the system on a chip, the chip is a greater portion of the manufacturing cost.

Among vital design choices is that of power consumption. For instance, in communications applications where equipment must run twenty-four hours a day, power consumption becomes significant and for telephone switching equipment with a twelve-year lifespan, the power consumed can cost more than the equipment. One solution is the sixty-four KB chip, where one circuit suffices where previously there were four. This means reduced square footage on the printed circuit board, which in turn leads to smaller cabinets, a decreased requirement for cooling, and lower power consumption.

There are choices to be made and priorities to be observed. In any organization, growth and survival depend upon the ability to sustain a dynamic, competitive, and profitable product line.

This reference is better exemplified when we look at the uses to which business and industry are putting microcomputers. A little less than fifty percent are new uses (Figure 4-3) from which spring a whole generation of products previously unknown to the market. Slightly more than fifty percent concerns the replacement of existing machines and devices which involves the risk of product obsolescence for most firms.

Interestingly enough, the replacement market itself is divided into three parts:

1. About fifty-two percent involves the replacement of logic circuits.
2. About thirty-two percent of microcomputers replace minicomputers, the kings of the 1970s. "The minicomputer," it was said at a 1980 symposium, "is dead. Long live the microcomputer!"
3. Significantly, about eighteen percent involves the replacement of controllers, and this involves the greatest danger for firms who let their product line slip into obsolescence.

THE NEVER-ENDING CHALLENGE

Greater density per chip, higher speeds, gate arrays, reliability, packaging, and power consumption pose never-ending challenges for the research physicist and design engineer. One such recent challenge is *very high speed integration* (VHSI) which involves the development of integrated circuits with 100 times the data processing capacity of existing devices. VHSI would vastly increase the capabilities of communications satellites, new

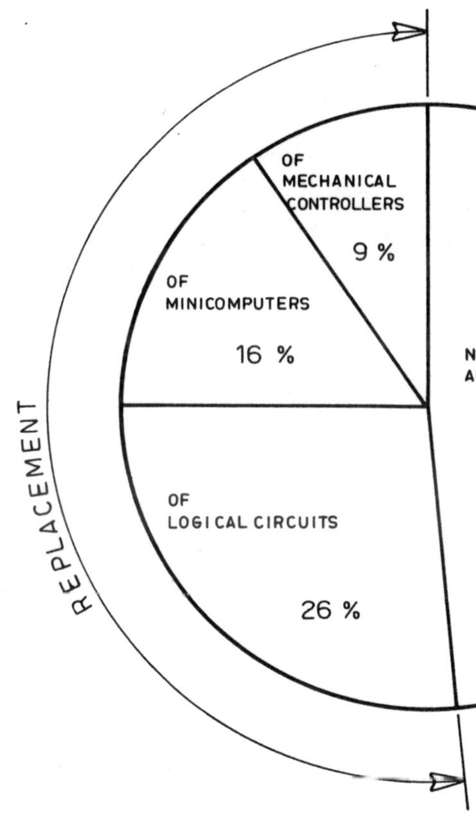

FIGURE 4–3 **Estimated percental use of microcomputers for new applications and for the replacement market.**

weapons such as the cruise missile, radar and aircraft control systems, and computers from mainframes to minicomputers and microcomputers. It may also produce important commercial spinoffs at the personal computer level.

Objectives for new R&D programs include formidable challenges:

- Pilot production of semiconductor memories capable of *storing two million bits of data*, compared with sixty-four KB in the best available (commercial) computer models.*
- Logic devices equivalent to a high-speed mainframe computer on a single chip.
- Significant aftermaths in switching speed—while increasing miniaturization.
- Development of semiconductor processing techniques and equipment capable of achieving lines as thin as half a micron—a tenfold improvement over today's standard.
- Creation of new software chip designs, and testing procedures to take full advantage of complex VHSI circuits.**

Researchers are banking on advanced logic and memory circuits to develop a fault-tolerant computer in which several powerful microcomputers will backup one another. Another line of technological development in which the Japanese are very active is Gallium Arsenide which is expected to conquer between five percent and ten percent of the market by 1986. Field-effect transistors (FET) are emerging as strong contenders for microwave switch applications in communications satellites.

The gallium-arsenide semiconductor is projected to be twenty-five times faster then silicon and will probably turn out fifth-generation computers responding to voice commands and reading charts and graphs, by the 1990s. The key to that feat may be the Josephson Junction device that conveys electrons faster than any other type through super-thin

*Both IBM and the Bell Labs expect to win the world race when the 256 K chip goes into production.

**Microelectronic chips that contain nearly a half million circuit elements and are hundreds of times faster than currently available devices, fall under the very high speed integrated circuits umbrella. These super-chips are as complex as 100 Los Angeles street maps printed on a thumb.

pieces of metal at a temperature of 270° C below zero. (While Fujitsu gears up to manufacture its HSMT or High-speed Mobility Transistor with gallium arsenide, both MITI and the government's Science and Technology Agency are financing the research needed to perfect the Josephson Junction in the race to beat IBM into mass production.)

With the exception of bipolar linear circuits which since the mid-1970s have been holding a steady twenty percent of the market, and the CMOS, other technologies come and go. The Schottky TTL has substituted the classical TTL (though at a lesser market share than the latter commanded in the mid-1970s,) and the HMOS is almost totally replacing the PMOS. Other bipolars are also being phased out.

(Let me explain in a few words the terms which have just been used. MOS stands for *metal oxyde semiconductor*, a development of the mid-to-late 1960s. CMOS, or Complementary MOS, followed in market introduction. It has not been a great improvement because it isn't high speed.)

(The PMOS and NMOS—respectively for P-junction and N-junction, have also been of the late 1960s in terms of laboratory work; as usually the market introduction came later. More important however is the 1970s development of HMOS (high-speed MOS) which is now actively in production.)

Figure 4-4 identifies the market share in units for different types of VLSI circuitry. The low end occupies about sixty percent of the total; the high and intermediate end, fifteen percent and twenty-five percent respectively, both of which will substantially increase. Bit-slicing occupies about five percent of the market. The cost ratio is significant—1 to 50 in favor of the low end. However, this ratio will change; the low end share will probably shrink to fifteen percent and twenty percent if money is the basis.

Market shares are also shifting at a higher-up level of integration. For example, microprocessors and memory chips are taking the market away from MSI and linear circuits. As hardware features and accumulated software bases grow, general purpose microprocessors or single chip microcomputers become the preferred choice over custom LSI circuits for an increasing percentage of applications, as mentioned in the reference to gate arrays.

Simultaneously, design methodology is changing. The older method of drawing circuit layouts by hand may not be entirely replaced by the computer—many parts of a large-scale integrated circuit are still hand-

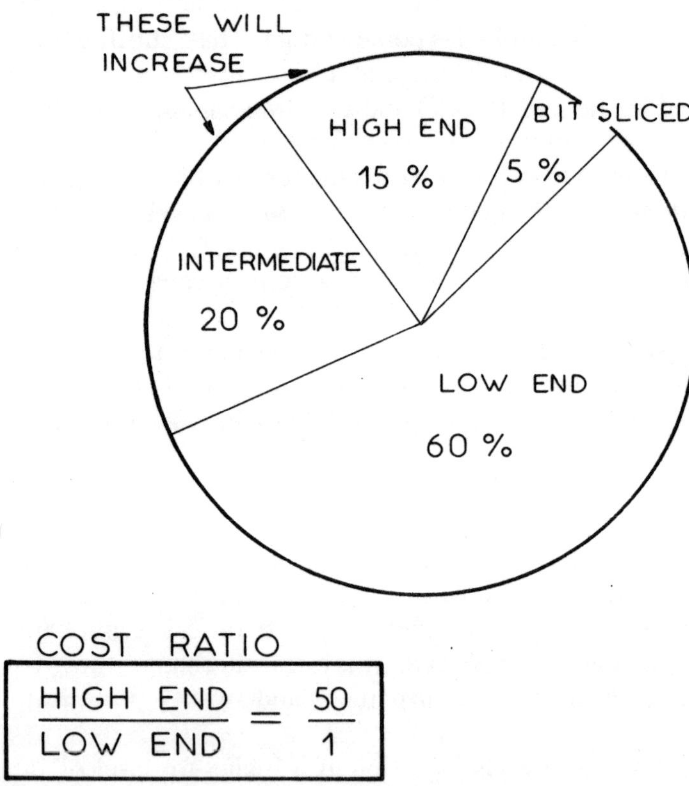

FIGURE 4–4 **Market share in units (not value) for VLSI circuitry.**

drawn before being submitted to the computer—but the computer-aided design of circuits has opened new capabilities manual methods could not afford. (We will return to this issue in Chapters 11 and 12).

For example, Fujitsu introduced in 1980 a new CAD-designed CMOS Family comprising four models which permit free selection of gate sizes best matching customer needs, from the medium-scale 770-gate model to the large-scale 3,900-gate model. These have produced brisk orders from manufacturers of industrial machinery and consumer products.

The 32-bit microprocessor is a product of advanced design techniques which provided at least half the incentive for its development, and market potential which, however, is still latent. Nevertheless, in regard to stimulating the latter, every time the price per bit is reduced, new applications are found, and the 32-bit processor is along those lines.

MICROMAINFRAMES

Intel calls its new chip a *micromainframe*, for that company has shown that a major portion of the architecture of a mainframe in the IBM 4331 class can be reduced to several VLSI chips. Its architecture emulates a large machine. It includes.

- an impressive addressing space (up to four Gigabytes),
- a virtual memory system,
- built-in floating point microcode,
- instruction execution speed that in some cases is in the IBM 4331-1 and -2 class, and
- a content addressable memory buffer to support an efficient virtual memory operation, much like the IBM translation look-aside buffer.

These features are not new; what is new is that IC designers are now fully conversant with mainframe concepts and have the technology to put it on several chips. The separation of CPU and I/O processors and the elimination of all interrupts from the CPU domain is reminiscent of the CDC 6000 architecture of the early 1960s. The memory management system resembles the Burroughs 5500 of the same era as if micro developments in general are following the same pattern of 20 years ago, except that size and costs are many times smaller.

These are significant departures from the 8-bit microprocessor which commanded the market of the 1970s and whose relatively limited capabilities—in contrast to the above reference—are outlined in Table 4-2. Table 4-3 outlines American manufacturers' models of 4-, 8-, 12-, 16-, and 32-bit microprocessors.

Six companies have disclosed designs of new 32-bit microprocessor chips following the announcement of Intel's iAPX 432, implemented with three chips. Bell Labs disclosed its one-chip 32-bit design. Hewlett-Packard's bit is implemented with more than 450,000 transistors on one chip. National Semiconductor's processor chip, separate from the memory management chip, incorporates more than 60,000 transistors.

Among vendors of the 32-bit microprocessor, Intel is using four of its iAPX 432 chips, though the adder is 16-bit. Motorola applies the 68000 with eight 16-bit data registers, and Zilog markets the Z8000 which has 8-bit registers that can be paired. In this sense, the true 32-bit processors do not yet exist and there are product designers who think that such processors

- are getting too big for many applications and
- require a memory management chip along with
- lots of software to make them run effectively.

The 32-bit microprocessors may also be an end point. A 4-bit chip was first, followed in order by the 8-bit, the 16-bit and now the 32-bit designs. Perhaps we will see 64-bit microprocessors, a possibility partially documented if we look at the mainframe industry which stopped at 32 bits as the architecture most suitable for the widest range of applications.

It is also likely that the 32-bit microprocessor chip will propel some of its producers into the computer software business. There are plans for supplying a complete operating system and a compiler for the Ada language. Such strategy aims to avoid having to sell systems products, as Texas Instruments and National Semiconductor have been doing, choosing instead to generate revenues from the sale of software. Intel will most likely follow this course.

TABLE 4–2

MICROPROCESSOR CAPABILITIES AT THE 8–BIT LEVEL

Intel 8080	*Rockwell 6500*	*Motorola 6800*
– one 8–bit accumulator	– one 8–bit accumulator	– two 8–bit accumulators hence, double precision (16–bit) arithmetic
– six 8–bit scratch registers *save storing intermediate results in memory *provide limited addressing capability *enable access to multiple lists	– no scratch pad	– no scratch registers
– no index register	– two 8–bit index registers	– one 16–bit index register (pseudo index register allows easy access to lists, looping)
– one 16–bit stack pointer	– one 8–bit stack pointer	– one 16–bit stack pointer
– one 16–bit program counter	– one 16–bit program counter	– one 16–bit program counter

TABLE 4–3

4-, 8-, 12-, 16-, AND 32-BIT MICROPROCESSORS

4–bit	*8–bit*	*12–bit*	*16–bit*	*32–bit*
Intel 4004	Intel 8008	Intersil IM6100	Intel 8086	Intel
Intel 4040	Intel 8080		Zilog Z8000	Bell Labs
Rockwell PPS–4	Intel 8085		DEC LSI 11	Hewlett-Packard
	Intel 8748		National IMP 16	National Semi-conductors
	Motorola 6800		TI 9900*	Motorola
	Zilog Z80**		Fairchild 9440	Zilog
	Synertek 2		General Instr.	
	Mostek 6502		CP1600	
	Fairchild F8		Motorola 68000	
	RCA 1802			

*The TI 9900 has been the first 16–bit microprocessor in the market.
**The Z80 object code is compatible with the 8080 – but the 8080 is a subset of the Z80. So, the Z80 is the first PCM at the microprocessor level.

AN ARSENAL OF OPPORTUNITIES

While we speak of computers, communications, and semiconductors as one, complex, and fairly integrated field, it is correct to state that semiconductor companies did not flourish only on the strength of the computer business. Computers are estimated to account for nearly one-quarter of the IC demand, but micro-based developments have penetrated every walk of life, and this has created a vast arsenal of opportunities for further growth and development in a dynamic and fast-growing industry.

Tables 4-4, 4-5, and 4-6 make this point by reviewing technological progress from 1950 to date, and also projecting some years hence. Tables 4-4 and 4-5 demonstrate how over a third of a century semiconductors have found their way into industrial applications, office and business systems, and communications.

As Table 4-6 shows, though semiconductors begin to infiltrate consumer items ten years after appearing in the numerical control of machine tools, the effect is no less dramatic. If a quarter-century span of their usage (1955-1980) brought robotics, we can expect equally impressive results from the semiconductor's domestication before this decade is over.

Indeed, people with insight in this industry have claimed that LSI and VLSI have progressed so rapidly that they will soon outstrip the user's ability to fully utilize them. We have these powerful tools, now what do we do with them? Potentially enormous markets in personal computers, consumer communications, household and automotive applications will emerge when designers and equipment manufacturers really learn what these markets need.

The spread of LSI from the electronics industry to a broad diversity of fields is based on merits of this technology:

- reduced product size and weight;
- lower power consumption;
- greater reliability;
- higher performance and speed;
- overall product cost savings.

In turn, this broadening assumes a significant role in the turnover to LSI technology. Large-scale integration has acquired a reputation for high

TABLE 4–4

SEMICONDUCTOR-BASED DEVELOPMENTS IN INDUSTRIAL CAPITAL GOODS

Developments in Electronics		*Factory Floor Impact*	*Process Change*	*Product Impact*
Late 1940s	Birth of Transistor			
Mid 1950s	Commercialization of Transistor	First Generation of Numerical Control (NC) Machine Tools (Vacuum Tubes)		
Late 1950s	Early Integrated Circuitry (IC)	Second Generation of NC–Transistors		
Early 1960s		Early Experimentation with Industrial Robots (USA)	Continuous Casting (Steel)	
Mid 1960s	IC Production	Third Generation of NC–IC		
Late 1960s	LSI Development	Fourth Generation of NC–Minicomputers		
Early 1970s	Microprocessor Development		Fully automatic Transistor Production	Automatic Pattern Knitting Machine
Mid 1970s	One–chip Microprocessor	Fifth Generation of NC–Mainframe Microcomputer Controlled Robots	Microcomputer based Continuous Casting	Microcomputer Controlled Sewing Machine (USA)
Late 1970s/ Early 1980s	VLSI Development		Power LSI Incorporated Motors	LSI in the Auto Industry
Mid 1980s	Pre-Josephson Technology		Fully automatic IC production systems	Microprocessor Controlled Vehicles

TABLE 4–5

SEMICONDUCTOR IMPACT IN OFFICE SYSTEMS AND COMMUNICATIONS

Time Frame	*Offices*	*Merchandizing*	*Technology for Communications*
Early to Mid 1950s			Electronic Switch Board Development
Mid 1960s	Electronic Facsimile Applications		Introduction of Electronic Switches
Late 1960s	Plain paper copier application	Electronic Cash Register Development	
Early 1970s	– Electronic Calculators –		
Mid 1970s	– Widening LSI Applications –		
	Word Processor	Point of Sales (POS) Equipment	Transaction Telephone
Late 1970	– Electronic Translators – Intelligent Copiers		Digital Exchange System Computer Based PBX Viewdata in England
Early 1980s	Design for Office Automation		
Mid 1980s	– Third Generation Online Systems –		
	Widening Applications of Office Automation	Online devices to Computer Resources	Wideband System for Offices and Homes
	– Decision Support Systems –		

TABLE 4–6

SEMICONDUCTOR BASED DEVELOPMENTS FOR CONSUMER ITEMS

Time Frame	*Passenger Cars*	*Precision Machinery*	*Consumer Electronics*	*Communication Devices*	*Personal Computers*
Mid 1960s	Regulator Development	Electronic Cameras			
Late 1960s	Electronic Automatic Transmission	Quartz Watches (Analog)			
Early 1970s	Anti-Skid Equipment				Microprocessor Based Calculators
Mid 1970s	Electronic Ignition	Quartz Watches (Digital)	LSI Controlled fully automatic Washing Machines		Hobby Computers
Late 1970s			Microprocessor Controlled Air-conditioners and Ranges	Videotex: Broadcasting and Interactive	
Early 1980s		Autofocussing Cameras	Application of Environmental Equipment	PCM Audio Equipment	Home Computers
Mid 1980s		Solid state Color Video Camera	Microprocessor control of most appliances	– Home Information Systems –	

quality and reliability backed by advanced computer aided design (CAD) systems, whose applications we will detail in Part Three.

Each wave of semiconductor products gives us new products, and new electronic devices using the semiconductor products. Granted, such products launched in the market have both new capabilities and limitations, but the often overlooked point is that such limitations have provided impetus for technology's next jump.

The replacement of the multilayer printed circuit by a *ceramic support* with circuit connections of very high density is a precise reference. The new industrial ceramics, developed over the past three decades, use purified chemicals found in clay, particularly alumina oxide. Alumina ceramics are almost as hard as diamonds; they provide excellent electrical insulation and offer high resistance to humidity and heat. These qualities make them useful as electronic insulators, cutting tools, bearings, nozzles, and chemical pumps, and now for semiconductor chips.

The ceramic package supports the chip structurally and provides hermetically sealed protection against moisture, heat, and other environmental hazards. Gold is another highly valuable product whose contribution to semiconductors is uncontested. Industry estimates suggested that the amount of gold used in the manufacture of electronic components in 1980 was just over 80 tons.

What is gold used for in microelectronics? Its resistance to corrosion and its high conductivity (its specific electrical resistivity is only 2.42 microhms per cubic centimeter) make it suitable for use in connectors, printed circuits, semiconductors, relays and switches. The familiar image of a microprocessor chip lying at the center of its packaging shows it surrounded by minute squares of gold. Fine gold wires run from the chip itself to gold pads which link the inner workings of the chip with the outside world. The entire microelectronics industry depends on gold for this infallible link. In fact, connection is the chief use of gold in electronic circuitry, which is why suppliers and buyers have searched hard for a replacement to shield the industry from gold's unsettling price fluctuations.

Figure 4-5 gives an example of a copper/gold spiral circuit, part of an ultra broadband microwave antenna for highly accurate radio direction-finding systems. Its diameter is four inches (roughly ten cm).

Considering the industry as a whole, the oldest and most obvious technique used has been gold plating. Spot plating, strip plating, and reducing the thickness of the gold layer have all been tried as ways of reducing the gold content while retaining its properties. There have also been attempts to dilute the amount of gold used by incorporating it in

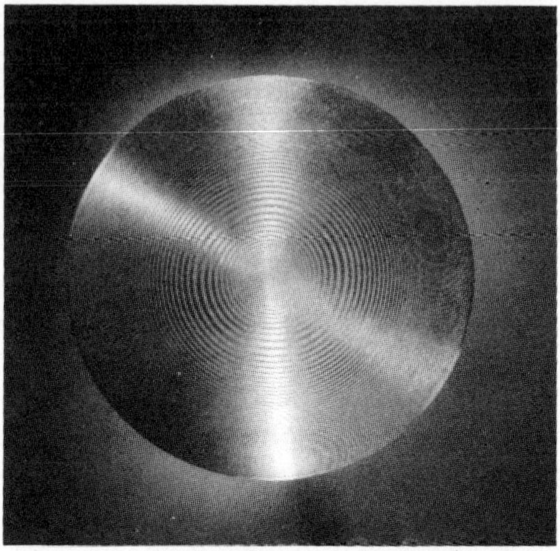

FIGURE 4–5 **Example of a copper/gold spiral circuit from a broadband microwave antenna.**

alloys with palladium or platinum, or by using non-gold alloys between tin, lead, and palladium. While such latter alternatives work reasonably well for ordinary commercial products, other materials than gold are simply not reliable enough nor do they last as long. Only gold gives a guarantee of repeatability in semiconductor products, and though most suppliers are experimenting with new alloys with a lower gold content or with copper and nickel, for critical applications—often defense work—gold is specified and demanded.

THE USER'S SIDE

Whenever we study a given product, and most particularly consider the market potential of this product, we should always consider the user's side. Microprocessors are employed to perform a flexible range of tasks; therefore, this range of capabilities must be carefully considered and established.

In matters of choice, the three top considerations are:

1. Software development tools,
2. Software development tools, and
3. Software development tools.

For example, we create economy of mass if we apply the same process to several applications fields, but we also increase overhead as the different functions have to be interfaced through software or microcode.

The next issue is hardware development tools. In-circuit emulation (ICE) provides an extension of the microprocessor into such tools. Even so, from an end-product designer's standpoint, the fundamental need is to thoroughly evaluate the software and language capabilities of the microprocessor to be chosen. We are going to pay over and over again for inefficiency—if such inefficiency exists. This fact has led many users to benchmark the microprocessor's compilers prior to selection, or to even write one on their own. It is not surprising that firmware costs contrasted with hardware costs have reached a 10 to 1 ratio in recent projects.

We have been speaking of end products. Which are they most likely to be? It is projected that products to be supported by microprocessors up to 1985 will largely fall into nine categories:

1. *Communications.* This is a major (and most likely *the* major) market for semiconductors. The business opportunity which is projected, however, will not be limited to physical goods but will also stimulate the need for new expertise in trained scientists and other professional personnel.

2. *Automotive.* To bring about cheaper transmissions to eliminate hydraulics, to decrease power consumption, and so on.

3. *Home Appliances.* To decrease energy costs by controlling power consumption during the day and making appliances more efficient.

4. *Home Entertainment.* To reduce prices and vastly increase applications perspectives.

5. *Computer-Aided Instruction.* We have reached a point where the computer-based contact hour costs less than the teacher's time. Along with uniform quality of education and better pupil motivation through computer graphics, this should open new vistas in CAI.

6. *Office Automation.* The objective is to increase office productivity and streamline operations.

7. *Factory Automation.* Through robotics we can improve blue collar productivity and improve product quality.

8. *Decision Support.* The goal is to improve productivity by enabling managers to interactively access a distributed database, and obtain a more effective presentation with the inclusion of color and graphics.

9. *Weapons Systems and Space Applications.* The Pentagon will be a frequent consumer of the next generation of semiconductors and systems technology, the more recent case being that of VHSI circuitry from which will be made machines of the mid-and-late 1980s.

Weapons of tomorrow will rely on sophisticated algorithms to choose targets and aim for the most vulnerable spots. For instance, the Wasp anti-armor missile being developed for the U.S. Air Force will incorporate densely packaged electronic components and new low-cost, compact signal processors. Its automatic target selection will free pilots from time-consuming target detection tasks, thereby increasing weapon delivery rates. Also, the *fire-and-forget* capability reduces the need for close approaches to the target, thereby decreasing pilot exposure to enemy defenses.

In the industrial world, an estimated 750,000 business-people are currently using microcomputers. Their purchases were often made in "hobby" shops, and frequently with their own funds. As a result, many businesspersons are learning to tackle computing problems by themselves by adapting desktop microcomputers to their own requirements, using packaged software without looking down at it as do many information scientists.

To curb the growth of clerical labor, semiconductors now propel the concept of office automation. The market is widely considered to be potentially huge, and does not necessarily refer to the sale or use of products offering only one function, such as word processing or telecommunications. What it does refer to are efforts by suppliers to build and sell multifunction integrated systems:

- PBX (Private Branch Exchange)
- Videotex
- Facsimile
- Small business systems computers

- Personal computers
- Word processing
- Data terminals
- Data storage devices
- Copiers
- Microforms, and above all
- Knowhow, and
- A good timing plan for implementation.

Timing is a big factor in the upcoming challenge for office automation. Another critical question is which companies in the vendor pack starting this race will cross the finish line.

5 An Information Policy

INTRODUCTION

TECHNOLOGY KNOWS no frontiers and can be friend or foe depending on our attitudes. To be competitive as a person, a company or a nation, we must feed our opportunities and starve our problems. Is this what we are doing? How keen are we in meeting approaching challenges? Trouble can be predicted; we have the means for projecting tomorrow's problems and opportunities. Do we take advantage of them?

The proliferation of microprocessor applications is not necessarily an evidence that we know what we do. There is an increasing need for a long-term information policy and for a plan to help in its implementation so as to sustain continuous market growth and product research in the international arena.

Such questions become increasingly urgent as American information systems companies see their customer-base abroad eroded through aggressive marketing by competitors, particularly the Japanese. Yet, we all know that semiconductors, microprocessors, databases, computers and communications are an indispensable part of business activities in all branches of industry—financial, merchandising, manufacturing—and that falling behind will have severe economic and social repercussions.

Even in home information systems, the microprocessor has long been more than a fad, though it still has far to go until it is common as radio and television. By that time, home computers will have changed considerably from their present roles. As a reviewer of my recent book on Interactive Videotex suggested, the home computer "will most likely be an integral part of domestic operations, automatically performing financial and social functions for the residents: As new functions are created and subsumed by the resident computer, life without its automated support may become difficult or even untenable. . . "

In Europe, as in America, billions of dollars are poured into ailing industries of yesterday while much more effort needs to go into propelling *compunications* (computerized communications)–the industry of the future. To many governments this is not a self-evident truth. In Europe, the Common Market Executive has still to devise a coherent information technology plan; each Government in the Community mainly buys its country's own compunications products, inducing several state-run organizations to the same. Makeshift solutions abound, such as the EEC Commission recommendation that each country open up ten percent of its compunications market to other member countries. Is this a policy for survival or an assurance for slow death?

Compared to measures adopted by the Japanese government, federal policies in the United States are not insuring a much better score. American computer companies have about eighty percent of the European computer market, but the Japanese are challenging both in Europe and the United States. Governments should surely know that the high degree of advanced technology involved and the many fronts to be faced at the same time by industry call for huge amounts of funds to be raised and properly allocated, and for a determined effort to capture a major share of the world market so as to feed a polyvalent industry.

To establish a viable base, we must build a knowledge-intense strategic plan. This is not accomplished by indecision nor by parties financed by trade unions, protecting crafts that became uncompetitive twenty years ago, or by parties whose loyalty is bound to great manufacturing companies whose businesses should be shipped to third world countries or radically revamped.

PREPARING FOR THE KNOWLEDGE REVOLUTION

Not only companies but entire nations will find themselves exposed to rough economical weather in this decade. Germany, until recently one of the foremost industrial states, faces a monumental task in attempting to reshape an economy concentrated in traditional, mature industries such as chemicals, automobiles, and mechanical and electrical machinery. This is one of many examples of prevailing conditions in England, France, Italy, Switzerland, and even the United States.

As with many other industrial nations, Germany does not have firm footholds in today's high-growth, high-technology industries, from electronics to biochemicals. Therefore, demand for Germany's prime exports is declining; there is increasing competition from Japan at the high-technology end, and from the developing countries at the low end.

The resulting exposure of German industry to increasingly severe business cycles is a matter of key concern to the country itself and to the other industrial nations.

The right preparation for the knowledge revolution starts at the education sector and calls for foresight, a firm program, and capital investments. Today, a state of the art computer science department costs $60,000 per researcher to equip, not including building and land. Understandably, companies working in the fringes of technology must have better facilities.

Not only a lack of strategic orientation but also the absence of necessary impressive increases in capital investment required to manufacture new technologies is limiting the number of countries and companies that can participate to the growth of technology-intense industry. We are going to see a trend in this decade reversing past capabilities in starting from scratch; we simply cannot initiate a new VLSI system as easily as we could work with a comparable technology in the mid-1970s, and the same is true for office automation gear robotics.

Yet, we must learn to live with the technology- and knowledge-intense environment toward which we are moving. Peter Drucker predicted in 1968 that by the mid-1980s one-half of the United States GNP would be dedicated to the production, distribution, and consumption of knowledge, and it has happened. The United States is running about forty percent of its workforce on this basis. This is a knowledge industry; a driving force in keeping the computer and the semiconductor business thriving is to promote the "knowledge worker." We are just beginning to enter the era where we are making significant tools for the knowledge worker, such as terminals through which he or she can look at several different aspects simultaneously, using the system to reach decisions, rather than just entering and receiving information.

Technology is a double-edged sword. It relieves humans of manual labor but also obliges us to continue to evolve and to update skills so as to avoid obsolescence; it propels companies toward broader business horizons, but also undermines their established bases, factories and sales networks till they crumble. If humans, industries, and nations are not prepared, the consequences will be grave; technology will be badly utilized, competitiveness will be lost, and costs will not have a corresponding benefit.

The industrial prospects for rich countries in preparing for the "Knowledge Revolution" is that large, trade unionized companies and brown-power industries (steel, automobiles, textiles, chemicals and rubber) should be moving out of the mainstream of their manufacturing capability to substitute robotics fabrication and knowledge-intense tasks. We must appreciate the fact that in all developed countries there is under way:

1. A sharp shift to skilled jobs requiring *higher capital investment* in new growth businesses.
2. A fast-growing need to *manage the productivity* of basic resources: knowledge, time, capital, and key physical assets, in that order.
3. An evolving fact of life that capital investment has become *inseparable* from the need for more *knowledge work*.
4. A not yet conscious realization that the productivity of people requires *lifelong, continuous learning*.
5. A basic, but not appreciated, reality that *knowledge* has to be *applied to all resources*: time, capital, key physical elements, and knowledge.
6. The realization that all this has to be done within a *properly projected* and well-coordinated *far-reaching plan*; day-to-day, short-lived solutions are of no avail.

We cannot match the longer-range vision of the Japanese through piecemeal, uncoordinated programs. In moving toward new, largely unknown fields of endeavor, such as compunications, there will be accidents—but accidents help those who are prepared. We have to be risk-takers, be willing to make mistakes, recognize them, and learn from them. We cannot stand still behind ill-fated protectionist barriers unless we wish to be overtaken by burgeoning reality.

AN INNOVATIVE TECHNOLOGY

Failures are basically the result of an absence of goals; if we don't know what we want to happen, we will be unable to utilize instruments of policy to work for an acceptable outcome. However, we do know that we cannot stand still while others erode our markets and take away our opportunities.

Here are some facts concerning growth industries:

- The United States currently owns about 45% of the world's installed information systems, compared with ten percent for Japan.

- Japanese computer companies control 75% of their home market, giving them 7.5 percent of the world market.
- Japan Incorporated hopes to reach about 20% of the world market by 1985, which some accounts assign a 30% level.
- In 1980, Japanese semiconductor manufacturers captured about 42% of the American 16 KB chips market, helped by a tremendous shortage of chips.

The trouble goes beyond these statistics and the trend which they suggest. Presently, in the United States and to a greater degree in Europe, the information industry is in search of a policy, and since this industry is the pivot point of all other sectors of the economy due to its high degree of expertise, this quite unfavorably affects all other sectors. Who will plan for an ordinary transition to the new environment? An unplanned third industrial revolution could cause much misery and endanger democracy itself.

We have to strip problems inherent to this transition to the core in order to find valid solutions. We must plan for the coming microprocessor revolution and foresee the resulting industrial and social problems, rather than leave them to blind forces. We must make sense from the conflicting elements.

Nobody should try to exclude microprocessor-based technology from products and manufacturing processes in order to preserve jobs. This would merely make products uncompetitive with those from other countries which are advancing correctly. If such an irrational solution were to be adopted, many millions of permanently unemployed would still remain so because their acquired skills would be made obsolete by the cutting edge of technology. That is how and why scores of people become mentally aged, insufficiently flexible to acquire new skills and, in the end, nobody really cares to give them this opportunity for renewal. Along with social and industrial problems, a technologically-retarded country would have far greater difficulties in keeping its unemployed at the standard of living to which they had become accustomed than an efficient, fully-automated economy. Society can now operate only by having information available to all persons. This has positive aspects, because the more we distribute knowledge the more we enrich our own knowledge.

This is so vital to understand that it bears repeating. It is an old principle that information and knowledge bring power. However, information, and most particularly knowledge, have these two special characteristics in contrast to physical assets:

- The more we share them, the more we have.
- If we stop sharing them, they decay and eventually become negative assets.

Personal effort, innovation, and productivity must be appreciated. Also, a combination of the informatization of society, reasonable leadership in developing technologies, lifelong part-time education for all, and a mind open to change can help us overcome the coming crisis, thus establishing ourselves on new and more solid ground.

THE MANAGEMENT OF CHANGE

If we fail to manage change, we will be overrun by coming events, but the management of change has prerequisites. Emphasis must be placed on research and development; training must become a vital part of our system; we must have the courage to abolish the compulsory retirement of anybody not yet senile, to preserve developed stores of knowledge; and we must assure an orderly transition to a leisure society, as work hours are bound to diminish. Nothing short of a well-thought-out plan can solve our present and coming social, cultural, economic, and industrial problems so as to guarantee the survival of our society through its own conscious transformation.

Advancing technology increasingly implies multiple changes in our thinking. Education offers an example. The 1980s will see the passage from collective to individual instruction through interactive microprocessors; the conversion of now-passive into active instruction because of the availability of computer supported media; the implementation of far reaching educational plans on a distributed basis; and the substitution of the school years blocked in early life with lifelong learning.

People-oriented drawbacks can only be overcome with imaginative approaches and people-oriented applications. At the same time, the strength of a nation hinges on its ability to shape sound strategies which target economic winners. Our entire philosophy of life should evolve: we have always thought that development is strictly economic; now we must realize this is erroneous, that development is above all human and sociological, and here is the greatest challenge in the management of change. As

Drucker was to suggest, we are living at a time of turbulence which makes our environment irregular and erratic, but underlying causes can be analyzed, predicted and managed. We must put a lot of thought into how problems are solved: at the beginning we may not even know a problem exists, only that we are confronted with something that calls for order to be made of it. But what *sort* of order?

Social puzzles and their inherent uncertainty are in the origin of turbulence, and we should appreciate that such turbulence is not only a time of hardship but also of great opportunity for those who can understand, accept and exploit the new realities. It is above all a time for leadership: managers can prepare themselves and their organizations for difficult periods through a continual appraisal of all operations under their control. Every product, service and activity needs to be put on trial every few years with questions such as:

- If we were not already in this product line, would we go into it knowing what we know now?
- How can we get out, or at least stop infusing additional resources?
- What are our alternatives? Are we ready for them? If yes, then:
- How can we take advantage of our strengths? How can we feed opportunities and starve our problems?

Managing in turbulent times requires future strategies to anticipate *when* and *where* the greatest changes are likely to occur, and *what* they are likely to be. Great changes will result from the collision between the delusions of decision makers and the advantages a realistic appraisal can offer. There is evidence of positive forces at work today, and just as great resistive forces. For those building a balanced future, the real fear is of damage that can be inflicted by the death throes of the old order unable to understand that turbulent times sweep away obsolete systems, concepts, and values.

The real lesson of the future is that it will be what we make it. Our actions and inactions will be decisive. The choices we reach individually and collectively will provide the ultimate answer to our destiny, and these choices will be that much better if we appreciate that a time of turbulence is a dangerous time because of the temptation to deny reality.

We have to be trained and informed, and our organizations must be lean and muscular, allocating our resources not by inertia and tradition but by opportunities and results. Resources must be concentrated: fragmentation inhibits flexibility. Corporate "weight control" is a fundamental step in difficult times; growth that results only in volume and fails to produce higher, overall productivity is fat—and any volume increase that leads to reduced productivity is both degenerate and precarious.

Furthermore, the time to ask the tough questions, to exercise radical surgery, to restructure and reorient, and to train human capital is not when an institution is in trouble but while it is successful. Success always means an effort of organized abandonment in order to reach new goals. To be successful, we must:

- isolate skill requirements for jobs of the future: knowledgeable people are a basic ingredient to profits;
- identify available skills and those to be developed through training; and
- match skills to new job requirements. A failure to do so lies in the background of many unsuccessful efforts.

When, for instance, we start using terminals in an organization, we should know that everybody will be affected. We have to manage people in this conversion process—there is no alternative to this basic need.

Among other considerations, the selection of trainers is critical to this process. Blue Cross/Blue Shield gave a good example of both a productivity increase through online claim management and of major planning failures involved in the initial changeover. At the beginning of 1980, prior to implementing the online environment, the claims handling operation for the State of Texas alone employed 900 people who largely worked batch. With the online solution, a 200-person reduction came into effect; another 200 jobs dropped by mid-1981. To make these savings feasible, Blue Cross/Blue Shield initiated a one-and-one-half year retraining program whose implementation was by far more complex than any other subsystem of the conversion to an online environment.

Experience in this sort of work was thin. Much was forgotten in the first phase of the conversion, and had to be corrected in the second. The vendor promised to help in a consistent manner, but the management of Blue Cross/Blue Shield claimed, "The manuals you get from the vendor are *not* user-oriented. And you have to rewrite them." There were 18 such manuals with 2,000 pages among them.

Another major task involved the hundreds of people to be retrained in keyboard skills. "Keyboard skills," management said, "keep showing up and you can't train everybody prior to the conversion. Yet, the topmost lesson learned from this experience is the need for plenty of support; don't pinch pennies . . . " Management also underlined the need to provide for contingencies, absenteeism, and time out.

The requirement to teach everyone on a consistent basis was given weight: "Don't teach them in different noncompatible ways. Integrate your approaches and do a very careful evaluation of the personnel under training together with the instructor." The advice emphasized the need to start the training process early enough, so that when Murphy's Law shows up ("Anything that can go wrong, will!") there is time to react. Contingencies must be provided for the unavoidable resistance to change and means of overcoming such situations.

It is necessary:

- to develop timetables of events;
- assign responsibilities;
- get commitments;
- establish feedback channels;
- promote team building;
- eliminate personality conflicts;
- describe (in writing) new positions;
- announce new titles and their responsibilities;
- establish salary grades and ranges;
- and install a production incentive system.

Wholesale training is badly needed (including the management level); higher caliber people are needed and must be recruited; new policies are called for and, with them, a new philosophy: "We are a different company now."

TOWARD AN INFORMATION POLICY

The 1980s are almost certain to be a period of high technological impact and true innovation. Practically every home in the industrial countries already has two devices needed for direct reception and transmission of voice, data, text and graphic information—the telephone and television. Other media such as newsprint will be greatly affected (Figure 5-1).

In the 1980s, the data processing manager will be a technology executive rather than a developer of software and hardware as he was in the 1960s and 1970s. He will have to heal many wounds resulting from the unplanned integration of systems, devices and services which occurred over the decades. With computer systems, we have acquired the bad practice to focus on machinery, as opposed to critically evaluating what technology does for businesses in which we are operating. Now we see some of the results by observing difficulties office automation creates in many central data processing organizations.

Users begin to realize that they may be drawn into "system traps" with quantitative information driving out qualitative information unless they seriously consider requirements and preparatory steps and develop a well-planned environment. Preparation requires a concentration of effort on end-user facilities, natural language access, and assistance in pushing forward the implementation of the most efficient technology. This, in turn, puts a premium on expertise.

The productivity of the knowledge worker should be a key ingredient in assuring that management is able to provide proper answers. In this regard, productivity calls for continuous learning. We must challenge the obvious: each individual should be constantly thinking through what he can do to improve what he is already doing. The key issue to the successful solution of any system has always been the people who will use that system. Today, this is being further magnified.

Furthermore, in some businesses, such as banking and insurance, the DP shop is, in effect, operations. The mismanagement of information, even the simple fact of falling behind technology, negatively affects income and earnings. Improvements can come across the board, from text and data input to decision support systems. In one bank, system upgrade has reduced the rejection of data input from as high as seventeen percent to less than half of one percent. (The equipment is programmed to provide margin calls for customers as well, and can handle hundreds of screens.)

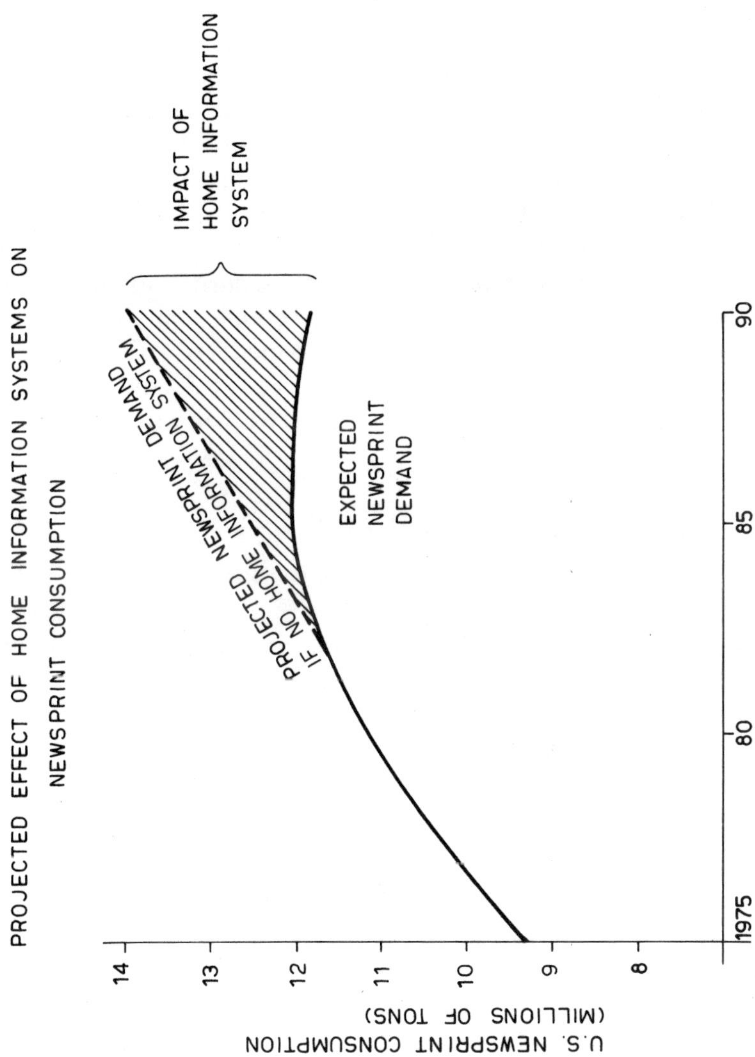

FIGURE 5–1 Projected effect of home information systems on newsprint consumption to 1990.

Yet, what is rarely appreciated is the amount of preparatory work necessary to get results. Hardware is becoming a less significant cost factor in most applications. This has an effect when we talk about the cost of solutions: there are many technical facts which need to be kept in mind. Cost/effectiveness definitely calls for an inventive vision of the future.

A sound policy must coordinate communications and information handling. As interest in information systems becomes more widespread, so will the need for coordination and integration. A host of requirements are imposed by the merging of computers and communications. In the foreground is the broadening user population; information is no more the subject of a scientific elite.

The latter reference underlines availability, security, and protection in gaining access to information resources. An equally important fact is that the information part of the GNP (including media people) represents about one-half the wealth of the nation and exceeds the contribution to national wealth of manufacturing/production. We cannot afford to be blind to these facts.

THE KNOWLEDGE WORKER

Today, the largest part of the United States workforce is composed of white collar workers: 44.8 million, as opposed to 29.5 million blue collar workers. "Knowledge workers" alone—those engaged in work pertaining to information—represent nearly one-half the labor force; they take home fifty-three percent of the nation's total wages; and are involved in forty-five percent of the GNP.

The emerging knowledge society is opening new social and creative horizons, but we must define:

- *Who* are the information workers? We must distinguish between "creative information workers" (who need specialized education) and "routine workers in the information sector."
- *Where* should information workers be educated? The prerequisite is to establish an "information discipline" so as to set goals and then, establish fields of study.
- *What* are the information functions? This calls for a flexible classification open to future developments and applicable to present goals.

- *When* should the skills of information workers be updated? Different levels of expertise in information handling are required at different stages of professional development, and we should clearly establish these stages.
- *Why* should access to information be reserved to authorized persons? We cannot implement security measures unless we answer this query, and we should also define who, when, and why a person is authorized to access the text and databases, and to which degree.

Capable, punctual answers to these questions call for: *a national information policy, an information freedom act,* and information *privacy and protection laws*. A great deal of legislation is needed on copyrights, evesdropping, electronic funds transfers, electronic mail, and a sorting out of conflicting policies and interests. In the United States, the communications industry is regulated, but not the computers industry. But where is the one beginning and the other ending?

In short, we need a set of principles to serve as guidelines, laws to cope with the pervasive, often elusive and penetrating nature of *information*. Our new legal structure should sustain the need for more knowledge work—the future of our society depends on it. In addition, while legislation and physical or logical resources which it regulates are so important, we should not forget that behind any worthwhile endeavor the key element is humanity. Microprocessors or no microprocessors, human beings are still the pivot point.

We must prepare employees with orientation, practice, and training: people fail, not projects. We should create a project environment that allows people opportunities to be successful. *Winning* means going from beginning to end with a goal, on schedule, within budget—and we should orient our people to future opportunities. A human being is human only to the extent to which he or she is not concerned with oneself but, instead, with something or someone other than oneself. This may involve work, a cause, or another person. With commitments, humans find meaning in life.

A person's search for meaning is the basic human motivation, one that keeps him alive and makes being alive have value. Such a person is capable of suffering when he or she sees a reason for it, as witnessed by political revolutions throughout history. A person who has not found meaning is most likely to take his life, even amid plenty. Moreover, we have within ourselves the basic tools for dealing with fears, frustrations and dangers: an inherent desire for reaching out, a sense of humor, and physical and emotional strength beyond that which most people perceive possible.

If we can give purpose to our human capital—a purpose consistent with the new environment in which people think, work, and operate—we can magnify human effort through computer power and systems. The data and text people use is more important than the programs we write.

The late 1970s brought text and word processing, but that is only the tip of the iceberg. In the 1980s, we are going to become involved in graphics, image formation, and new voice capabilities. By the end of this decade, diverse technologies will coalesce, and this will require polyvalent executives able to handle the developing systems. Management both in industrial companies and financial institutions must recognize the need for compunications not so much as an abstract service but more as an in-house resource. This calls for an educational function and a coordinating process that disseminates technology for the benefit of humanity.

PART TWO

Designing, Manufacturing, and Interfacing

6 The Wafer

INTRODUCTION

THE DESIGN of circuits can be enhanced with the aid of computers determining the most space-conserving layout of the circuit elements. Computer-aided approaches help prepare a set of masks, each containing the pattern for a single layer. This is usually done by first generating a multifold enlargement of each layer which is checked, corrected and regenerated until it is perfect.

Precision in the manufacturing process has also become of utmost importance as costs are mounting in setting up a production process. Today, a complete new manufacturing line costs up to $40 million, and semiconductor companies have to be increasingly selective about new products and new markets. Motorola, for instance, is reducing the number of different logic families it can profitably produce, while industry leaders have warned that unless firms are able to improve their profit margins, very few will be able to afford the development and capital equipment costs to produce state-of-the-art VLSI circuits.

"Changing boundaries on the floor plan of a chip is like changing the boundaries of a country. It requires a lot of negotiations and diplomacy" suggested Dick Gruen of Intel. A whole new branch of science: *Reverse Engineering* is being developed by the Russians in their effort to emulate the best Western technology can provide: taking a chip apart through the electronic microscope, then reconstructing it.

The time is long passed when the designer of a microelectronic device would study the behavior of his proposed circuit by building a breadboard prototype from discrete components. Instead, the circuit is represented on CAD equipment by a mathematical model whose characteristics are investigated with the aid of a computer. The model, in turn, must be based on an accurate description of electrical properties of the individual circuit elements.

Computer-aided design has been the leading agent (along with research into the physical properties of materials) in making VLSI possible. As the elements recede ever further from human contact, verifying those properties becomes increasingly difficult. Computer-based approaches help solve this problem: a main advantage of simulation is in that the designer can change a circuit element through software support and can immediately observe the effect of the modification on the behavior of the circuit. Thus, one requirement for continued progress is the need for improved models of circuit elements.

Furthermore, the entire manufacturing process must be projected in all its stages and properly followed step by step with design and manufacturing considerations, and also with quality statistics. We will follow concrete examples in Chapters 11 and 12 when we speak of CAD and its applications.

At this point, we shall study the main phases characterizing the process of fabrication. Figure 6-1 outlines four main phases in the product cycle of a chip, each followed by the proper testing procedures. At the top is the chip on the untested wafer; its relative cost may stand at $.10. Next comes the testing phase, and here yield plays a key role in defining the resulting cost; a single chip may cost $1.00. Next is packaging, again followed by testing. The cumulative cost may be $1.50.

From this point on, the application to which the packaged chip will be applied plays a significant role. Assuming a printed circuit board will be used in a computer assembly, the added value will most likely push the price to $2.50. Sharing the cost of backpanel wiring, cabinet and power supply, the total value will finally rest a little below $3.00.

THE PHOTOMASK

The purpose of the above introductory discussion has been to present in a nutshell the manufacturing and assembly process, and also to underline that when we speak of semiconductor design and fabrication, automated approaches have played a key role in results obtained to date.

The design of circuits will be typically carried out with the aid of computers to determine the most space conserving layout of the circuit elements. This layout is used to prepare a set of photomasks, each containing the pattern of a single layer. Evidently, the work must start with a conception, that of the new circuit.

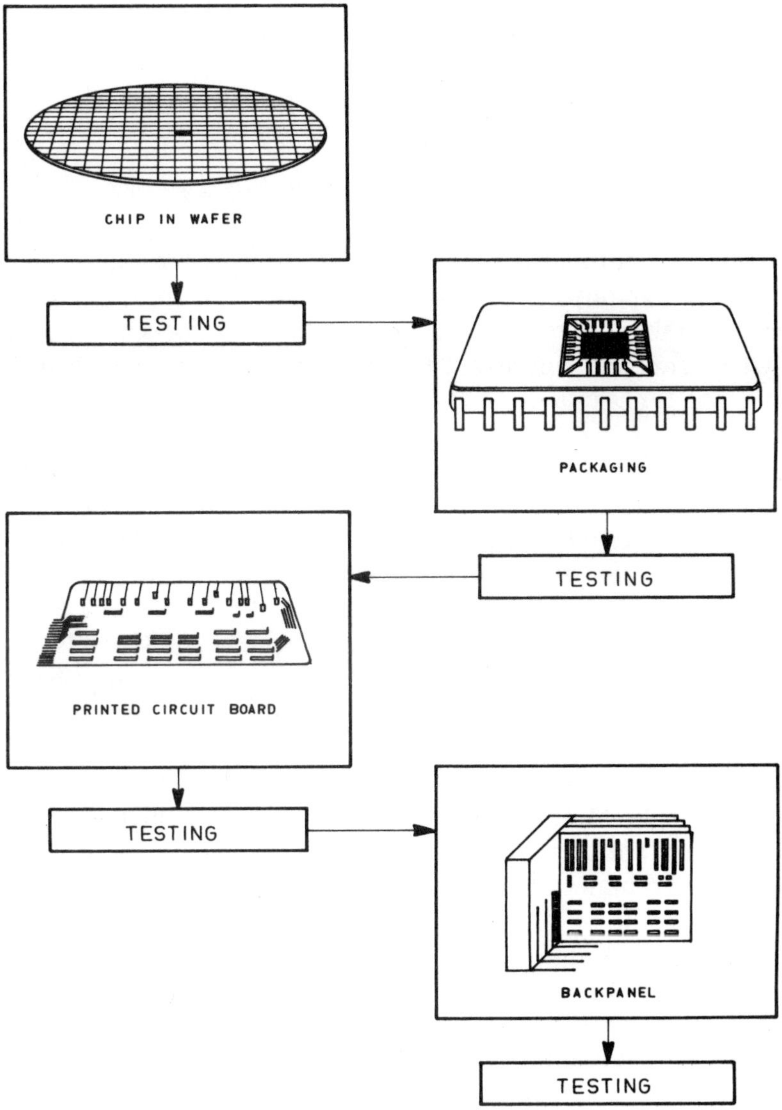

FIGURE 6–1 **Four main phases in product cycle of a chip: starting with the chip in wafer; testing; packaging; testing again; printed circuit board; testing; computer assembly; and final testing.**

The preliminary specification of design elements and fabrication processes will be typically conducted with CAD equipment to provide design and layout of circuits. Two outputs are of key importance:

1. The generation of an optical reticle which will lead to master masks made by the step-and-repeat method, and
2. the pattern generation by electron beam.

Figure 6-2 outlines the manufacturing of LSI. Working copy masks for photolithography are prepared; the isolation, polysilicon, oxide-removal, metal and overcoat masks are the five processes characterizing the first layer. Each will affect the oxydized silicon wafer, respectively creating isolation, gate definition, contacts, interconnection, and bonding pads.

Following the latter processing step, emphasis is placed on probe testing, sectioning, the handling of the individual dies, packaging, the production of a sealed package, and final testing. The complexity of these steps make it evident that a well-planned systematic solution is required; the models must reveal not only how the element works but also how it is to be made. Continued progress in microelectronics depends to a sizeable degree on our ability to predict the properties of a transistor from our knowledge of steps taken in its fabrication. Let us look into this process.

The product to be finally delivered to IC manufacturing is a very thin circular slice of crystal—the wafer. Wafers must be highly polished and extremely flat to produce functional circuits—the chips. However, if we wish to obtain a high density on chips and also to improve end quality, it is to the wafer that we should focus our attention.

Dopant atoms (impurities) are introduced into the wafer through diffusion or ion implantation. Either process modifies the electrical behavior of the crystal in localized areas where the atoms are introduced. Defining the areas of ion implantation (or diffusion) and controlling their relationship to other regions of the wafer are prerequisites for the construction of transistors, diodes and resistors, the components of an integrated circuit.

Many thousands of transistors, diodes, and resistors are built into the wafer. Once this is done, very fine metal lines are deposed on its surface to act as electrical interconnections between components. With such complexity in the basic design, we can easily understand why quality

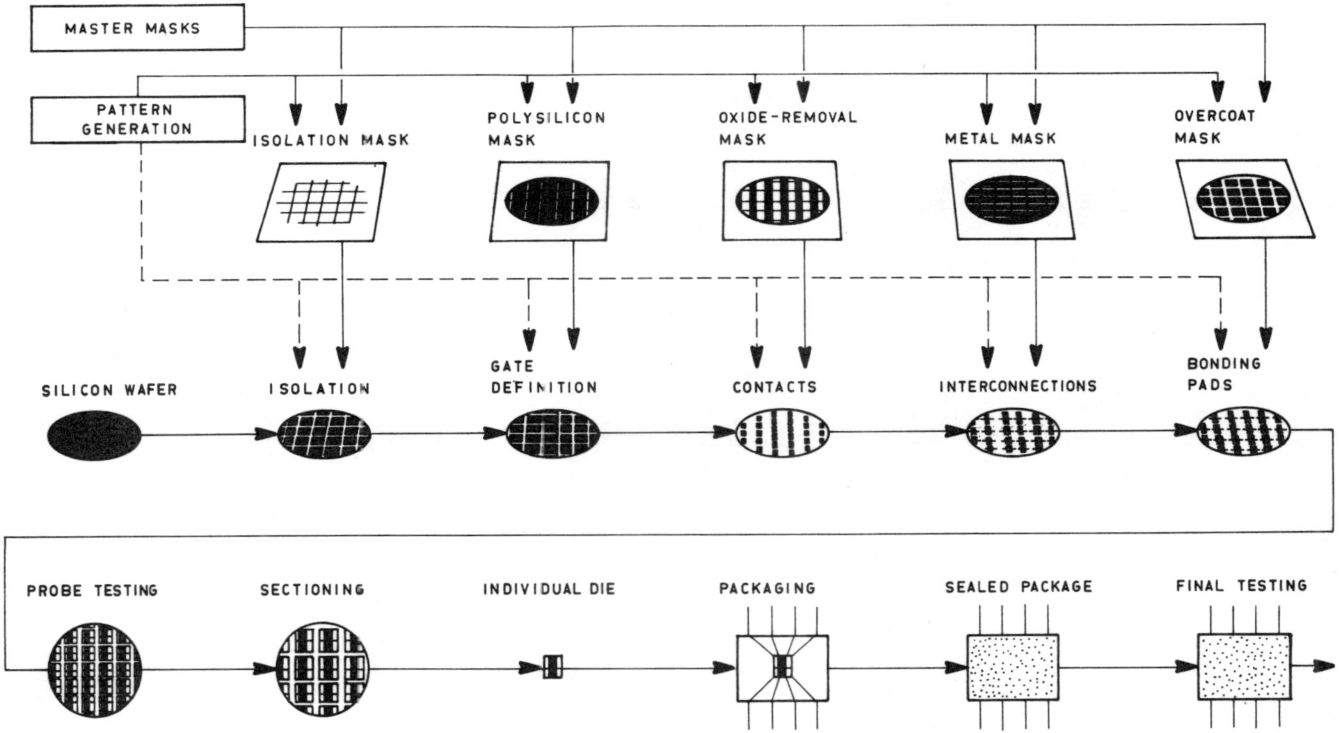

FIGURE 6–2 The making of large-scale integrated circuits, from the isolation mask to final testing of the packaged product.

control is a very important activity, and so is precision: a region misplaced by as little as 0.00005 of an inch can cause a critical failure in the IC.

A wafer diameter will typically vary between four and six inches, and each of the larger circuits on it may be 0.20 to 0.30 square inches in design. This suggests that hundreds of ICs can be manufactured on a single wafer.

However, limits exist, largely depending on the state of the art. Figure 6-3 presents the evolution of the wafer's diameter and size during a 12-year period (1969-1981). Two tendencies can be observed: first, the manufacturable wafer diameter increased during this period from two to six inches and, correspondingly, die size increased by about two-and-one-third inches; secondly, there is always a difference between the maximum possible die size and the economical one. Thus, the photomask is one of the most important technical constraints in making increasingly more complex semiconductors which can support a greater number of functions than the preceeding generation.

The photomask is the catalyst of the whole process. In the manufacturing process, it is positioned against the coated wafer, with ultraviolet light projected through its clear portions. When, following this operation, the wafer is dipped into a chemical solvent, the photoresist is dissolved in those regions that have been exposed. Where there is no photoresist, the glass is etched away and all the remaining photoresist is stripped from the wafer. The wafer is then placed in a furnace with a very high constant temperature containing a gas with a concentration of the desired dopant atoms. The very high temperature causes the atoms to diffuse into the wafer at those locations where there is no glass, a process which demands a significant amount of accuracy.

The culmination of the design phase is a complete set of correct masks. The plates are then delivered to the wafer fabrication facility where they will be used to produce the desired sequence of patterns in a physical structure.

A manufacturing facility typically receives:

- silicon wafers,
- process chemicals, and
- photomasks,

and processing is automated to a significant degree. A typical small facility employing 100 people can manufacture several thousand wafers per

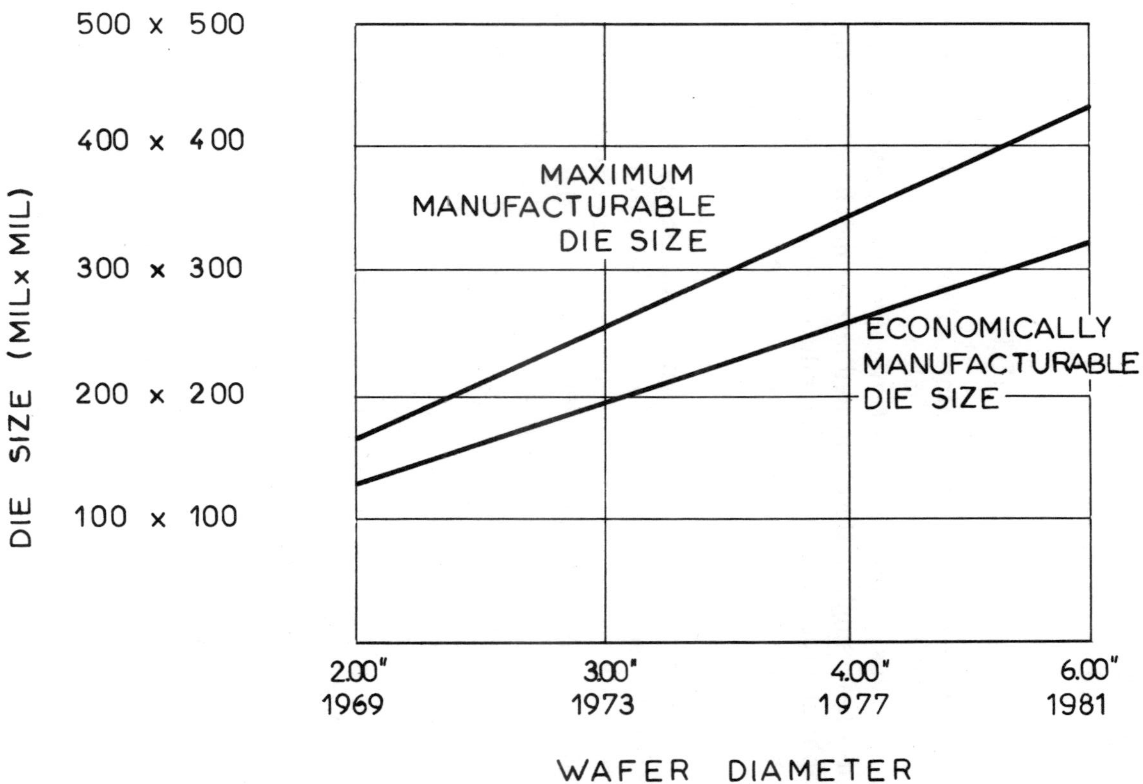

FIGURE 6–3 Evolution of wafer diameter and die size over a twelve-year period (1969–1981). Note the difference between the maximum and manufacturable die size, along with the trend toward larger wafers and dies.

week. Assuming there are 100 working circuits per wafer, such a plant can produce ten million circuits per year. (The inside of a wafer fabrication facility must be extremely clean and orderly; because of the smallness of the structures being manufactured, even the tiniest foreign particles cannot be tolerated.)

PRODUCTION YIELD

Let's look once again at fundamentals. Since circuits on a wafer are very small, many can be fabricated side by side simultaneously on a single plate of silicon. Thus, each photomask (typically a glass plate about five inches square) has a single pattern repeated many times over its surface. A photographically-reduced image is reproduced hundreds of times in a step-and-repeat process to yield a set of final-size master masks from which a large number of working plates are copied.

The technology of photolithography has undergone several changes. As projection lithography has replaced contact lithography, the number of defects has decreased, while the availability of masks of higher quality has helped to steadily reduce the size and cost of microelectronic devices. New methods of lithography are being developed, resulting in a tenfold reduction in the size of individual circuit elements and a hundredfold reduction in circuit area. Gradually, as the cost decreased, electron-beam lithography was introduced into the fabrication of wafers and a new generation of more complex microelectronic circuits has been born.

Electron beam machines direct a stream of electrons to fabricate computer logic chips. One equipment, made by IBM, interconnects circuits on up to 2,000 high density chips per hour. This is the fastest production rate reported for the lithographic electron beam process.

To appreciate the contribution of computer-aided approaches in circuit and wafer design, we should recall that integrated circuits offered improved reliability, lower power consumption and reduced size over earlier electronic components. Man-made approaches would have been prohibitively expensive because it was very difficult to design ICs and to project their manufacturing engineering by such methods. Even though these circuits were quite simple by today's standards (as they contained twenty to thirty transistors), costs were high and their applicability rather limited.

The structure of an integrated circuit is complex both in the topography of its surface and in its internal composition. Each element of such a device has an intricate three-dimensional architecture that must be reproduced exactly in every circuit. The structure is made up of many layers, each a detailed pattern, some layers lying within the silicon wafer while others are stacked on the top.

The dies bearing the finished circuit are first fastened to a metal stamping. Fine wire leads are connected from the bonding pads of the dies to the electrodes of the package, a plastic cover is molded around each die, and the units are separated.

As we will see later, the wafer-fabrication phase ends with an electrical test. Each die on the wafer is probed to determine if it functions correctly. Defective dies are marked with an ink spot to indicate that they should be discarded.

The manufacturing process consists in forming the stated sequence of layers precisely in accordance with the plan of the circuit designer. In so doing, a dual goal must be observed: high reliability and the lowest possible cost per electronic function performed.

Key features of a manufacturing process in microelectronics find their justification in terms of these goals. For instance, the fabrication of many circuits at a time to take advantage of the economies of mass production; the reduction of circuits to the smallest possible size; and the greatest possible simplification of processing technology.

Many developments in the manufacturing of microelectonic circuits aim to guarantee that progress in cost reduction will continue. Virtually every stage of processing—from photolithography to packaging—will be thus affected.

Design and manufacturing engineering must run synchronously to assure a competitive edge. Their coordination has been the driving force behind shrinking costs which decrease by a factor of two every eighteen months or so. In a broader sense, these results have arisen from ingenuity in designing circuits and the adoption of efficient technological processes for producing them. This duality can be seen in the background of the continuing miniaturization of circuit elements and their interconnections, as well as the gradual elimination of defects in various fabrication steps and greater yields.

For more than a decade, the main technological barrier to achieving more functions per circuit has been production yield. More complex circuits result in larger devices and a greater probability of defects, so that a greater percentage of the total number of devices must be scrapped. It is only reasonable that when the cost of defects exceeds the cost saving in subsequent assembly and test operations, the cost per function increases rather than decreases. In this sense a cost/effective design is a compromise between

- high assembly costs incurred at low levels of integration, and
- significant scrapping costs resulting from still unknown factors at high levels of integration.

As a result, technological developments have concentrated primarily on increasing the production yield either by reducing the number of defects or by reducing dimensions.

PRECISION IN FABRICATION

The pure single-crystal silicon wafers that bear circuits are currently three or four inches in diameter. As one of the basic economies in the manufacture of microelectronic circuits is the simultaneous fabrication of hundreds of circuits side by side on a single wafer, the challenge stands at this point.

In order to attain a greater economic scale of mass production, manufacturers are processing as many as 100 wafers in a batch. After a wafer has passed through the fabrication stage it is sectioned into individual dies, or *chips*, each a complete microelectronic circuit. Of course, not all circuits work. Defects in a wafer cannot be avoided, but a single defect can ruin an entire circuit. A scratch only several micrometers in length can break an electrical connection, and since it is both physically and economically impossible to repair defective circuits, they are simply discarded.

After the tests, at the end of the production line, the completed circuit must undergo one last operation—packaging. It must be placed in a protective housing and have connections with its environment. There are many types of packages, but all are much larger and stronger than the silicon dies.

Precision in fabrication is necessary well before the wafer is sectioned to separate the individual chips, usually by simply scribing between the chips and breaking the wafer along the scribe line. Precision is also necessary when good circuits are bonded into packages and are connected to the electrodes leading from the package by fine wires. As the packaged circuit undergoes an exhaustive series of electrical tests to make sure it functions perfectly and will continue to do so for many years, precision is again at a premium.

Neither reliability nor cost/effectiveness can be built into the chip at the end of the line; both, along with functionality, must be projected at the drawing board or they will not exist at all.

Since a higher level of integration is a prerequisite to low cost, our interest in VLSI is understandable for it will be the dominant microelectronic technology of this decade, surpassing old barriers of competent density and circuit speed. As microelectronics is a batch process technology, putting more functions on a chip results in more product per dollar; the result is an accelerating entrance of microelectronics into product fields formerly cost-prohibitive, provided fabrication problems are resolved in an able manner.

The drive for greater component density is stimulating research into submicron techniques to avoid the optical diffraction limits imposed by today's contact photolithography method of circuit patterns. For example, direct writing E-beam uses a computer-controlled scanned electron beam with a wavelength shorter than that of light. Other areas of development include projection, x-ray lithography, dry processing, automated wafer production, and computer-aided modeling. As a result, circuit densities of up to a half-million transistors on a single chip are foreseen, along with new super-speed circuitry. The semiconductor industry has tested D-ECL circuits (dielectrically-isolated emitter coupled logic) with delays of 170 picoseconds. Experimental devices have also shown gate propagation delays of less than 200 picoseconds at extremely low power levels (picojoule). This technology is now being applied to very high speed and low power large-scale integration for space-borne applications. However, the key here, as elsewhere, is precision.

If we wish to obtain the needed precision and optimize processes, the final plans giving the exact positions of various circuit elements should be made with the aid of a computer. Typically, the designer will work at a CAD terminal, placing and moving circuit elements while observing the layout magnified several hundred times on the visual display of his workstation. The information specifying the pattern of each layer of the integrated circuit will be within easy reach with all modifications updating the engineering database being automatically executed by the machine.

The goal of an optimal layout is to achieve desired functions in the smallest possible space. At each stage of this process, including the final one when the entire circuit is completed, the layout is checked by means of detailed computer-drawn plots. Since individual circuit elements can be as small as a few microns, the checking plots must be greatly magnified. Usually, plots are 500 times larger than the real size of the circuit.

Through such approaches, the time required to complete the task of circuit design is greatly shortened while, by automating trivial tasks, project engineers can devote their attention to more imaginative functions. With computer-assisted approaches, time and brainpower vary greatly with the nature of the circuit. The most difficult circuits to design are microprocessors. Other devices, such as static memories with a largely repetitive pattern, can be projected and laid out more quickly, in some cases in only a few months.

Usually, in a CAD system, when the design and layout of a new circuit is complete, the computer memory contains a list of the exact position of every element in the circuit. From that description, the set of plates (photomasks) is prepared, each holding the pattern of a single layer of the circuit. An engineering database is created, assisting the design of the product under study and also available through interactive processes to manufacturing engineering and other specialists.

Computer-aided approaches are instrumental in the reduction of dimensions of basic circuit elements, enabling us to pack more complex circuits into a given area. (Improvements in the resolution of the photoengraving process have also contributed to this end.) Reduction in size of circuit elements not only affects cost but also improves performance. Delays are directly proportional to the dimensions of such elements, so the circuit becomes faster when it becomes smaller. Furthermore, power is reduced within the circuit area.

At this time, no one can say with precision where physical limits lie. The prevailing hypothesis is that the linear dimensions of circuit elements can be reduced to about one-fifth their current size before fundamental limits are encountered, but this has still to be proven.

PROJECTING A MARKET STRATEGY

Many companies have been established to serve the needs of integrated circuit producers. They supply everything—crystal silicon, computer-based design aids, automatic test equipment, and special tooling. In addition, a host of firms specializing in IC production supply their clients with memory chips and microprocessors.

Competition proceeds in regard to functions supported on a chip (see also in Chapter 4 the discussion of the micromainframe), reliability of the devices, and costs. Price reductions are necessary to develop the market, but this may be insufficient, for markets can also be lost.

It was not the companies that were in the forefront of the vacuum tube industry that developed its successor, the transistor. Of the ten leading American producers of vacuum tubes in 1955, only two are among today's top ten United States semiconductor producers, and the majority of these companies were formed after 1955.

The rapid growth of this market has found existing companies too busy expanding their horizons and altering product lines to which they are committed. In an industry whose price decline per unit is an impressive twenty-five percent a year, the motivation for research and development is clearly high—technological advantages must give companies this cost margin if for no other reason than that of survival. In support of this are design strategies which we considered in this chapter, starting with emphasis on the wafer.

As I have repeatedly stated, cost advantages alone, while highly necessary, are not the entire answer. Also of significant importance are reliability, supported functions on a chip, and marketing strategy. Both functionality and reliability of the device are part and parcel of engineering premises, while marketing strategy is closely related to its end usage which in turn brings into perspective sales engineering. These are reasons why a lack of steady effort can have catastrophic results; a year's lag may put a company at a significant disadvantage with its competition. Product, manufacturing and marketing development is a critical part of strategy, and obsolescence is an inescapable fact of life.

In general, two manufacturing strategies are available:

- constant performance, which is a *low cost* strategy, and
- *constant cost*, which is a high performance strategy.

Theoretically, a good approach is to make flexible manufacturing equipment and upgrade it functionally as new technologies become available, but this has practical limits. Changes in chip technology bring new needs for capital investments and intensify the search for new solutions to manufacturing processes. As a result, the leading producers of integrated circuits spend approximately ten percent of their sales income on R&D. The return on such successful investments can be great, but so is the penalty for failure.

7 Quality Assurance

INTRODUCTION

RELIABILITY IS not built into the chip at the testing level; end-use reliability is (or at least *should be*) the concern of the design engineer at the early design phases. What thorough tests at the fabrication level are doing is to assure that the manufactured product *conforms to specifications*.

To be successful in quality assurance, we must have a goal from original design to production and delivery. Why are we building a certain device? What is our goal? Communications is an example: AT&T expects a life cycle for its equipment of at least twenty-five years. This level of dependability is built into the device at the CAD level, and then tested in manufacturing. To achieve this at low cost requires imaginative approaches, highly qualified personnel, and efficient training policies.

When we speak of semiconductor manufacturing, we should be aware that new approaches are necessary for hardware testing so as to overcome the problem of accessibility to high-density electronic components. With LSI (and more so with VLSI), the power of reaching the individual component—gate or flip-flop—is lost. *Controllability* thus becomes a crucial factor. The black box approach can be used for testing by establishing a protocol at the chip level on the basis of input and output variables which can be studied (see following section). However, this means testing 10,000 to 100,000 elements simultaneously.

To be successful, we must have a valid methodology. The most expensive instruments will be useless unless we know how to handle feedback. Figure 7-1 illustrates an emphasis on corrective action; without it, product quality will be lost.

A wafer is probe-tested to determine the good circuits; as we said, defective circuits are marked with ink spots. Individual dies bearing good

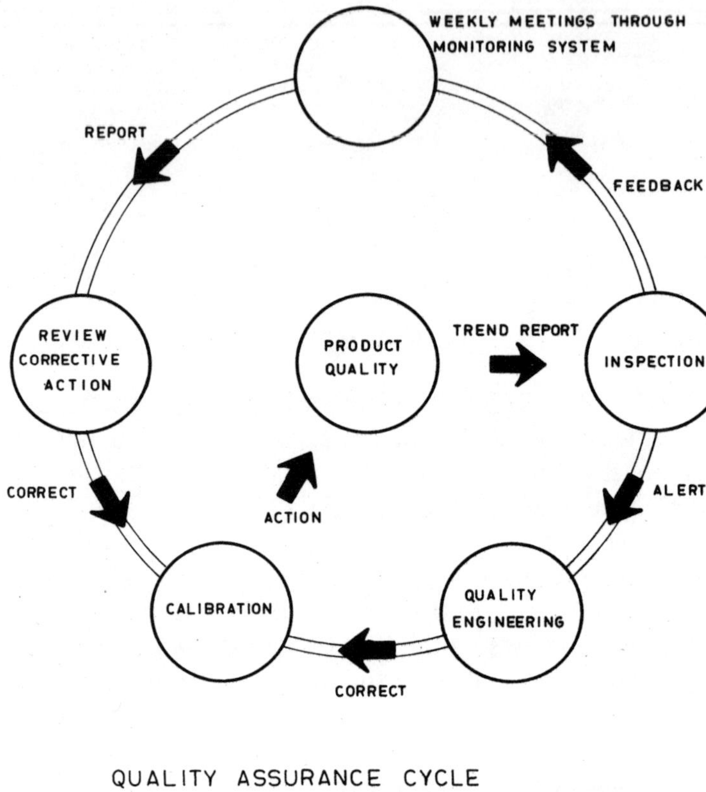

FIGURE 7–1 **A quality assurance cycle exemplifies the methodology necessary to guarantee the observance of product specifications. Outgoing quality can be no better than the applied control action.**

circuits are selected from the sectioned wafer and assembled into packages. Then, a test is performed to ensure that the packaged circuit works properly.

Once circuits are separated by breaking the wafer into dies, each chip must be handled individually. From this point, the cost of any process such as packaging or testing is not shared by hundreds or thousands of circuits. In fact, for integrated circuits, testing costs often dominate the other production costs—and that is why they have to be properly considered even before their inception.

THE BLACK BOX APPROACH

Black box testing should not be confused with simulation as the two methods are rather opposite. With simulation we describe the inner workings of a system: If we consider the three key elements—I, input; S, structure; and O, output—then simulation studies *output* as a function of input and structure. By contrast, a black box analysis guesstimates the structure as a function of input and output. Besides, what a black box is to one person is a known function to another; for instance, the washing machine is a black box to a housewife, but known to its designer and (presumably) to the repairman.

Simulation (a working analogy) both resembles and contradicts trial and error. It contradicts in terms of the systems approach which is taken, but it resembles in the sense of successive approximations to the design of inner functions. As such, it can be comparable to a black box analysis (Figure 7-2).

The approximation of a simulator can be estimated (or verified) through a steady measurement of the simulator's output, and its comparison to data collected from real life. Our hypothesis in relation to a black box is, first of all, that it has a function; that is why we are interested in studying it. Given this, we examine its mechanism (without opening it up) by observing its output.

The two following examples of a simple I/O protocol lead first to the conclusion that the black box is an *inverter*, and secondly suggest a *time series*:

I/O Protocol

I	*O*	
I	O	Inverter
O	I	
I	O	Time Series
O	I	
:	:	
I	I	
O	O	
:	:	
I	O	
O	I	

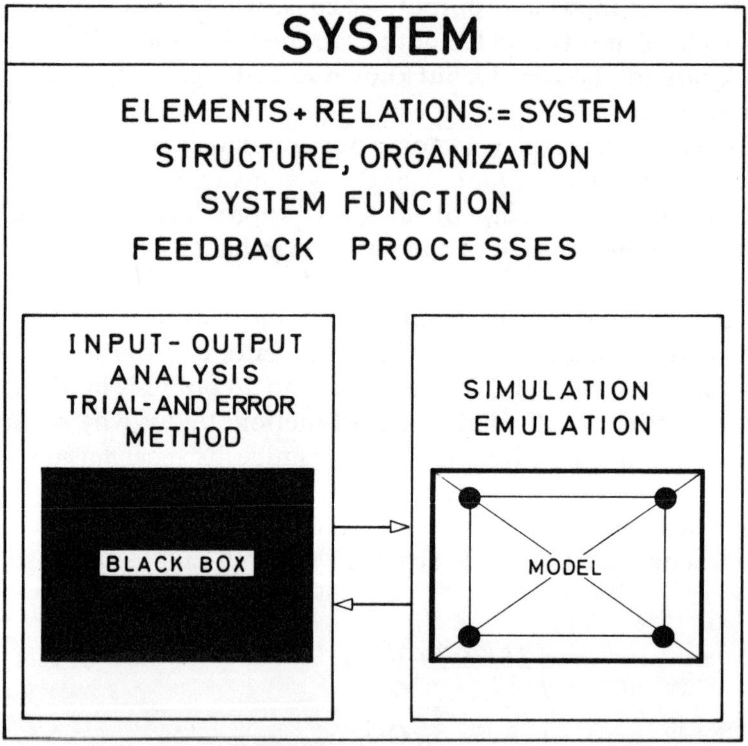

FIGURE 7–2 **Systems are composed of elements and relations; they have structures and provide certain functions, and can be tested either through simulation or the black box approach.**

Of course, the testing problem with VLSI is much more complex than that. The objective is to calculate product quality assurance though we know we are far from ideal testing conditions. Approaches can be combinational or sequential. We:

- give a stimulus (input) of, say, a 2^{10} (1024) order of magnitude,
- study the response (output), and
- try to guess the inner workings through the 2^{10} patterns.

Using a combinational approach, we register the output, compare it to expected (projected) values, create a test database, and accept/reject according to preestablished algorithms. However, we also know that a black box can be indeterminate.

Sequential testing is more complex, because results are determined by the status register. For example, say there are 100 memory elements to perform arithmetic and logical (ALU) operations; thus, we have 2^{100} possible single statusses with which to cope. We must establish the test pattern. Still, such a graph is a partial representation of all possible solutions (Figure 7-3).

Another possibility for test data is to take failure statistics from the ALU of older machines—which correspond to the ALU we project today—and use these data as an approximation of failure statistics for the device under study. We must, however, realize that technology and structural design would have a different impact on the results.

To recapitulate, black box experimentation for testing is an euristic approach which generates a test sequence. Given the complexity of the process,

- the handling of a number of "test vectors" can only be done by computer, not by hand, and
- it requires a test strategy.

The test of a system (and subsystem, device or component) calls first for defining this system; then, formulating a hypothesis; selecting a "typical" portion; administering the experiment; observing and recording quantitative results; subjecting these to a test procedure; and, on the basis of the outcome, deciding if the object quality level is met.

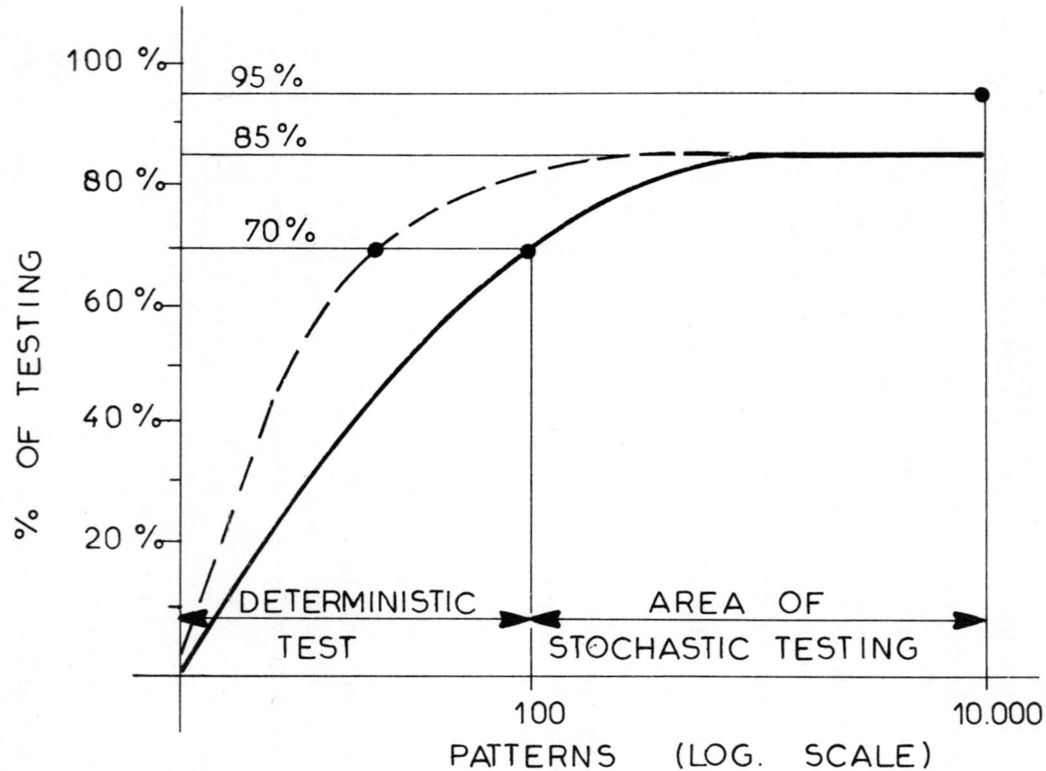

FIGURE 7–3 The test pattern should be established as a representation (even if a partial one) of possible solutions.

The answer obtained from tests poses two questions:

1. Does the design meet functional objectives? (This family of tests concerns design verification.)
2. Does the component part meet specifications? (The aim is fault detection.)

The object is quality assurance, with a significant role played by diagnostics. Euristics enter into the picture in that they constitute an approach to the "discovery" of a problem solution by providing plausible and fallible guesses as to the next best course of action.

QUALITY MEASUREMENTS

Before the advent of LSI, testing of pieces, subassemblies, assemblies, machines, and systems was based on established theories.

- Manufacturing was an assembly operation.
- The smallest piece received the most attention.
- Emphasis was on assembly; all assembly parameters were tested.
- Measurements were made in OQL (outgoing quality level).

However, quality procedures have changed with LSI and VLSI: the smallest item is the chip; circuits have often not been tested when the chip is manufactured; many parameters cannot be measured; quality is a function of process integrity; and new measures to be used must project outgoing quality extrapolation.

This brought the QM (quality measure) standard. A test becomes an "environment" which causes manifestation of:

- a fault (physical defect) and
- a failure (observed manifestation).

The impact of simulation on system testing is demonstrated in Figure 7-4. Two lines are followed: one for software, the other for hardware. The former is much more complex than the latter, and we have the lesser experience. For both, the objective is to allow dealing ahead of time with problems which might be presented.

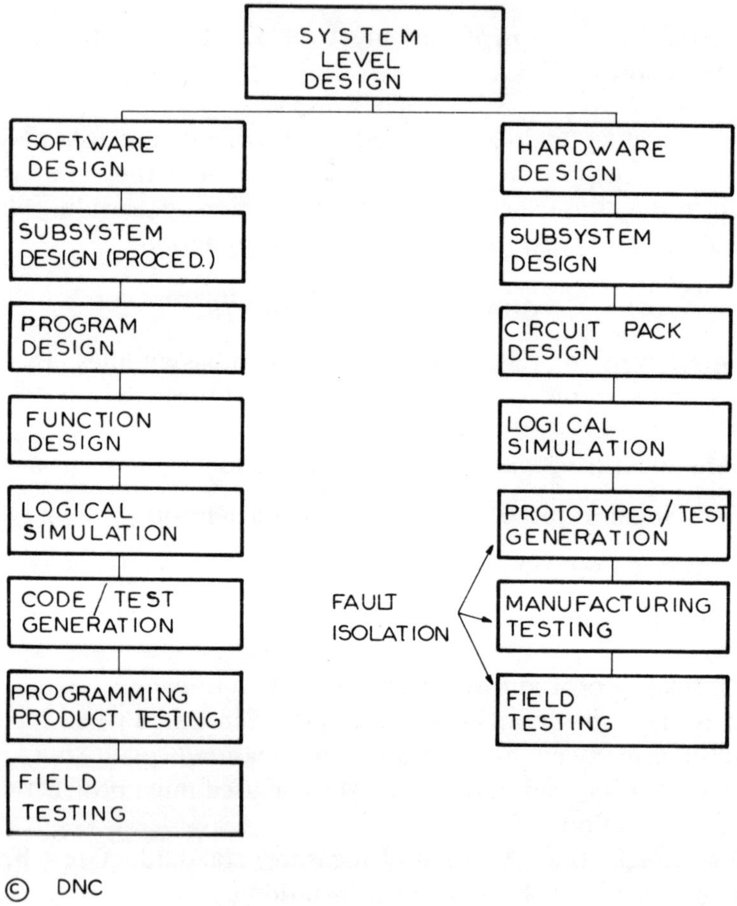

FIGURE 7–4 **A simulation procedure at system level, with discrete paths for hardware and software. The goal is to permit dealing with possible problems before they arise.**

This figure concerns systems testing, but the methodology is just as valid at all levels: subsystems, assemblies, components, simple devices. Computer-aided design is one means which can be effectively used for the suggested experimentation. Through simulation of complex functions, IBM's advanced Engineering Design System (EDS) has speeded the development of more than 100 products. Over thirty large computers support EDS throughout the company.

Electron microscope scanning of newly-designed computer circuits is one of many quality control measures taken prior to production to assure the performance and reliability of products. Generally, the testing

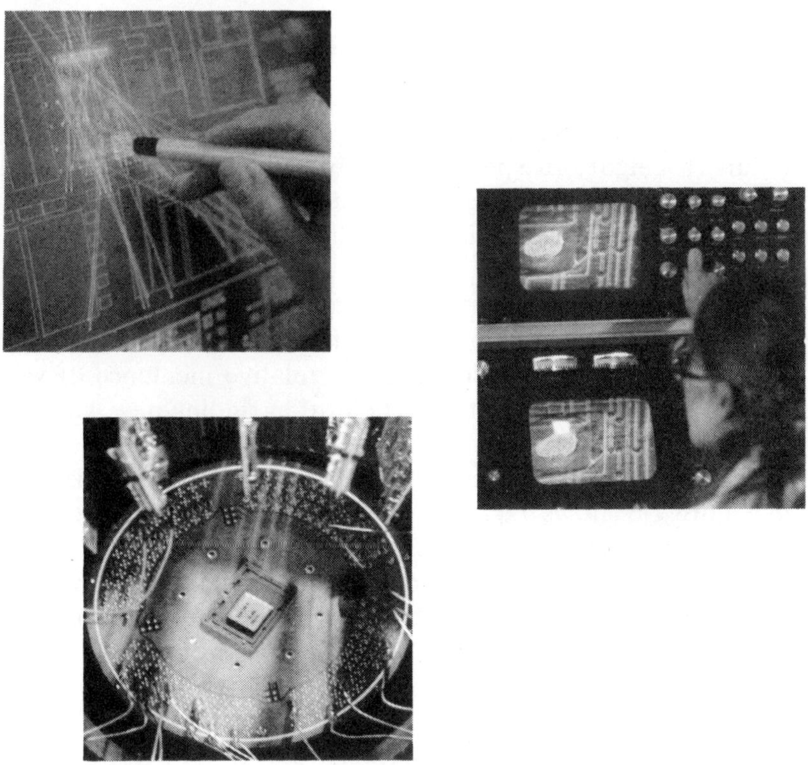

FIGURE 7–5 **Three examples of product testing: (a) simulation of complex circuit functions; (b) electron microscope scanning; (c) experimentation through specially designed equipment.**

of complex functions of logic and memory circuits for future computers is speeded by specially designed equipment that permits quick computer analysis of the circuit.

We have spoken of black box testing through the generation of a stimulus and response mechanism. Speed is at a premium; if we have a ten nsec/test machine to make a 100 percent test procedure of a 10 x 10 array, we will need 2^{100} or 400 trillion years. This dramatizes the fact that with VLSI we cannot exhaust the number of combinations. This methodology is used to:

1. Use sampling,
2. Test Gates
3. Associate an I/O protocol, and
4. Identify faults.

Thus, eighty-five percent coverage means that the test procedure produces failures for eighty-five percent of all modelled faults. The procedure ascertains fault modes, builds a fault model, generates exercises, counts failures, and *justifies* (finds values that will set assigned conditions).

A computer-based testing machine can quickly test each circuit, move to the next one, and perform the quality testing without human intervention. They can also keep accurate statistics on the number of good circuits per wafer, their location and the relative incidence of various types of failures. Such information is helpful in finding new ways to improve the yield of good circuits.

Quality costs have to be ascertained in a properly organized, valid manner. Figure 7-6 shows a quality cost methodology of general applicability in industry, but integrated circuits are a special case. The testing methodology of the latter must respond to technological tendencies without upsetting cost effects. It must answer the prerequisites of system performance:

- increased complexity,
- more efficient algorithms, and
- more accuracy,

and must guarantee test accuracy: speed of operations, real fault coverage, and relationship of test coverage to qualities. Test theories are still weak

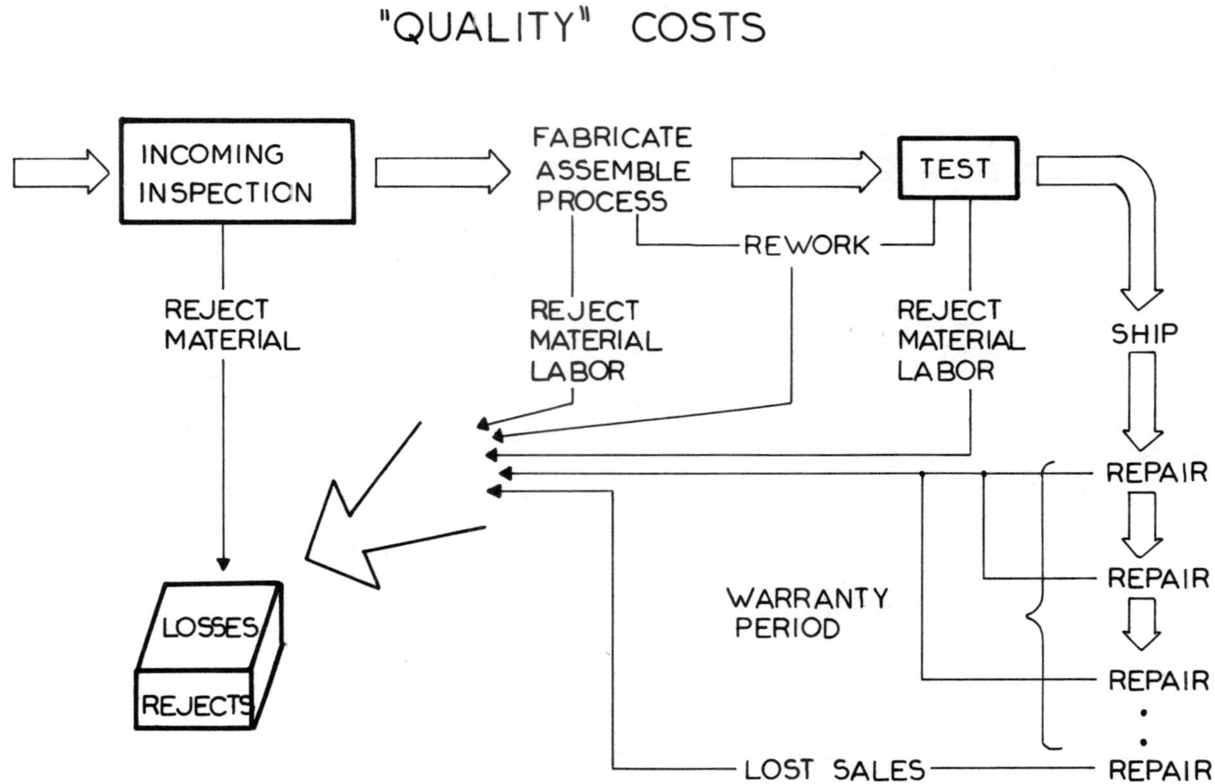

FIGURE 7–6 A quality-cost procedure of general applicability for industry. It is advisable to quantify results step by step.

in this area, though operating characteristic curves help control the consumer's and producer's risk. Furthermore:

- components and systems must be designed for testability, and
- cost considerations must be fully observed.

International competition now focuses on product quality and in this, too, the Japanese seem to have a lead. "Failure rates for Japanese-made chips are so low that we hardly have to test them," said John A. Roth, vice-president of manufacturing for Northern Telecom. He also noted that other manufacturers measure semiconductor reliability by counting the number likely to fail every million hours, but in Japan, the preferred unit of measurement is failure in one billion hours—a clear reflection of high confidence.

A recent study by one Northern Telecom manufacturing plant indicated that from May, 1979, to February, 1980, the failure rate of chips purchased from Japan was .008 percent. Chips from three major United States suppliers failed at rates of 2.1, 4.3, and 10.3 percent, thus failing 260 to 1,200 times more often than Japanese chips.

Secondary tests on chips that passed the first test and had been *burned in* were equally revealing. Only 2.2 of every million Japanese chips were defective. In stark contrast, 171 to 306 of every million United States chips failed. The failure rate for Japanese chips in this case was as much as 1,000 times less than for United States chips.

THE CONSUMER'S RISK

Quality defects will soon become evident in subsequent applications, and the further down the line this occurs, the more costly the restorative operations, and plenty of actual examples exist to support this statement.

One such case occurred in late 1980 and early 1981. It involved a mainframer we will call "X," and one of his semiconductor suppliers we will call "Y." The history of Y's chip problem can be briefly described as follows:

- At procurement time, X's large-scale systems circuit engineering evaluated the component parts; almost all tested good.

- When failures showed up, there was a burn-in of 240 devices for sixty-five hours, and thirteen failed. At this time, vendor approval for Y was revoked.
- The failed chips were sent to Y for analysis. Failure analysis indicated ionic contamination as the cause of failure.
- Y's presentation to X indicated that parts would self-heal after 1600-2000 hours in the mainframe operating environment. (Ionic contamination would be driven to the glass passivation layer and trapped.)
- X engineering decided to purge all field spares.
- Yet, field failure during December to January 1980/1981 continued at a high rate. Some of the failed systems exceeded 1600 operating hours.
- Y knew the ionic contamination problem through its product line. To improve outgoing product quality, the company purged 1,000,000 parts out of forty-four million.
- As field failures continued, X engineering decided to purge all operational units of chips in its product line.

This particular mainframe design uses 405 parts per system which are distributed on thirty-two boards. Twenty-five among them may use Y's products alongwith those of two other semiconductor manufacturers; of these boards, some have forty parts, others only two (seven boards never had Y chips).

Thus, the replacement of an average of twelve boards per mainframe meant about one-half those containing Y chips, and thirty-five percent of those of the machine. (In actual United States installations, a range of nine to fourteen percent is observed). However, plans made by engineering for worldwide installations led to the conclusion that it will take some time to replace and recycle the boards with Y's components. The adopted tactic was to use extra sets of boards as replacements. Technically, this solution is acceptable, but financially, the whole affair was disastrous.

In any type of production there exists consumer risk and a producer risk, respectively known as Type I error, or "a," and Type II error, or "b." (Figure 7-7). Operating characteristics (OC) curves were developed

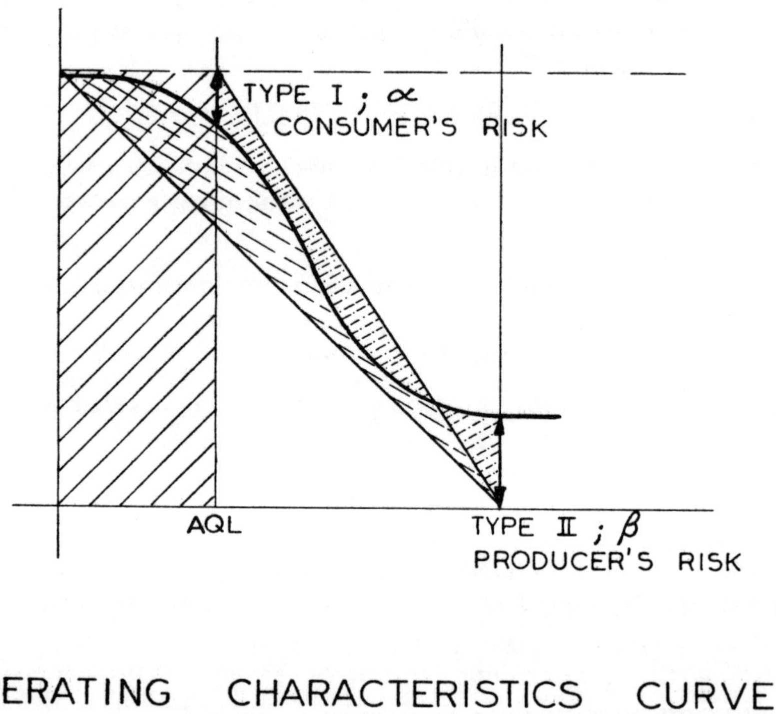

FIGURE 7–7 Operating characteristics curves: producer's risk and consumer's risk.

during the war at Columbia University, in a research project under Professor Uri, as part of the Manhattan Project. They have been in steady use since then.

To avoid falling into the trap of this X/Y case which we considered, it will be wise to do two things. First, institute a tough quality-acceptance procedure by the purchaser which should be computer-based and use all available algorithmic approaches, such as OC curves, t-test, X^2-test, and reliability tools. Second, formulate a solid contract binding the supplier to this procedure, and most particularly including a system of demerits and chargebacks.

In regard to the end user, drift due to faulty semiconductors is always present. The mainframer's design and reliability engineers may assure him that, "No system stress is expected to be created by drift because of this problem. Once these problems are out, this system should be among the most reliable in the field. . . " Nevertheless, the user should be sure to include reliability clauses in his computer contract.

Table 7-1 presents performance data from July to December, 1980, for the computer model in the X/Y case. The data regards only CPU and reflects on total operating hours and Mean Time Between Unit Interruption (MTBUI)—a new measurement which concerns "Unit Interruption" as opposed to "System Interruption." Notice that the number of CPU reporting problems includes both the aforementioned Y failures and other reasons. There was an evident improvement in November after corrective action, followed by a relative drop in December.

In the United States, the factory quite closely recorded all failures in the installed equipment. For every unit, an audit was conducted in which

- defects were reported, and,
- item-by-item, results were brought to the department of origin to analyze faults.

TABLE 7–1

MTBUI (July to December, 1980) relative to CPU Performance

Month	*Jul., Aug., Sept.*	*Oct.*	*Nov.*	*Dec.*
CPU Operating Hours	7.566	6.402	6.381	3.418 hours
MTBUI	378	377	798	570 hours

The number of installations reporting CPU problems within this technical auditing inspection is identified in Table 2. Table 3 contrasts MTBUI for machines with and without the Y chip. Mean time between unit (CPU) interrupt is four times better in the latter case.

TABLE 7–2

DPS 8/20, 8/44 SITES REPORTING CPU PROBLEMS

Third Quarter 1980	5 of 13 total (38.5%)
Fourth Quarter 1980	11 of 17 total (64.7%)
CPU Interruption Data Analysis/Interrupt Summary (34 total):	
Suspect Signetics 663 IC	26
All Other	8

TABLE 7–3

DPS 8/20, 8/44 CPU INTERRUPTION DATA ANALYSIS
PERFORMANCE SUMMARY (17.221 HOURS)

Condition	*MTBUI*
* Current	506 hours
* Less 663	2.153 hours

TESTING VLSI AND SOFTWARE

We have seen for more than a decade falling semiconductor prices per bit of storage and switching gate. As a result, we often fail to appreciate that total cost is composed of manufacturing and test cost—and the more complex the functions per chip become, the more the latter increases.

There are two products related to computers and communications for which this statement is true: VLSI and software. For both, our testing procedures are still rather rudimentary, in need of both qualitative and quantitative improvements.

There exist similarities between VLSI and software. First, complexity increases non-linearly as the number of components increases; second, to guarantee all logical and physical paths, one must test all of them which is a virtual impossibility; third, more than fifty percent of the cost is dedicated to correction. (Testing costs once trailed design and manufacturing costs; then the ratio became 1 to 1; now testing costs *exceed* other costs.)

Testing costs are one reason why, with LSI and VLSI, though unit prices decrease sharply, the cost of a board grows along with the functions it performs. The difficulty in performing quality measurements is particularly troublesome; when a fault cannot be located, the whole board is dropped. At the same time, software costs progressed to the point of exceeding by far the hardware costs.

Current research on the quality aspects of the semiconductor technology reveals that

- design verification and fault simulation for hardware provides a base for software development and testing, and
- there is a good possibility of verifying the impact of faults on maintenance programs.

As discussed throughout this chapter, the use of simulation for fault location involves *detection tests* (mainly for learning purposes), the identification of *symptoms* of different kinds of faults, and the transfer of fault tests to Automatic Test Equipment (ATE). This calls for a sound methodology to help

- calculate fault *signatures*, and
- find the best match between actual fault behavior and a signature.

A *fault signature* indicates a faulty circuit, but for predictive purposes it must correspond entirely to the identified *fault behavior*. Such a signature should mirror the effect of the fault on the circuit's good behavior. This technique was extensively used with SSI, but LSI and VLSI require improvements. An example is the *guided probe*—comparing faulty behavior to good behavior—while assuring that it does not incriminate a whole collection of components due to extensive feedback.

Fault simulation is an alternative method being developed into a new, broad area of activity. It involves:

1. *Parallel simulation* (for instance, test the computer word as a whole).
2. *Deductive simulation* (that is, associated to a fault list). In this case, the "fault list" acts as an *entity*, but in the worst cases complexity is an exponential function.
3. *Concurrent simulation*, acting on the fact that during circuit simulation only a small number of faults are simultaneously active.

The idea is to trade "space" for "speed" and obtain some data compression. The tradeoffs are more storage requirements and the fact that inactive faults are not simulated (though the simulation level can be elevated), while timing faults can be easily and economically simulated.

The deductive method is faster than the parallel method for large circuits. The concurrent method is faster than the deductive one but requires a simulation hierarchy.

8 Engineering Premises

INTRODUCTION

CHAPTER 6 made a reference to the great assistance CAD can give to the design of discrete components, starting with those of the wafer. While a VLSI will always require CAD assistance, the latter is by no means limited to wafer design; an equally relevant activity is that of printed circuit board layout studies.

Printed Circuit Boards (PCB) are named for circuitry which is not connected by wires but by copper-foil lines, or paths photoprinted onto the board. Parallel to the trend toward increasingly greater circuit density is the one for larger boards, fewer layers, higher accuracy, and greater resolution.

Board development is a parallel to the expanding use of integrated circuits which, in a few years, expanded from very expensive yet rather simple designs used in avionics and weapons systems to inexpensive but complicated circuits which have found an excellent market from games and personal computers to large-scale systems of all kinds. The design of a printed circuitry board requires much repetitive work involving:

- component placement and routing,
- the reproduction of the same component in many locations,
- the addition of annotations and dimensioning,
- the design checking and other control activities,
- the production of bills of material,
- updating of the design/database, and
- thorough, complete documentation.

Improvements made in engineering products can be technological, structural, or both. While research in physics has and is making great strides, it is just as true that superimposing structural and technological advances can help better results which we obtain (Figure 8-1). However, not all structural changes are productive; some may lead to erroneous or suboptimal solutions which, at the level of complexity we are speaking of, can only be fleshed out through experimentation.

Interactive terminals allow for experimentation, the immediate visualization of schematics, the production of artwork masters, and the generation of finished drawings, all of which are parts of a valid solution. In this sense, CAD helps solve some of the bottlenecks in the *manufacturing* cycle, automating time-consuming and error-prone tasks, reducing time leads, improving quality and, thereby, having a significant cost impact.

THE PRINTED CIRCUIT BOARD

Printed circuit boards (PCB) range from 1" x 1" to 15" x 20" square. Typically, however, dimensions between 5" x 7" and 10" x 12" are preferred. Such boards may contain one or two chips per square inch of surface, on one or both sides. While two-sided boards are common with chips mounted on one side, multilayered approaches are widely used with computers and communications, systems where the circuitry is complex.

One of the major problems in PCB design, once the schematic and board geometry have been decided, is to place the components of the board in a way that minimizes the total wire length. The designer must take into account a variety of gate and discrete component packaging alternatives, while avoiding physical constraints. Compatibility, physical/logical characteristics and error probability require many iterations, this being both a demanding and time-consuming task when done manually.

The placement of integrated circuits on a board must guarantee a good signal route, stretching all related interconnections to maintain signal continuity. Optimization can be achieved by defining the location of all IC components, the wiring between them for interconnection purposes, the in/out pins, and the test points.

Figure 8-2 demonstrates automatic recognition of design charts for printed circuit boards. These photographs, obtained on a pilot machine, show examples of (a) an original image detected from the image-input unit; (b) the symbol and connective direction extracted by symbol recognition; (c) the line network by image representation; and (d) the final result by combining b and c. Credit for this presentation belongs to Fujitsu.

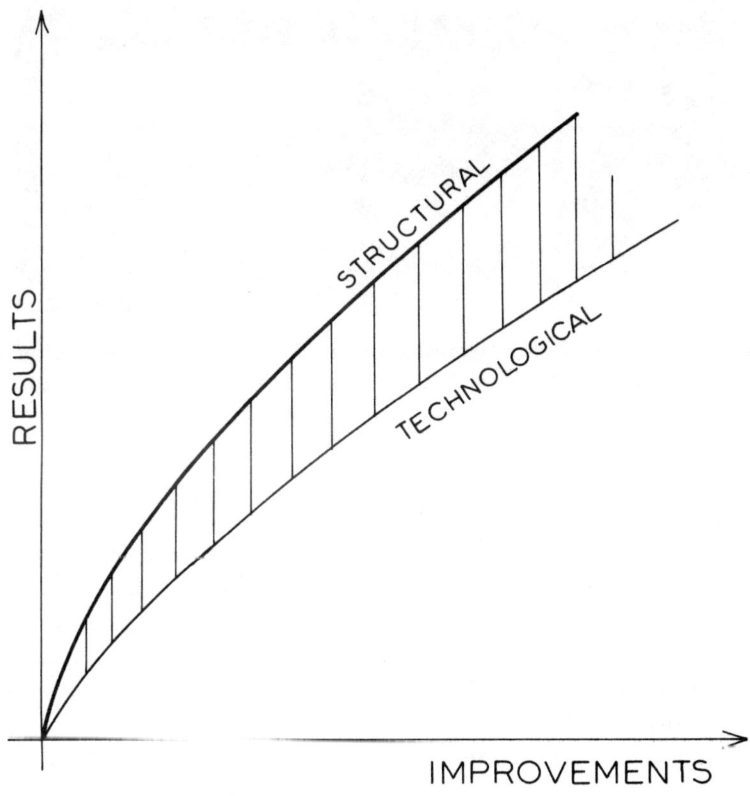

FIGURE 8-1 Improvements made in advanced products so as to obtain better results can be both technological and structural.

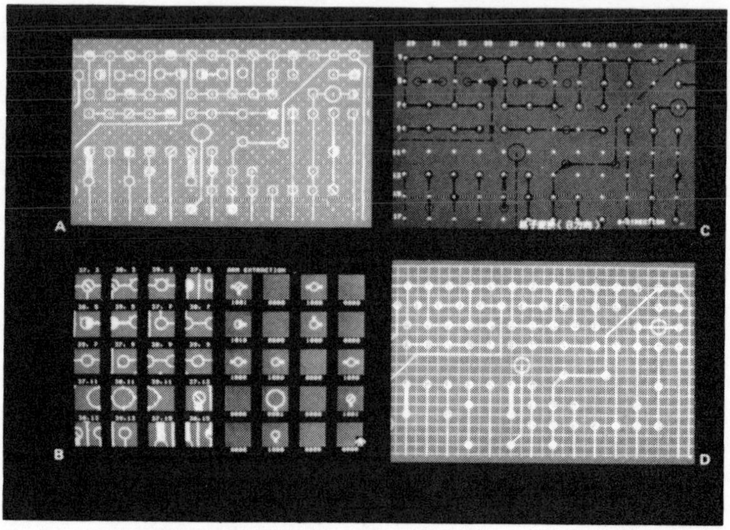

FIGURE 8–2 **Automatic recognition of design charts for PCB: (a) an original image; (b) symbol and connective direction; (c) line network; (d) final result.**

CAD capabilities are instrumental for avoiding repetitious work on PCB and in providing a checking aid for the designer. Automatic comparisons can thus be made between the PCB net list and the schematics to check interconnections. Errors are annotated through software support, and can be interactively corrected. After correction, signal nets are automatically listed and posted to the schematic in a process which assures consistent documentation and a pruned final design.

When the electrical considerations are satisfied, mechanical route quality can be verified through a separate checking process: controlling geometric design rules, comparing the board's physical characteristics to constraints, and fleshing out errors which can then be corrected interactively. A CAD approach can help the designer to automatically extract non-graphical information from the database and produce a variety of textual documents from point to point wire lists to the bill of materials.

Yet, while computer assistance will definitely improve quality, it is not a substitute for the fundamental requirement of setting clear goals. Our first task as designers is to project the software and hardware aspects of the application, and then proceed with system definition (Figure 8-3).

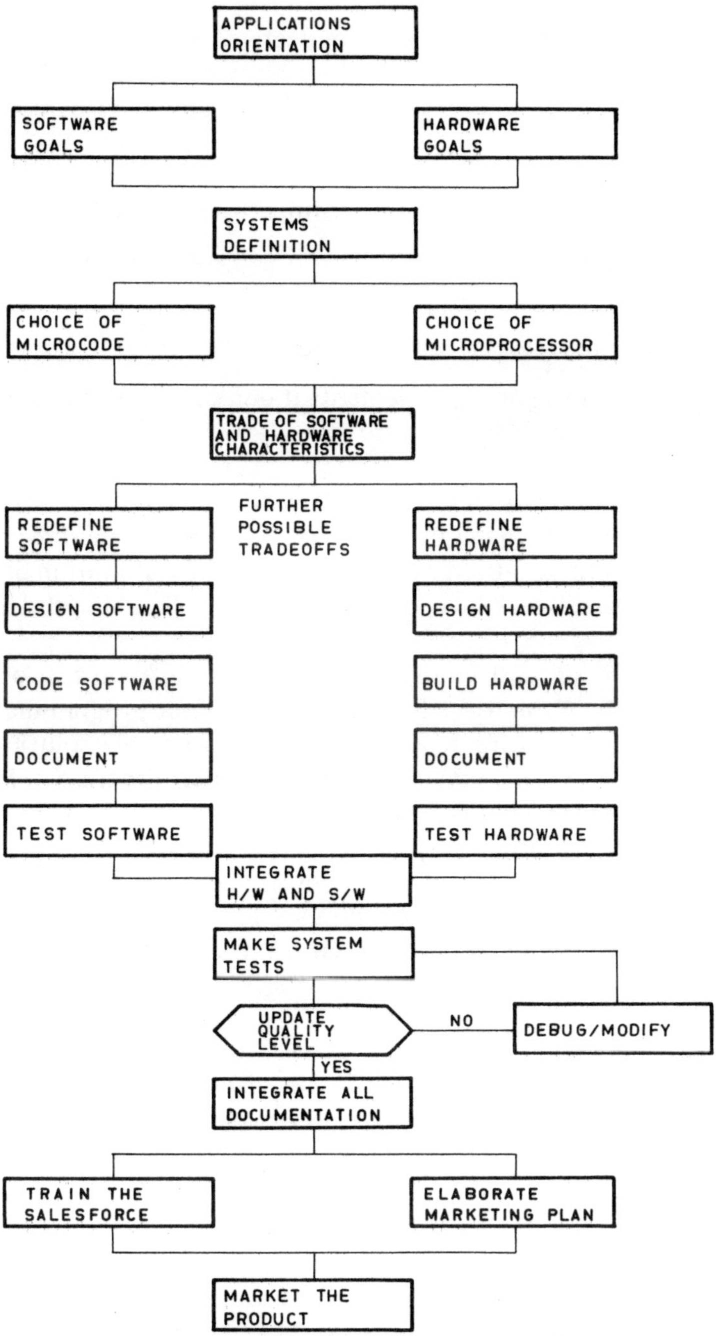

FIGURE 8–3 A procedural flow chart.

Microprocessors may provide innovative approaches to equipment design, but engineering premises call for answers to a number of critical questions, and this should be done at the initial phase of orientation prior to PCB design:

- What functions are to be performed by the PCB?
- Is the projected microprocessor-based solution cost/effective for these functions?
- Is the expected performance sufficient to meet the objectives?
- Can the board and the elements it contains be subjected to specified environmental conditions?

A fundamental design criteria is how to select among commercially available off-the-shelf elements. A major challenge with microprocessors and integrated circuits at large is the tremendous proliferation of custom-made designs—an issue which relates directly to that of printed circuit boards.

The "cure" of custom-made approaches has historical origins. In 1971, work with calculators advanced the idea of the programmable chip. From that came an entire generation of programmable solutions, so in the beginning there were only a few types of microprocessors. However, the need for improvements brought mutations; by 1974, there was a proliferation of LSI circuits, and an expert counted 140 types in 1977.

The differences between custom-made VLSI and standard microprocessors are basically that of economics and flexibility. A rational design calls for a functional structure, but often sophistication complicates rather than simplifies. Furthermore, to a significant degree, circuit costs are dominated not by the cost of the IC but by other system costs such as fans, power supplies and PCBs. Little can be done by way of dramatic cost reductions unless new techniques are employed.

HIGH AND LOW END

To have a factual and documented basis for selection, we first need to know our system's requirements and then to look carefully at what is available in the market, from 4-bit to 32-bit chips. Such choices are bound to be tentative; semiconductor specialists agree there is no end in sight to the improvement of computer technology at the component level. There may be quite a time-lag, however, between the availability of technology and its insertion into equipment.

In Chapter 3 we classified microprocessors according to the BPW criterion, which is always in the background. In Chapter 4 we took a different approach, looking at them from the viewpoint of final use:

1. Low-end (controllers)
2. Intermediate (general purpose)
3. High-end (minicomputer-like)
4. Bit-slice (for emulation).

Characteristics of the low end are: four to eight BPW; binary capability only; minimum of chips; programming ease; small number of instructions; no memory-intense design; no high speed; limited arithmetic; simple interrupt; good I/O usage; and on-chip timers (for realtime processes; this is a key feature).

The intermediate, general purpose microprocessor is basically characterized by: eight to sixteen BPW; larger memory than that of the low end; higher speed; a flexible I/O structure; more sophisticated interrupt features; fairly good software; sound arithmetic and logical functions; and a fairly complete instruction set. There must also be caution in the level of system functions; if these are too audacious, the processor runs the risk of either being unresponsive to the market or being supplanted by cheaper technology, and if too conservative, it cannot be priced in a competitive way.

The last remark is just as valid about the high-end microprocessors. Typically, they feature: sixteen and thirty-two BPW; a full instruction set; high-speed functioning; large memory handling capability; flexible addressing; and the support of rather sophisticated software packages.

Finally, bit-slice microprocessors lead to a line characterized by expandable bit-slice mechanisms (we may have 32-bit microprocessors by 1983/1984 at the high end); a very high speed; microprogrammable capabilities for emulation; a sophisticated microcontrol; and high performance I/O.

Other important considerations in terms of choice are system partitioning and pin limitations. If the entire microcomputer will fit on one chip, then system partitioning presents no problem. Otherwise, we must divide the system into several chips and partition the registers, the arithmetic and logical unit. This introduces chip-to-chip transition delays of approximately 150 to 200 nsec, an issue which computer-aided approaches help optimize.

The transition delay problem can be solved by the pipelining technique, or by chips with a larger number of pins. Pin limitation is therefore a major factor in the design of the control section of the unit. Technology and costs suggest using larger pin packages so as to minimize the chip-to-chip transitions.

Still another fundamental criterion is cost. Further cost reductions call for better techniques to be employed. Microprogramming architecture using RAMs and ROMs represents a means of reducing the design, manufacturing and field service cost of digital processors; it yields a simplified board layout; requires fewer connections, allowing for simplified cabling; and makes feasible a faster system design time.

Quality should evidently be evaluated along with cost. At the wafer level, one parameter for judging quality is the number of defects present on the surface at the end of processing. If in the course of time this number decreases, it is possible to make circuits with increasingly large surfaces, correspondingly complex logical functions and good return. Quality at the PCB level however, calls for more attention to detail; the layout should be more refined, a reason why ways have been searched to solve at the chip level some problems encountered in board assembly. In this sense, a solution has been found to get away from very small elementary logical blocks, so that in the same silicon area it has been possible to progressively collect more elementary functions. Such contributions are significant, for in planning a highly complex logical circuit it is necessary to bear in mind both the functions which are attainable *and* a logical plan which allows for large production volumes able to amortize the project's expenses.

Manufacturers are very much aware of this fact and increasingly focus their design and fabrication capability on mass-produced items. Figure 8-4 comes from Fujitsu (annual report to the stockholders) and includes examples on the current product line: (a) a variety of optical semiconductor devices; (b) semi-custom-made LSI; (c) +5V single power 64-bit MOS random access memory devices.

A trend has been developing away from making circuits on order (those which would totally satisfy the requirements of a particular client)

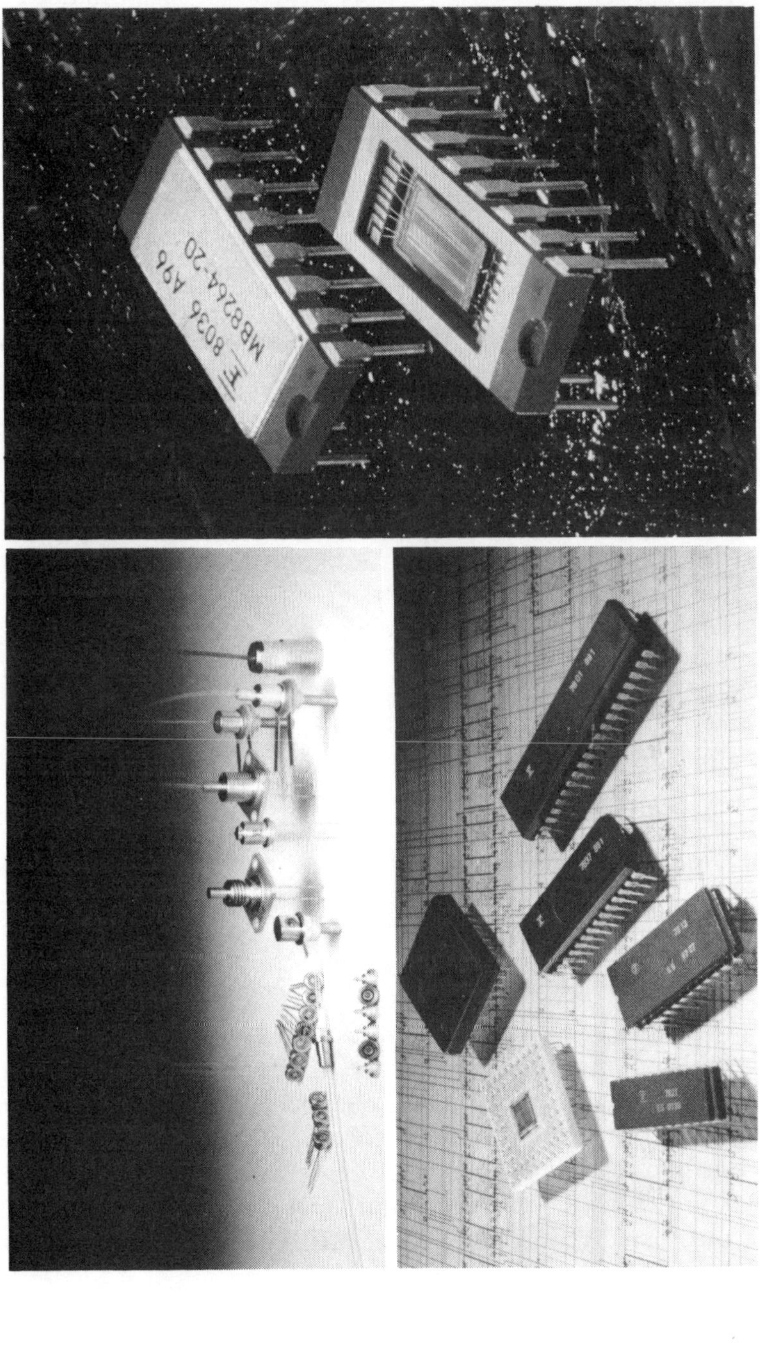

FIGURE 3–4 Examples of a current product line: (a) a variety of optical semiconductor devices; (b) semi-custom-made LSI; (c) +5V single power sixty-four KB MOS random access memory.

toward the creation of polyvalent circuits, which can be specialized by single users specifying only the final presentation, that which corresponds to the last level of metalization.

The success of proceeding this way is bound to the quality of choice of subject functions: making the right guess was easier (and more spontaneous) with serializers for use in line transmission with integrated modems, with multiple drum registers, and with pocket calculators. This task is now much more sophisticated, especially since the microcomputer was born, capable of program execution.

MICROPROCESSORS AND MICROCOMPUTERS

The circuitry we have been discussing is that of microprocessors which defines one or a very small number of chips that handle CPU functions including the instruction set, eventually RAM and ROM capabilities, and peripheral interfaces. It is a "machine within a machine." Its preprogrammed logical features are microprogrammed at the bit level. This can take the form of ROM/PROM or, if RAM, driven by another larger unit such as a minicomputer or a mainframe.

Among other functions, microprocessors are used to build microcomputers. This term defines a single board computer concept and includes:

- the microprocessor,
- some memory support,
- peripheral interface devices,
- I/O capability, and
- a support for programming functions.

Early processors had no standalone capability; this is still true to an extent. Looking at the microprocessor from this more limited perspective, we can see it as the component of a channel, a disc drive, a camera, a sewing machine. In this light, the microcomputer is a more complete system; it has input; output; an ALU of up to a fraction of one MIPS; memory (even multilevel); communication capability; interrupt features; display(s); a bus (usually of less than one MBPS); and is programmable by the user.

Still, a microcomputer is no complete system in the sense that we think of mainframes which are typically programmed by the user (or specialist); are able to drive other machines (minis, peripherals, terminals); possess full I/O faculties; have a central memory (CM) of "n" megabytes (eight, sixteen, twenty); drive a multilevel external memory (usually discs, tapes, mass storage); are supported by sophisticated software (from OS to VS and networking); and have a CPU of "n" MIPS and a bus of two, three, or more MBPS.

In choosing microprocessors, important considerations are the chip family, type of design, speed, precision, vendor support, price, and other faculties (power, instruction set, interrupt structure). The instruction set must be examined in terms of supported features: decimal mode, hardware multiply/divide, block transfer, autoincrement/decrement, string manipulation, bit testing, and I/O instructions as such. Whatever the instruction capabilities of microprocessors, they will be reflected in microcomputers, controllers, and terminals. Chip differences are often visible in the end product, and may exist in die size, voltage requirements, power consumption reliability characteristics, package size (pins), the on-chip clock, index registers, address modes, flag bits, general registers, pipelining architecture, the type of supported instructions, and other standard requirements. Memory refresher, decimal adjust, exchange instructions, block transfer/search, relative branch, test bit, explicit I/O instructions, restart capability and so on are examples of differences in chip design.

Microprocessor support chips can have parallel or serial I/O, a programmable interval timer, direct memory access, and controller functions (for video unit, keyboard, floppy disc, and so on). They can also support logical issues such as mathematical functions. They may offer software tradeoffs: program speed for memory size, loops and subroutines able to minimize program size at the expense of program speed; functional computation algorithms, and faculties for repeated computations when ninety percent of the execution time is spent on ten percent of the program. With such choices available, serving end use goals is both a feasible and complex task.

Another critical design characteristic is the memory system. Among issues to consider are the memory read-access time, the write set-up time, address and data drive capabilities, address space usage, and ROM, PROM, RAM, and I/O placement. (In regard to the programmable read only memory (PROM), it is proper to consider if it is field programmable, and if the fuse can be restored once blown (EPROM). Hence, can the memory be erased and preprogrammed, or is it only factory programmable? What if the program is likely to change?)

Random access memory (RAM) comes in two different versions—static and dynamic. The dynamic are larger (64 KB and must be refreshed); the static are smaller (8 KB and no refresh is needed). The technologies used may be:

- CMOS (800 ns access)
- MOS (450 ns access)
- Bipolar (fast, 50 ns access)
- ECL (very fast, 20 to 30 ns access).

The access time is calculated between the application of the address and the obtaining of stable valid data.

We have spoken of off-the-shelf microprocessors in contrast to traditional, custom-made logic designs. This, too, may present both advantages and disadvantages. Among the former, significant cost reductions are possible, modifications are not possible, additional functions can be readily implemented, and it is feasible to take advantage of the functionality incorporated in microprocessors and their support chips. Disadvantages include the fact that high-speed applications are difficult, data integrity is not easy to achieve with commercially available microprocessors (as they do not carry internal parity), testability is restricted due to the lack of access to internal components and that testing is becoming more difficult because of increasing VLSI complexity, and finally that development tools, test equipment, and training costs are a significant investment.

Advantages and disadvantages can be properly balanced if functional requirements are clearly defined. These typically include the interface to the system to be controlled (inputs, outputs), and the data flow to and from the system:

- formats
- precision
- calculation
- accumulation.

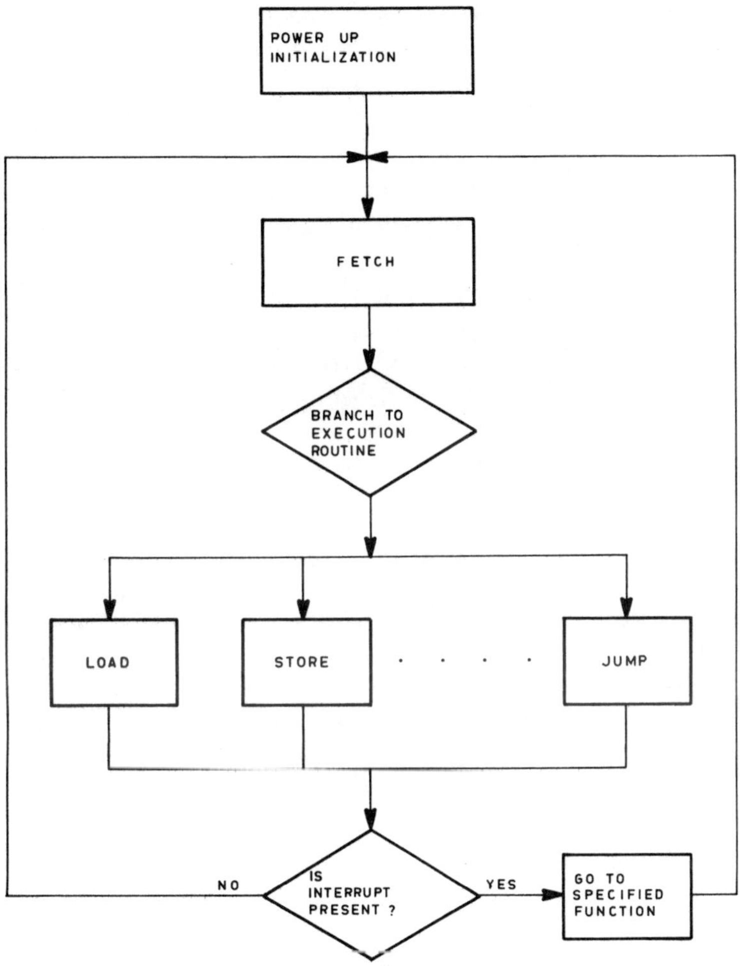

FIGURE 8–5 Example of an instruction set microprogram flow chart which can help the applications designer.

Equally important characteristics are the interface to the operator for realtime or for maintenance, the interface to a remote site for communications and data transfers, the sequence of events, safety features, and logical capabilities. To study the latter, the applications designer should ask the microprocessor manufacturer for a complete and well documented instruction set including microprogram flowcharts (Figure 8-5).

It is also well to consider the impact of available I/O devices on projected applications, evaluate the simplicity and flexibility of alternative microcomputer structures, and weigh the I/O features for alternative microcomputers which might be useful in a specific environment—handshaking on I/O ports, controllers for specific I/O devices, a versatile interrupt structure, a programmable timer, and so on.

To do so in a learned way, the designer must first establish the demands of his applications perspectives, and consider what jobs are likely to take most of the microcomputer's time. He must also evaluate the software features of several microcomputers which might be useful in his case: addressing versatility and efficiency, the subroutine structure (depth of testing and parametric flexibility), and the ease of flag testing and of packing and unpacking data words. All of these considerations are necessary to ensure a successful product.

MEMORY DEVICES

The correct choice of magnetic recording media can save money by improving system performance. The time a program waits for data to appear in main memory is, in part, the visible impact of memory supports on the system's throughput. To determine which media (floppy, bubble memory, tape, disc, mass storage, or some combination of these) should be chosen, the following questions may be useful:

1. How is the storage to be used?
2. How fast will projected use need access to data?
3. What are the tradeoffs between faster data access and lower storage costs?
4. Are the data storage needs large or small?

When storage requirements are small, bubble memory may compete with the floppy disc, particularly with the drop in prices projected over the next three years. Similarly, when storage requirements are small, cost is at a premium, but random access is important so floppy discs compete successfully with cassettes. These are generalities; the solid rule is that in each case, the designer should examine what technology can offer and at what cost.

Keeping with the example which we have given, between a 250 KB capacity of a floppy disc and a 2.3 GB capacity of a main storage disc exist four orders of magnitude of difference. Where will this large capacity be used? The very large databases towards which we are moving will need it; this will become apparent as broadband communications capabilities to be supported by optical fibers and satellites will call for massive storage media.

With memory devices, we should remember the very large ratio which prevails in supported circuitry. It ranges from the stated 250 KB of the single density floppy disc to the 2.3 GB supported by recent announcements in fixed disc capability, and beyond. An example of this "beyond" is the mass memory on cartridges introduced in late 1974 by IBM which is becoming a field of fairly intense competition (Figure 8-6 shows a mass memory unit by NEC; it supports up to 236 GB).

Another subject worthy of attention when we speak of memories is the substitution process which is going on all the time. Bubble memories did not sustain the growth projected in 1977; they have, however, some unique characteristics which should help them achieve a comfortable position in the market. They work much faster than disc memory, have no moving parts (therefore being more reliable), are cheaper than semiconductors, and have the added ability to retain stored data when power is absent.

One of the initial problems with bubble memory was that technology proved difficult to master. The early manufacturers—Rockwell International and Texas Instruments—were relatively late in developing supportive electronics needed to make bubble memory easy to use as discs (roughly half the cost in a memory system is this supporting circuitry). This oversight cost a couple of years in market acceptance, and made things tougher with the falling prices of both semiconductors and discs. Forecasts now indicate, however, that the market may grow tenfold by 1985, with a distinct possibility that bubble chips will take over all disc applications up to two MB.

For minicomputer and maxicomputer systems, this market segment of less-than-two-MB storage devices accounts for no more than five percent of disc storage sales, but the impact on personal and pocket computers can be tremendous. Anyone who tested the response time of bubble memory against that of the floppy can understand the reason.

Competition will be fierce. Rockwell International has left the bubble memory field, but there is a rush of other entrants: Intel, National

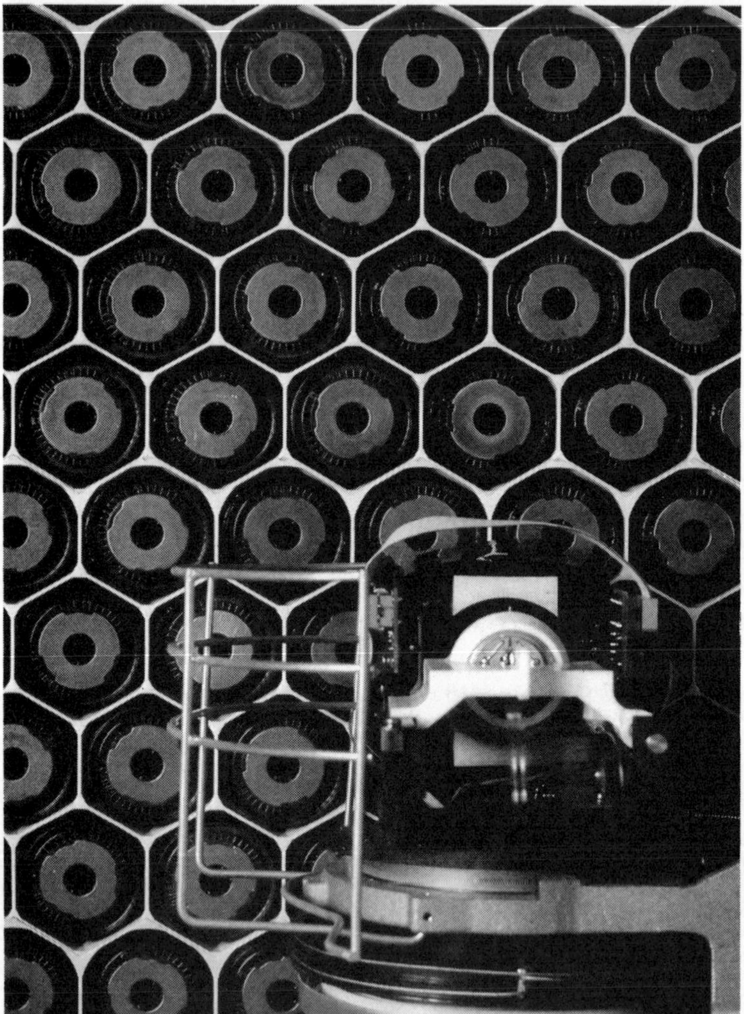

FIGURE 8–6 A mass memory unit by NEC. IBM and CDC are also among the leading competitors in this expanding field.

Semiconductors, Motorola and Hitachi. To cope with the floppy disc's removable and store-away characteristics, both TI and Intel are introducing removable bubble cartridge systems, and other advancements are in sight. That is why, with the price of bubble memories expected to drop significantly during the next couple of years, this is an important storage device to watch.

Technological advances are the main reason why older storage solutions fade from online access and are retained, to a large extent, as I/O possibilities. This is the story of magnetic tape which, with newer systems, primarily serves data interchange. A reel of tape can be easily moved from one system to another, and tape provides low cost data backup. However, magnetic tape has the basic limitations of slow access time because processing of tape files is done sequentially, and mounting and dismounting tapes (and cassettes) delays the operation of the whole system.

To alleviate the problems of online data availability inherent in magnetic tape, hard discs are generally used, resulting in reasonably fast access rates and higher transfer speeds. When using disc storage, data is accessed and transferred in milliseconds rather than seconds as with tape. Not only is system performance improved, but communications costs are reduced.

The main tradeoffs, then, between magnetic tape and disc packs are cost/access and cost/bit stored. For example, to locate a random record on a full reel of tape would take an average of 72 seconds, assuming a 200 inch-per-second search speed. The time to locate the same record on a full 200 MB discpack is 30 msec to 80 msec (depending on design) and access time is independent of the location of the record. This is particularly significant if the system operates in an interactive environment.

For applications that require small data storage, "floppies" are favored. The main appeal of the floppy disc as compared with cassettes/cartridges is its quick access time—one to two orders of magnitude faster than the cassette. Also, this is a random access device which offers better reliability (than the cassette), and is reasonably standardized while the cassette is not. A disadvantage of the floppy disc is its cost per bit for offline storage; floppies can cost two to three times as much as cassettes for the equivalent amount of storage capacity.

As stated, a fundamental criterion in choosing memory supports is storage capability. Also, we have steadily sought high speed, low cost, random access bulk memory almost from the inception of computertime. Keep in mind that a single floppy today offers about one-fifth of what was "large capacity" supported by initial bulk memories around 1960 (on the order of fifty MB).

With an access time of about 300 msec at a cost of 0.1 cents per bit, the bulk memories opened new applications and methods of data processing. Similarly, floppy discs have been instrumental for introducing the concept of a local microfile, but their response time (even if better than that of cassettes) is too long as compared to that of bubble memories. With a price drop projected for the latter, their instantaneous response should give them an unbeatable advantage.

9 Interconnecting and Interfacing

INTRODUCTION

We have stated that the basic difference between a microprocessor and a microcomputer is that the former is a machine within a machine while the latter should be looked at as a complete system. Such a system has the ability to effectively incorporate a number of units, such as memory modules and peripherals, which will communicate with appropriate drivers (software routines) through a bus.

The bus-structure approach to design is popular with microcomputers as it has been considerably simplified by using a standard interfacing discipline (software and hardware) for all devices. In general, a microcomputer architecture calls for connecting the central processor, memory modules and input/output through a set of busses. There are three major sections in the total bus structure:

- address,
- data, and
- control.

A fourth section will eventually be that of the power supply. Whatever its end use, a section will typically consist of a number of lines which may be circuit wires etched on a printed circuit board, soldered wires between connectors into which circuit board modules are plugged, or ribbon cable. As previously stated, the component parts of the microcomputer are physically packaged on one or more printed circuit boards, the number and type of functions supplied on a board varying with the type of system and the manufacturer.

On each board, the data bus ensures that information being handled is transferred from one subsystem to another. Signals used to control the addressing and data transfer functions are carried on the control bus; such signals concern precise conditions: read from memory, write to memory, address present, data present, and so on. The address bus is used to specify the memory location or I/O port at which data is being read or written. The power bus distributes power from the power supply of the system to the various subsystems of the microcomputer; several DC voltages are required.

Not only is interfacing and interconnecting very important in microcomputer design and implementation, but it can also be very costly. The Sharp company recently announced a 4-bit pocket computer which has programming capability (Basic); a twenty-four-dot matrix rolling writer displaying characters and numerals; full alphabetic and numeric keyboard; memory safeguard; playback functions; automatic power-off; and both data and text capability. A 16-digit printer/cassette interface is also available (and soon a line controller).

IMPLEMENTING AN INTERFACE

Interfacing practically means connecting the microprocessor with the external world and its own internal memory units. This makes it feasible to build up the central component, plug the busses and the clock, and link the whole to outside devices. In such an approach, the starting point is the ALU and the clock; the latter will assure that the right functions follow one another at the right time. The next most important consideration is the means for the interconnection. A transfer mechanism will ensure that the contents of one or more of the registers will be communicated to the entity which expects to receive them.

The more intelligent the device, the greater will be the need for paying attention to the interconnecting capabilities. A very simple microprocessor is typically non-intelligent, unable to make decisions. We can attach this to a display capability, but this will not change the content. To make the unit more intelligent, the ALU must generate conditional operations—for instance, Jump and Branch—and we must provide the parts necessary for their execution.

A more intelligent unit will be conditioned by procedural steps created at the CPU level, such being the result of a control procedure. In the example given in Figure 9-1, lines (a), (b) or both can influence decision. In early microprocessor designs, the decision mechanism resided

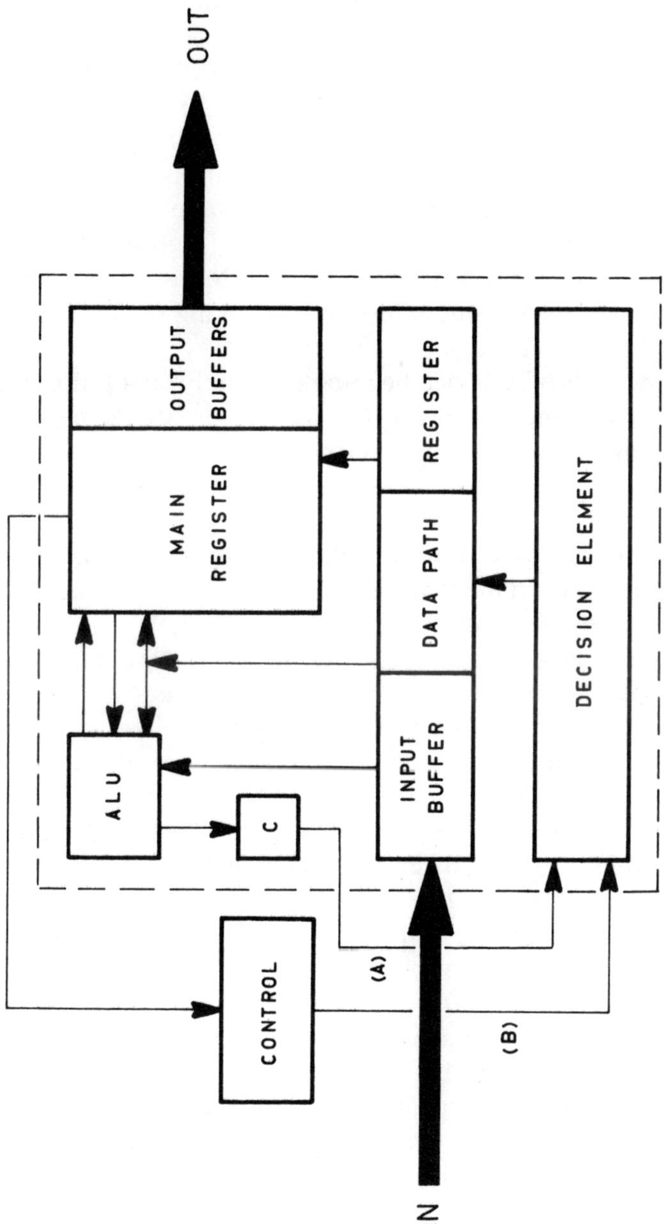

FIGURE 9-1 Procedural steps created at the CPU level: lines (a), (b) or both can influence decision.

on another chip, but more sophisticated approaches eventually included many functions, some affecting the program counter unconditionally, and others doing the same under certain well-defined conditions.

For instance, in this same example, path (a) might be a "carry" condition following the sum of two digits; path (b) the result of a comparison, an aftermath of an operation such as Add and Subtract. For example: Change content of the program counter *if* the content of register A = 1. More complete systems than the elementary ones shown in Figure 9-1 take the structure of a "stacking computer" (Figure 9-2), which has multiple building blocks, a bus line, hardware loops and programming capabilities. We will have a quick look into stacking requirements when we speak of data transfers.

As the functions of a device become more polyvalent, the attention paid to interfacing should increase. In any and every design, we should carefully look into the handling of data and commands, their distribution, and access to memories. These are fundamental considerations, and the most basic of native instructions of any microprocessor serve them. In other words, while the instruction set will vary from one microcomputer to another (and from microcomputer to macrocomputer), some fundamental operations will always be present, such as interfacing.

Another issue in interface studies is buffering. A complete design involving the coupling of different circuits and devices calls for appropriate buffers. It is the designer's task to optimize buffer space to keep the system coordinated: the time of the CPU and that of the rest of the circuitry must be balanced. Indeed, buffering between machine components is much more than a matter of balancing the speed. Code conversion is another example, but the buffer can also help between different lines of supply. (Though an entire line may come from the same supplier, a one-manufacturer dependence is *not* always advisable. Nippon Electric, for example, makes its projects spec-to-spec (not pin-to-pin) compatible with those of other manufacturers so that they appeal to customers who choose multimanufacturers dependence.)

Other reasons for buffering (and trapping) are for interrupts and the assurance of priority handling, but I/O is the area of the largest variety in terms of design and supply. Depending on the manufacturer and designer, there will be different associated registers to I/O.

Interfacing becomes increasingly important as sophisticated buyers acquire microcomputers from outlets such as stores; professionals learn to use microcomputers at the office and at home, hooking them to ap-

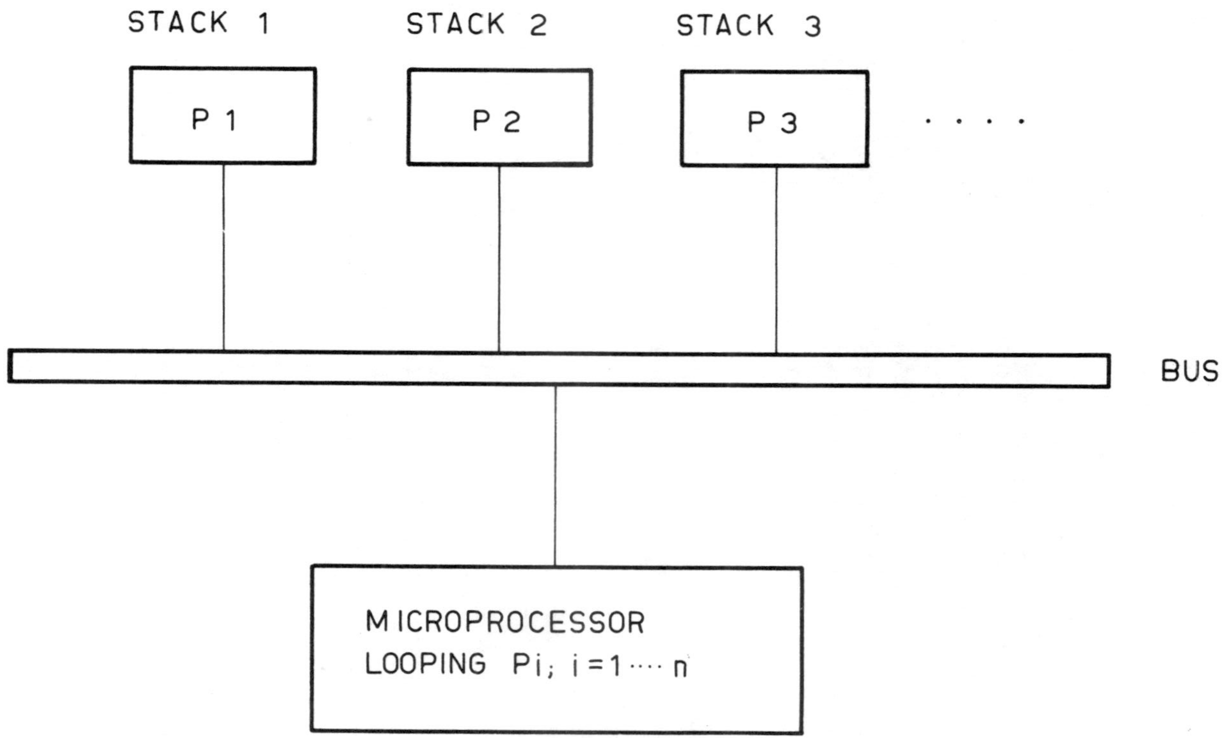

FIGURE 9–2 A stacking computer based on a building block principle with stack programming capability (needs also channels to multiplex).

pliances (thus pressing for better interfacing faculties); vendors begin to sell on a quantity basis without precise knowledge of the end use; and microcomputers are becoming increasingly powerful, such as the new 32-bit micromainframes. Eventually, some interface problems will surface, demanding solutions at the microprocessor level.

HANDLING DATA AND ADDRESSES

The interface work performed for microprocessors has a great deal of similarity to microcomputer interfaces with one exception–the limitation of the number of pins due to the packaging. The solutions adopted for packaging restrict the width of the data communications channels. With the narrower channels commonly found in microprocessors, lines are often multiplexed between data and addresses. Such multiplexing does not significantly complicate the design of interfaces, but it does slow transfers when compared to a system where both data and addresses can be transmitted over dedicated lines.

Another interfacing technique common with microprocessors is the memory-mapped I/O. With this approach, interface registers are treated as special locations in the memory address space, with the interface devices connected to the memory bus so that no special I/O lines or I/O instructions are required.

Design approaches vary both as a function of technology and in relation to the product line of the supplier firm. Products of the semiconductor companies include single-chip computers that combine the CPU, control circuit, memory, and I/O in a single integrated circuit package. Sophisticated approaches are required as microcomputers intrude on the more complex applications that are the domain of the mini after a number of improvements to their design.

The emphasis herein on interfacing is because this has been one of the most important early processor limitations. To overcome it, many microprocessor suppliers developed special interfacing chips corresponding to their devices. The latter provide, in a single package, all necessary logic circuits for a general-purpose interface. The individual interface chips are identified to the system by the use of address select lines externally wired to specify the address of the subject chip. Programmed data transfer operations are the most common microprocessor I/O techniques, but other types of interfaces are also being used. In this sense, the design of microcomputer interfaces and I/O channels is strongly tied to that of central processors.

Special instructions and control signals are provided for testing the status of peripheral devices and for transferring data to and from these points. Most microcomputers tend to provide one "read" signal and one "write" signal with an instruction for each. Both data and device status are transferred, and the program determines the status of the addressed peripheral device by examining bits transferred over a status report. (Most svstems use interrupts in dealing with peripheral devices.)

There are three basic forms of communication between minicomputers and microcomputers and the outside world:

1. programmed data transfers (PDT),
2. direct memory access (DMA), and
3. interrupts.

PDT is the technique of transferring information between the outside world and the programming registers in the microcomputer's ALU. This requires the program to explicitly indicate and be involved in each data transfer.

DMA does not concern the ALU in data exchange operations, but instead transfers data directly between the I/O unit and memory. In this sense, transfers are initiated by instructing the I/O controller as to the characteristics of the transfer operation: the number of words to be transported, starting memory location, and external control codes. Upon initiation, the transfers proceed without further program involvement until completion of the operation. The program being executed by the microcomputer may continue but is slowed in execution by contention with the DMA transfers for use of the memory system.

Interrupts are connected to the transfer operation as they constitute a means by which the outside world can signal the controller of the microcomputer that an event has occurred. The interrupt faculty does not itself transfer any data to the computer memory; it only signals the occurrence of an event. Upon receipt of an interrupt, the controller can inform the program currently being executed of the event by transferring control to predefined locations (interrupt vectors). These serve to identify the particular interrupt being processed by having separate vectors for each interrupt line. If only one vector serves all interrupt lines, facilities must be provided for program interrupt identification.

Figure 9-3 outlines how a microcomputer interface and memory system is usually organized: higher order bits of the address field are decoded to select blocks of the memory array, and lower order bits serve to identify bits within these blocks. Data is written into or read out of the illustrated places by the data bus, while the control logic serves (in terms of data transfer) in holding I/O data and in other operations such as refreshing circuitry if the memory is dynamic.

INPUT, OUTPUT AND DATA TRANSFER

With most microcomputers, the I/O is organized into ports—small groups of I/O lines that are read or written in parallel between the CPU and the I/O unit. The number of lines of bits in a port is usually the same as in the word-size of the microprocessor. Most microcomputers can be equipped with plug-in subsystems that contain the logic for several I/O ports, with addresses decoded to select specific ports.

- For inputs, the ports are usually sets of logic gates that route input signals to the system's data bus.
- For outputs, the ports are sets of latches into which signals from the data bus are stored.

Though the BPW is important in the data transfer function, the need for sophisticated I/O capabilities was not present in early 4-bit microprocessor chips (Intel's MCS-4, and Rockwell's PPS-4) as they were primarily used in dedicated computing systems characterized by rather slow-throughput situations.

As the design emphasis shifted toward a generalized applications approach, it promoted the development of chips able to handle I/O control besides processing functions. This marked the beginning of the second generation of microcomputer technology (about 1973) with 8-bit n-channel systems such as the Intel 8080 and Motorola MC 6800. Such processors, together with matched memory and I/O circuit interfaces, form a completely self-contained microcomputer family of chips. The 8080's accumulator and its associated circuitry have been moved into the ALU to speed up the operation of the processor. Data transfers between memory and ALU on the internal data bus are therefore not required for arithmetic and logic operations. With 8080 memory, information can be transferred from the internal bus eight bits at a time, while 16-bit transfers can take place from the address register. The organizational improvements of the 8080 yield a number of additional new features.

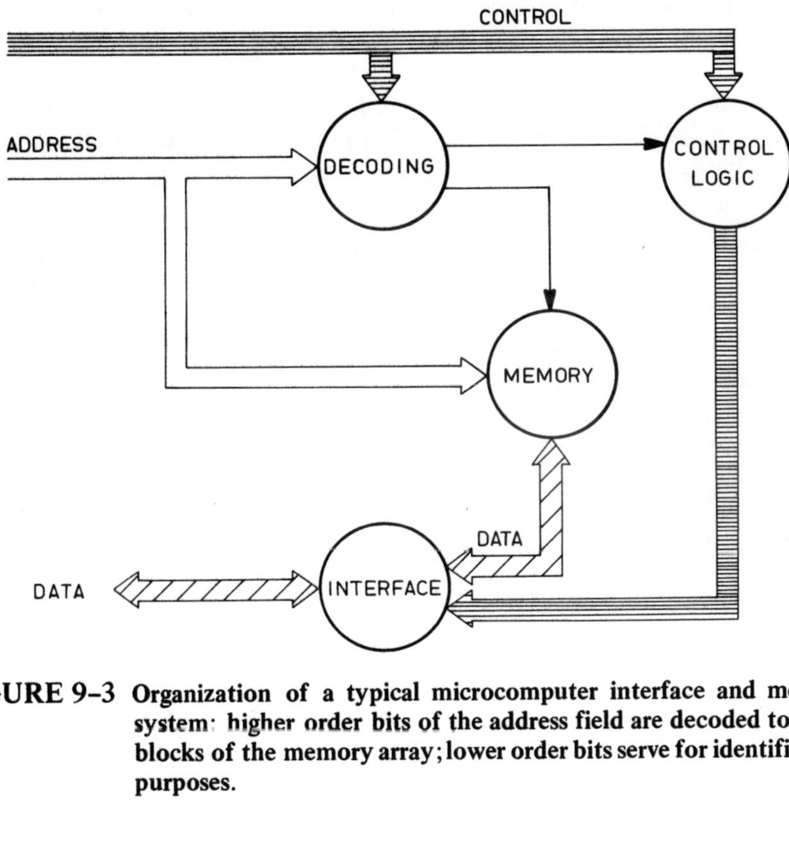

FIGURE 9–3 **Organization of a typical microcomputer interface and memory system: higher order bits of the address field are decoded to select blocks of the memory array; lower order bits serve for identification purposes.**

A still further development is the SOS (silicon-on-sapphire) technology for increased speed, which helps define the third generation of microprocessor systems. New instructions allow the contents of any register pair to be stored and retrieved by being pushed-into or popped-from the top of the external memory stack. This is a fast way to save the machine status after the interrupt has been serviced. The stack can also be used as an extension of the internal registers. Other new instructions permit easy manipulation of addresses and the memory stack, since the registers and stack pointer can be incremented and decremented with sixteen bits in parallel.

The stack concept was introduced at the beginning of this chapter. This is an area of memory reserved by the system (or user) for temporary storage of data in a last-in-first-out (LIFO) mode. In actual design, a stack pointer is a register able to store the next available location in an external push-down/pull-up stack, thus allowing to store and retrieve data in a known sequential order without regard to specific memory addresses (reentrant coding).

Design-wise, the stack is made always RAM: it is the "first page" of the memory and operates as the last in/first out buffer store. With each write operation, the pointer decrements, and with each read operation, it increments. The stack is automatically used for:

- return address (two bytes) for subroutine calls,
- return address (two bytes) for interrupt service, and
- status register (one byte) also for interrupt service.

The stack may also be used for saving accumulator and/or index registers before interrupt or subroutine operations, and transfering values for the main program to subroutines. Care must be taken so that stack storage does not exceed the allowed number of bytes.

Microprocessors will soon offer interesting and very competitive high-function solutions in network environments. When we speak of distributed information systems, it is not the minicomputer that will necessarily offer the user the most attractive alternative. More and more often, it will be the microcomputer, but for this to become a reality, a number of logical and physical functions must be supported.

An example of this is the software aspect of microcomputer interfacing. This is different from that encountered in larger systems; microcomputer operating systems are designed so that it is relatively easy to add device drivers (operating system routines that deal with the device interface) for "foreign" interfaces. Furthermore, the trend in peripherals is toward more intelligent devices that can, through hardware, provide some functions traditionally assigned to the operating system software. One good example of an intelligent peripheral is the data communications multiplexer (DCM). It supports multiple communications connections between the computer and external devices by employing transfers between memory and the communications lines.

The DCM uses tables describing each communications line and attendant memory buffer areas so that transfers can take place with a minimum of software intervention. The operating system initializes each line by transferring table information and instructions to the DCM, and then is not involved until completion of a transfer. Instructions usually reflect designating conditions such as end-of-transfer conditions (by specifying message length or end-of-message character), location and size of memory buffers, and desired characteristics of communication such as parity, speed, or character length. Such instructions typically involve general operation conditions, including:

data movement,

arithmetic and logical functions associated with transfer activities,

shift and rotate,

branching,

status inquiries, and

stack operation.

They also involve memory addressing, make use of on-chip registers, call for an interrupt capability, require service routines and an adequate instruction set, and most likely involve other functions reflecting the job requirements. Figure 9-4 illustrates the I/O and data transfer section of a microprocessor (Mostek Z80) sandwiched between the CPU and the peripheral interfaces.

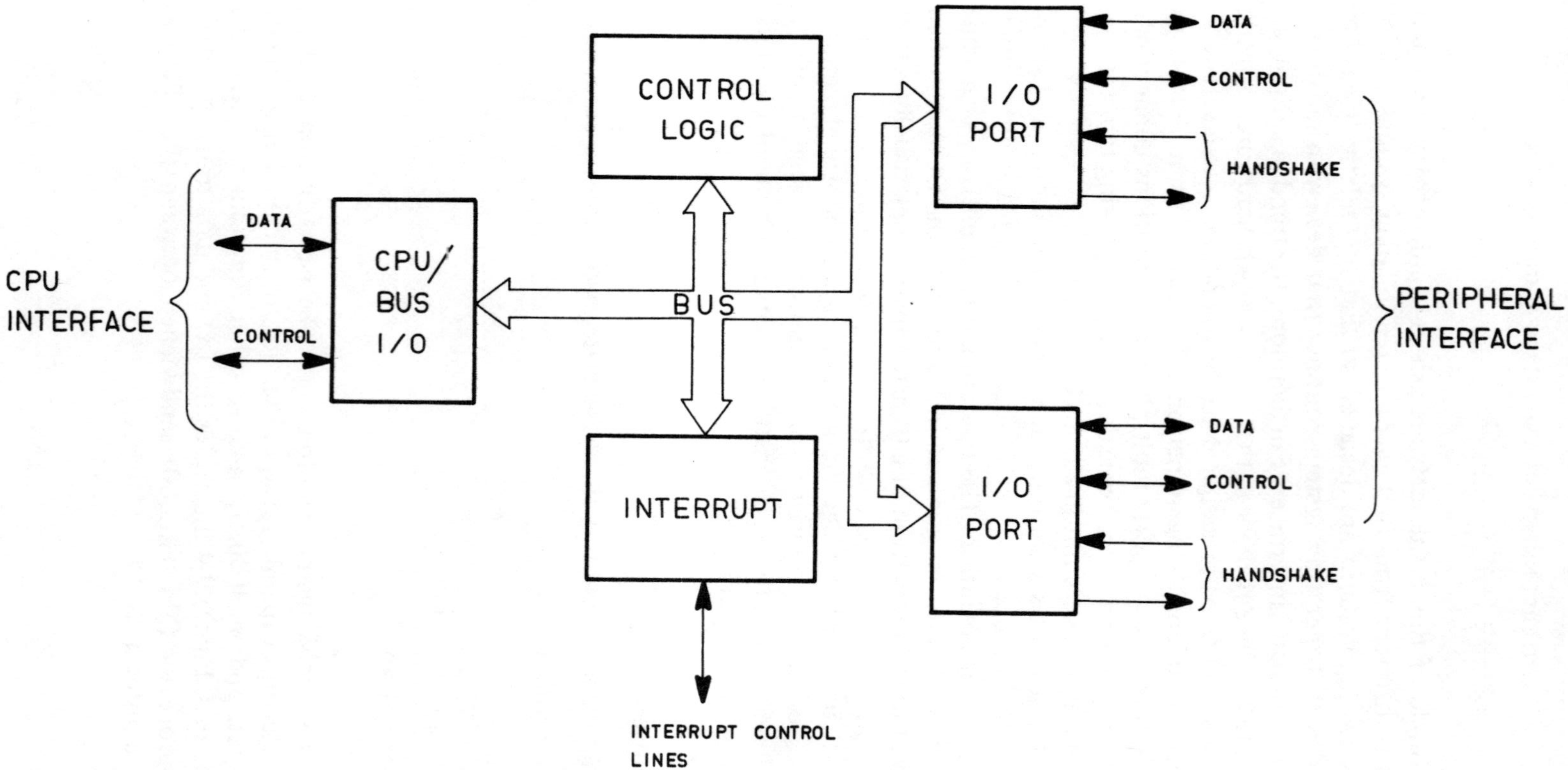

FIGURE 9–4 The I/O and data transfer section of a microprocessor: port structure; external data and control busses; handshaking; and internal bus reference.

FUTURE DEVELOPMENTS IN INTERFACING

Since the primary function of an interface is to support devices attached to the CPU, it is up to the designer to assure that there will be no developments in the foreseeable future to upset the balance he has established. Which future developments are worth keeping in mind in the current state of the art?

The semi-analog I/O on chip for special purpose applications is a case in point. Figure 9-5 presents a simple microprocessor-controlled process. It can be extended to mini-DIS (distributed information system), assuming the all-digital role of larger machines (Figure 9-6). Applications-oriented microprocessors for appliance control, automotive applications, and telephony (intelligent lines, multifunctional sets) are other references.

Among important questions pertaining to the near future are: Will the current definition of microprocessors retain its validity? How soon will programmable microcomputer networks assume tasks of larger computer systems, and to what extent will this be done? Is the von Neumann concept good for microprocessor design, and do we really need the structure this approach suggests?

The answers to such questions raise the problem of general architectural approaches, basic design philosophy and goals, status, limits to and alternatives of microcomputers, and the need to obtain quantitative and qualitative results. Ten factors influence the answer to the question: "what can the microprocessor offer?"

First, the answer depends to a large extent on the generation of devices to which we refer; more performance, greater complexity, better packaging, and more registers are in the future. Yet, it is always possible that at any time standard microprocessors may not offer features a user wants, as the user's need for functions steadily increases. For instance, floating point implementation is a difficult issue under present technological conditions, but current microprocessors have OS-type capabilities to manage their own resources.

Second, an increase in performance can be obtained with totally new architecture, rather than extending the lower end of a current one. However, cost/performance tradeoffs are not always clear, and radical changes might invalidate large investments. Compatibility limitations are not the only issue in such decisions; changes in design at the hardware level have software fallouts: new microprocessors may have features the

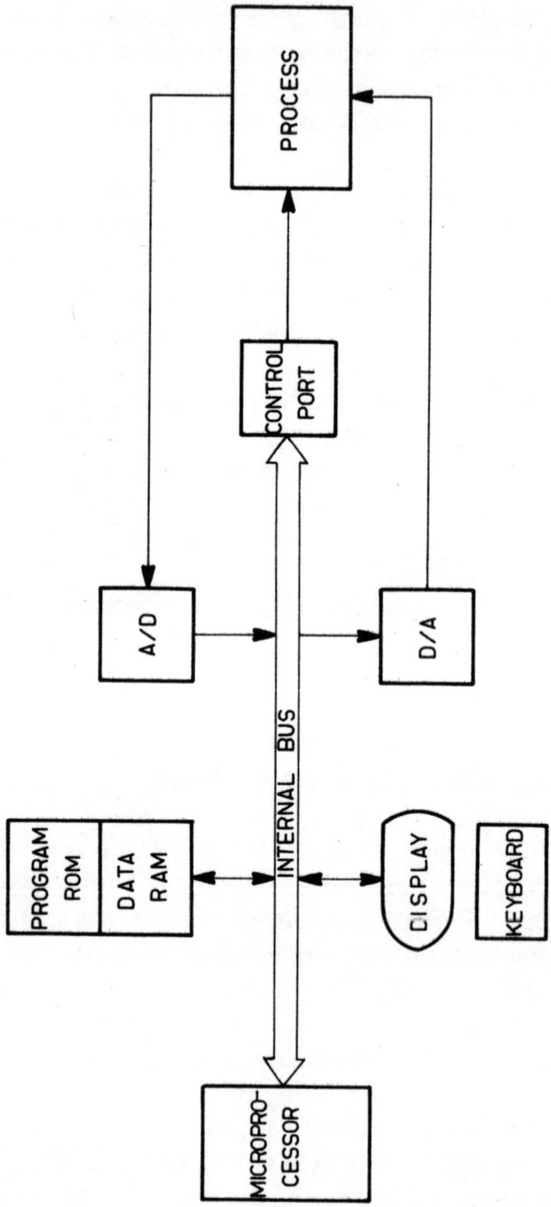

FIGURE 9–5 A simple microprocessor control structure, including analog-to-digital and digital-to-analog interfaces.

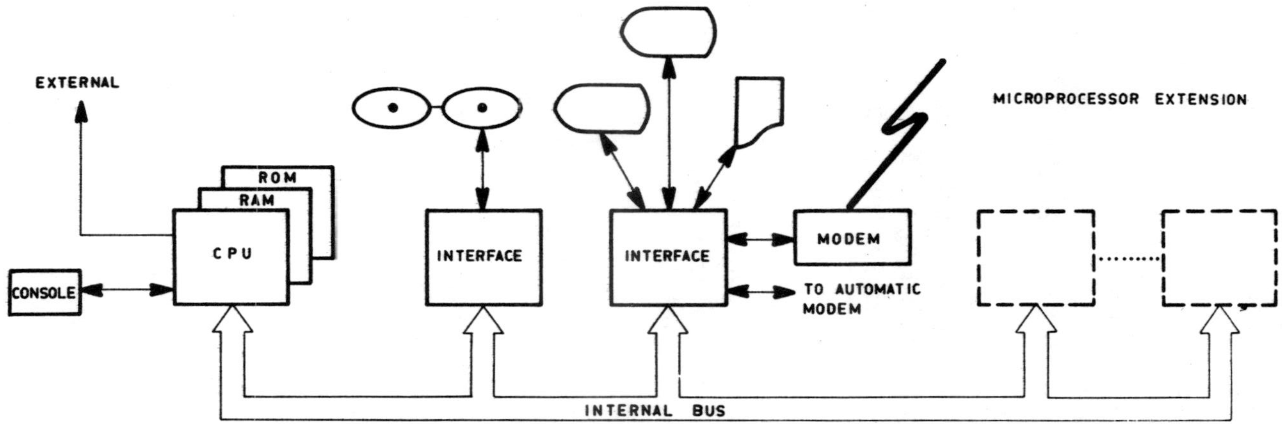

FIGURE 9–6 A more complex structure leading to a microcomputer capability. On the same bus are included internal and external interfaces; CPU; RAM; ROM; disc possibility; video terminals, hardcopy, modems; and a microprocessor extension faculty.

old programs do not account for, or some marginal capabilities of old devices may be dropped. Tradeoffs of registers and features is a constant in design.

Third, the evolution of technology has a great impact. A flexible approach is to offer internal instruction sets with a range of different implementations; but design changes are often radical. Moving from the four KB to the sixteen KB chip led to the cancellation of the bus relevant to the 4x4; and the same is valid with the change from the sixteen KB to the sixty-four KB chip.

Fourth, the "end cost" impact of steady technological advancement must be studied. Chips will eventually sell if not for cents, then for a few dollars. Even at very low cost levels, the cost inherent in complexity will be evident, and there will always be a market for simpler devices at still lower costs.

Fifth, design architecture raises important questions: How does data revolve around the chip? How should we make it? Which functions should be included? Design architecture also brings up considerations of cost/effectiveness, and often calls for a departure from established concepts.

Sixth, new architectural approaches will be influenced by DIS requirements, which will become evident in developments in distributed applications and networks. In all probability, the end user level will be most exposed to radical twists as we search for approaches which are user-friendly, require minimum training, and ease both maintenance and on-call duties.

Seventh, local (internal) network systems, combining voice, data, and image within various institutions will impact on microprocessor technology and design. Internal distributed environments using data communications principles may become commonplace, and may use microprocessors, nanoprocessors, and even picoprocessors. As a result, new applications perspectives will unfurl while the new generation of manufacturing equipment in more established industries will broaden the range of applications for nanoprocessors and picoprocessors.

Eighth, improved I/O performance requirements will impact on architecture. This can be viewed as an internal network situation, and will lead to computer companies becoming peripheral-rather than CPU-oriented. Peripherals may eventually account for about seventy percent of their total business. In this sense, I/O-oriented nanoprocessors will be introduced to unload many details the micro-CPU is now handling (as with IBM's 34 and S/1). This is one good reason why it is important to keep the I/O bus separate from the memory bus.

Ninth, as will be discussed in the following chapter, programming languages will have a significant impact on architecture. The designer starts with a simple machine language for the microprocessor, then users want Basic; the designer gives Basic, and users want Cobol and Fortran. Furthermore, existing languages (Pascal included) do not address problems of the microprocessor; there is at the moment no universal language for such devices. Yet, the language problem is real, and so is the OS problem. (The latter becomes apparent as more and more microcomputers are substituting minicomputers.)

Tenth, there is the changing market perspective. As microcomputers penetrate new markets, they find their real basis of growth and expand their applications. When this industry started, we were not sure which markets would accept our devices. Market response will have a great impact; it has always been thus.

10 Firmware and Microcode

INTRODUCTION

THE DEVELOPMENT of firmware is a combination of hardware and software approaches. In 1951, Maurice Wilkes wrote an essay on microcodes; seven years later, in 1958, IBM introduced the 1620 with table look-up instead of a hardware arithmetic unit. These are the earliest known references on these subjects.

In the late 1960s, the rationale for firmware was a blending of hardware and software characteristics. Ten years later, in the late 1970s, firmware advanced through the fast-spreading use of microprocessors which provide vertical and horizontal approaches to emulate other machines, provide program portability, and make the system more flexible.

Behind the effort toward a merging of software and hardware solutions are that:

- Hardware is an inherently simple and fast medium, though computer hardware may look complex to the user.
- A software machine is slower, more complex and upset by changes, though it may look simpler to the user by the way it affects his environment.
- There are other characteristics to be noted: Software is information and, therefore, essentially intangible; it can be transferred over telephone lines, so it's physical state is inconsequential; its value is not on the medium, it is stored—which is worth a few dollars—but in the skill and knowledge involved in its makeup.

The problem with a software machine is that it is open to well-known failures and is also more difficult to test and maintain. So, users

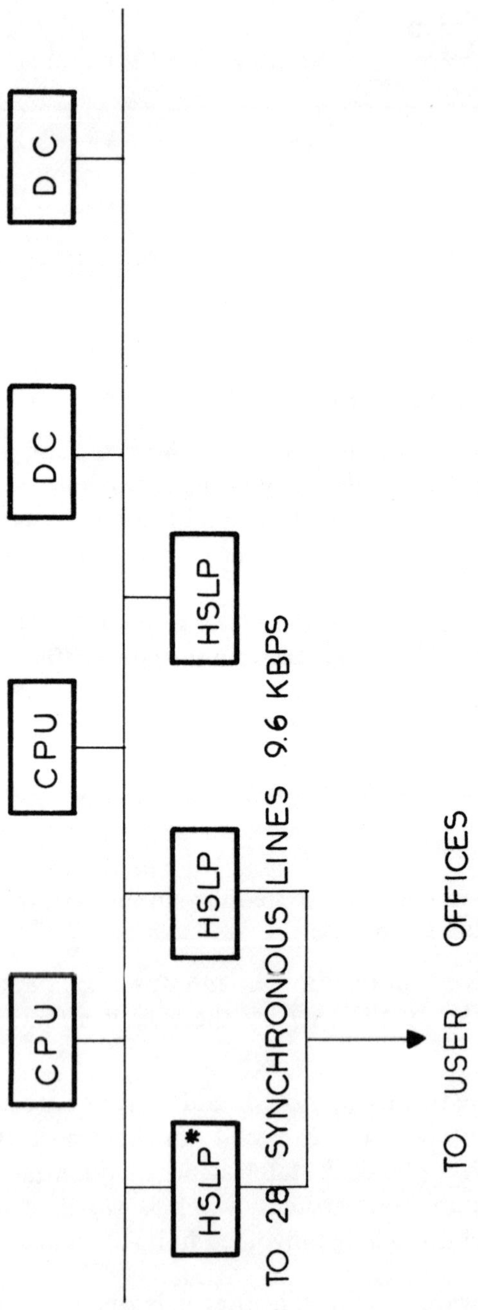

* HIGH SPEED LINE PROCESSOR

FIGURE 10–1 Node backup in the Northern Telecom structure. Microprocessor devices are assisted by software.

are more willing to go for firmware, such as pocket computers which require a solid-state/firmware approach, and so will the upcoming intelligent communications lines.

Working with inexpensive semiconductor technology is much more attractive if we have appreciable development in communications such as an intelligent data transfer with store and forward, text-data-voice, and error detection/correction capabilities. Figure 10-1 demonstrates a node backup in the Northern Telecom structure; with microprocessor devices assisted by solid-state software, this and similar solutions may become basic modules in the construction of local and other networks.

MICROPROGRAMMING

Microprogramming yields a reduction in the time needed for arithmetic and logical operations of a system, and also results in a more modular, structured organization. The control portion of a non-microprogrammed processor contains counters, special flip-flops and decoding networks. With microprogramming, a regular memory organization replaces most of this, with the result that architecture becomes more structured, fewer alternatives exist for implementing functions, and many special gates are removed.

Although the cost of a microprocessor with microprogramming may be greater than that of a comparable system using conventional hardware, increased complexity in a microprogramming solution is not as costly as comparably conventional approaches. In other words, while for relatively simple architectures conventional systems are cheaper, for more sophisticated systems microprogramming is more attractive, and this is mainly a matter of economics.

There are other advantages in favor of solid-state software solutions. For example, microprogrammed microprocessors are geared for diagnostics. Good-sized portions of such devices can be checked effectively, and control states can be tested under microprogrammed conditions that cannot be controlled by the machine language programmer. Changes to correct logic errors can also be made more easily by altering microprogrammed instructions.

A basic principle is that firmware emulates the software machine, and this emulation is impressive. In lower-order functions (simple instructions or codes) and non-complex hardware characteristics (registers,

ALU operations, and so on), the emulation is referred to as *vertical firmware.* An emulator mode operation is presented in Figure 10-2. The user views the emulated engine and does not necessarily concern himself with the original processor. He should, however, understand how the emulator works.

Emulation has been used with considerable success in the late 1950s and in the 1960s with software, but emulation by means of a stored program slows the machine significantly: quite often the ratio is 1 to 10, and even the most effective software emulator ever written (IBM's PRINT of the 1950s) had a ratio of 1 to 2. Microprocessor emulation, however, does not present such serious reductions in efficiency.

For an example of lower-end functions, let us assume that the hardware machine permits add and invert operations: through firmware we can emulate multiply and substract operations. If the machine permits all operations on a binary basis, we can emulate through firmware decimal and/or hexadecimal operations. Assume we have a machine which can only do elementary operations, and we want a machine which does complex operations. Through a programmed matrix solution, using several elementary operations, we obtain a machine slower than the original but able to perform more complex operations.

This is an example of vertical firmware. In the case of *horizontal firmware*, we distinguish between an *internal* and *external* machine. The internal machine has microinstructions, and is very simple. The external machine operates on these microinstructions through a microprocessor-implemented microprogram (Figure 10-3). In the latter case, the hard-

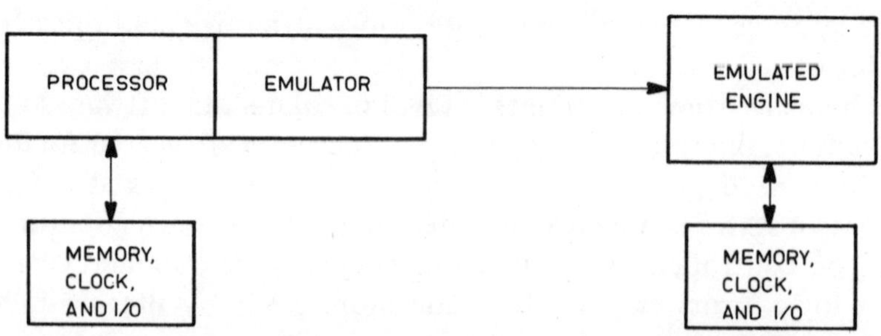

FIGURE 10–2 An emulator mode operation. The experimenter can view the emulated engine without necessarily concerning himself with the original processor.

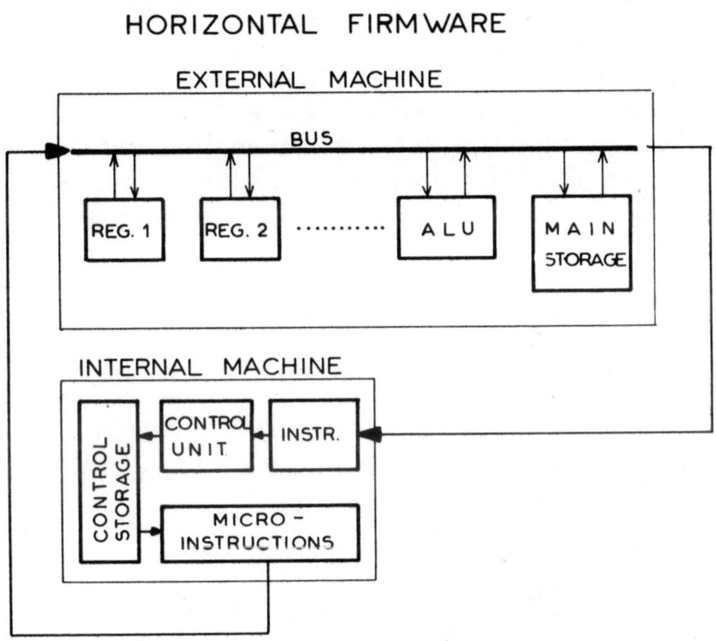

FIGURE 10–3 An example of horizontal firmware. The internal machine has microinstructions and is very simple. The external machine operates on these microinstructions through a microprocessor-implemented microprogram.

ware characteristics are not emulated, but this gives a great freedom of choice. By changing the microprocessor and the microprograms, we can radically alter the external machine, whereas the internal machine remains the same.

Instructions of an internal machine are activated via planned microinstructions. The resulting instructions are those of the external machine which, in turn, can help implement a distributed internal structure. Also, with reference to the bus structure, microcode permits bit-level addressing for greater efficiency.

It is evident that the low cost of implementing vertical and horizontal solutions has produced a propensity toward a greater utilization of available facilities. Several manufacturers keep the most frequent instructions at bit-level execution, then proceed with microcode approaches.

The following are general advantages of internal and external machines:

1. The internal machine is very simple.
2. Microprograms are part of the external machine.
3. The fact of a simple engine allows greater reliability.
4. The larger engine is flexible: by changing microcodes, we can make various types of equipment.
5. Continuity of development is provided.
6. Facility to change microcodes and thus confuse competition—hence, strategic capability.
7. The possibility to affect modular changes in terms of technical and structural considerations using the microcode as interfacing.
8. The instruction set remains *invariant.*

The last advantage enhances software probability. For instance, between 1964 (IBM 360) and 1979 (IBM 4300), technology has greatly changed, but the instruction set of both machines has remained basically the same. Apart from program compatibility which is a major advantage, as far as usage is concerned, what the programmer sees is the external engine; the internal machine is reserved to the designer of microprogramming modules.

TRADEOFFS AND THE OS CHALLENGE

Through firmware, the designer has an excellent capability to enhance standard functions, and to equip them with necessary protect-and-restore faculties. This can also be done with software but, as stated, other things being equal, the resulting engine is slower—though in either case, the programmer does not need to be concerned with the implementation of such faculties. Software solutions, however, largely affect processing time and performance (Figure 10-4).

Multiple virtual storage execution by microcode and software has given the following results (which serve a double purpose by demonstrating the greater efficiency of firmware solutions and casting some doubt on end efficiency due to MIPS):

By microcode	*By software*
1 instruction	56 instructions
70 cycles	332 cycles
70 cycles/instruction	6 cycles per instruction

The MIPS are higher in the software case, but performance is greater in the microcode solution. As a rule, instructions must be microcoded that have the higher "product" in cycles saved times repetitions per second.

Function	*Cycles Saved*	*Repetitions per sec.*	*Product*
X	25	40	1000
Y	50	5	250

Let us recapitulate. Microprogramming capability provides the needed means so that software design and programming practices can change in some aspects, the conversion toward software being aimed at reducing software costs per instruction. By microcoding functions which until now have belonged to software, the delineation changes between software and hardware. This is particularly valid for a number of utility macroinstructions (data moves, I/O), for language compilers, and for operating system primitives.

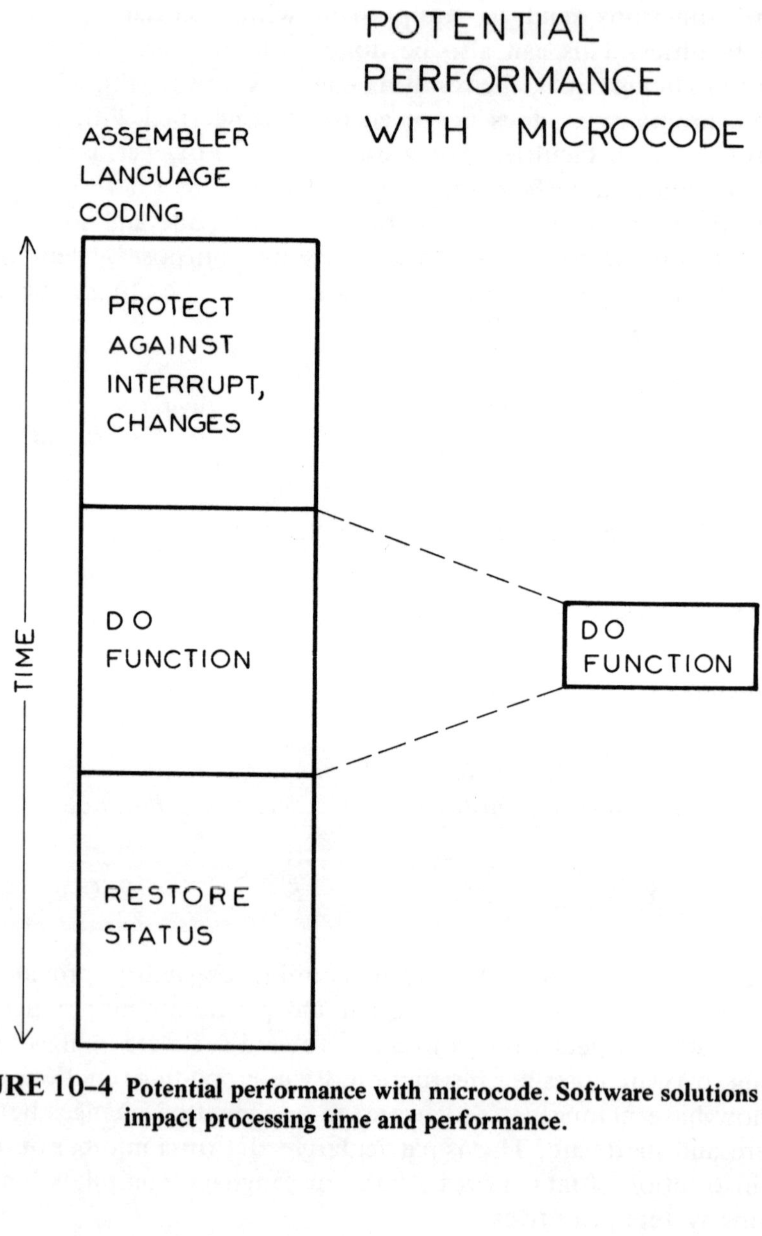

FIGURE 10–4 Potential performance with microcode. Software solutions largely impact processing time and performance.

Software should be reserved for those types of processing, data storage and transfer operations that change frequently during the product life: the primary impact of VLSI on software mainly deals with substitution capabilities for those functions which are unchangeable or change very slowly.

Another important impact is in software design. The design of operating systems (OS) and, in general, basic software is based on two prime considerations–its functional capabilities and the number of tradeoffs between conflicting constraints, namely speed of execution and available space. Particularly since OS design must consider the data load imposed on the system (Figure 10-5), microprocessor-supported functions allow tradeoffs toward a faster code execution.

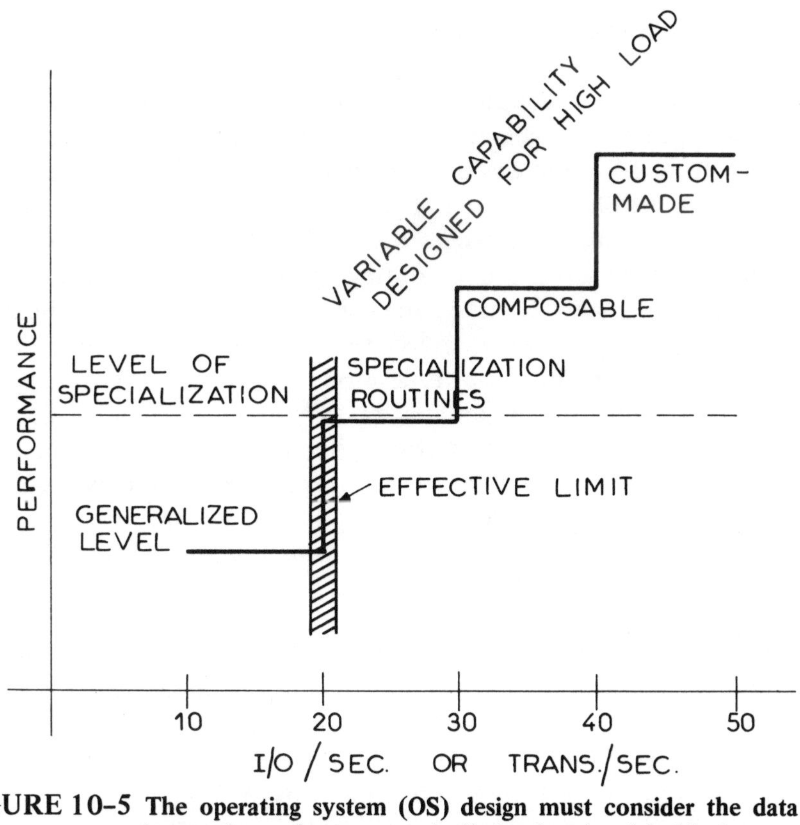

FIGURE 10–5 **The operating system (OS) design must consider the data load imposed on the system. A distinction is advisable between the general level and a variable capability designed for high load according to requirements.**

It has been observed that the supervisory overhead of the operating system does not grow linearly with the power of the computer system, but rather exponentially. If we increase the power of the processor by a small amount, we will not get proportionate increases in throughput; more likely we will get approximately the square root of the improvement in processor power in throughput. However, if the cost/performance benefit of the bigger unit tends to disappear in software overhead, the conversion of this software into firmware returns part of the lost power, and microcomputers are well-suited to benefit from this conversion.

Whether we use micro, mini, or maxi equipment, we certainly need a supervisory function to multiplex the system's resources to satisfy the competing demands of various tasks. The goal then is to minimize resources consumed by supervisory effort through the technological innovations made feasible by microprocessors.

There was a time when the general purpose computer system was composed of slightly more than a processor, a channel, a local communications controller, and peripherals. Then, software became a necessity. From 1964 to 1973, the general purpose computer had an operating system whose prime function was the control of I/O, a file storage capability, and running multiple streams of batch processing. Separate programs did timesharing, transaction processing, and monitoring, but since 1974, manufacturers have advanced operating systems which incorporate in an integrated simultaneous mode the capability of running applications programs in batch processing, transaction processing, and timesharing. This enables programs in these three modes to work with a single integrated database run by a data management program which has become, in many cases, the focus or center of a general purpose computer system. At the same time market perspectives radically changed, new design approaches appeared for the acceleration of system operations. This is the case with cache memories (Figure 10-6) which were first introduced in mainframes, then migrated toward peripherals (intelligent disc drives with cache, logic over data).

Microprocessor-supported approaches allow a distribution of intelligent functions throughout the computer system and make available to the designer the possibility of locally supporting capabilities which in the past needed to be mapped into central memory. Hence, over the last few years we have observed the distribution of functions in making some 3M faculties (multiaccess, multiprogramming, multicomputing) self-sufficient

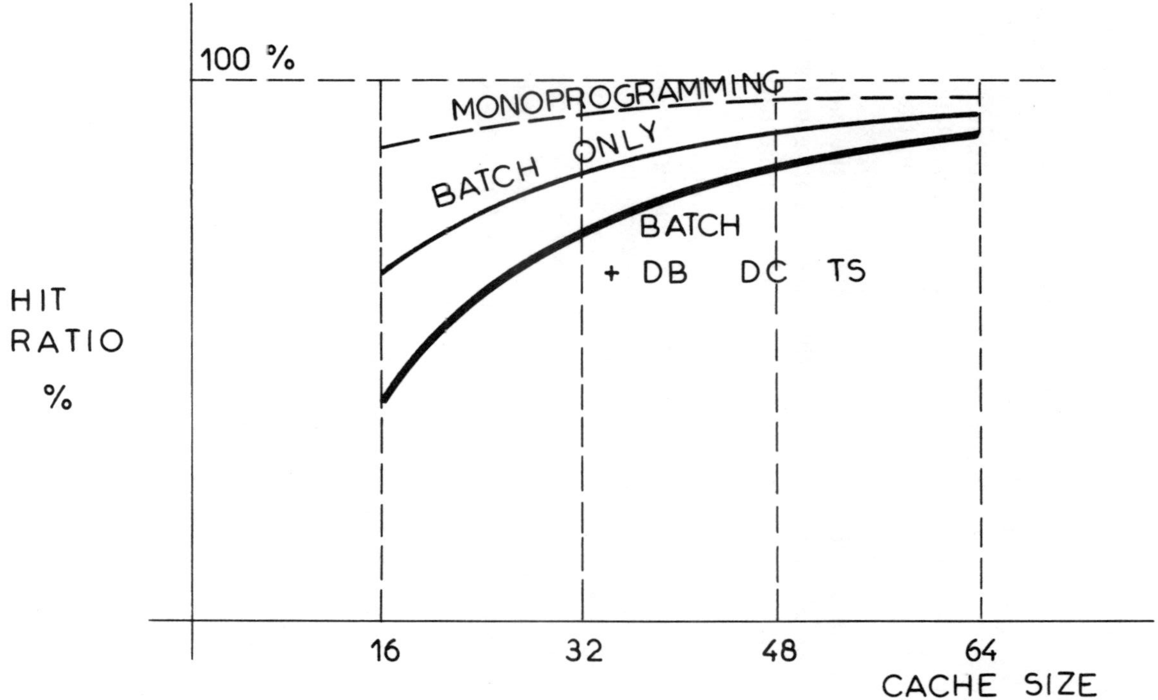

FIGURE 10–6 Cache memories have had significant impact on machine performance. As they work on the expectation of a piece of data demanded by the CPU, the hit ratio increases with larger cache sizes. The impact is much greater in a complex environment which includes databasing (DB), datacomm (DC), timesharing (TS) and batch.

with their own intelligence, and development of standalone microprocessors capable of being linked to one another through a communications capability.

The next big challenge with microcomputer systems has a precedence in the early 1960s and early 1970s. It may be coincidental, but the microcomputer appeared at approximately the same time as the general purpose operating system in the mainframes; so we should view the operating system rather than the microcomputer's hardware as that which made the new machinery challenge the old. Ten years later, firmware and solid-state software are playing a similar role in the fate of microcomputers.

In conclusion, we should be building into hardware the most basic functions and provide in microcode those which are repetitive and stable. Software must be reserved for functions which are non-repetitive, non-stable, new, or in evolution. If our aim is to convert OS to microprocessor-supported functions, all operations which are highly repetitive must be done by microprogramming; for instance, the first level interrupt handler, which receives interrupt and memorizes registers—even if the latter has traditionally been software-supported. The paging mechanism: the interface between modules, and elements which help keep the OS proprietary are other examples of this same reference. Evidently, such choices are not only influenced by technology and efficiency, but also by strategic competitive considerations.

PROGRAMMING THE MICROCOMPUTER

Useful as it is in its implementation with computer devices, microprogramming is not answering all requirements for machine instructions. Microprocessors must be endowed with a valid implementation language which will have a hardware impact (memory size, system speed). Basic choices must be made in this regard: high-level languages are faster to develop but require more memory; assembler-level languages are longer to develop but make better use of available memory.

The assembler program exists either resident to or on an external computer system (cross-compiling). Its goal is to translate mnemonic code into machine language, allocate storage, compute absolute or relocatable addresses from symbolic addresses, insert library routines, and treat symbolic code for macro instructions. A higher-level language works much faster in program development than an assembler language (as far as the programmer's time is concerned), assures some machine independence, is easier to learn, and lends itself well to structured programming. Among the higher-level languages available with microprocessors are Basic, Fortran, PL/M (Intel), Pascal, APL, and some others.

Starting at the most fundamental level of a computer language to be implemented by a microprocessor, we distinguish:

- *Machine languages* whereby the computer is programmed directly in a binary mode. For example, a binary program for an 8-bit processor may be:

```
11   001   001
10   110   001
10   001   011
01   100   100
00   000   000
```

- With an *assembly language* each statement is replaced by a symbolic code:

```
ADD   R1,   RO
STO   R1
JMP   100
```

- *Higher level language* statements correspond to several machine language instructions:

```
X = (Y*A) **B
```

Higher languages are converted by a compiler (or interpreter) to machine language. The compiler interprets entire programs at one time and is not required to be resident in the computer at run time. The interpreter processes the source program one statement at a time; it is slower and less efficient than the compiler, but easier to use. Compilation can be done through a resident system or a host system.

The resident system produces the object code that runs on its own processor. Tests are done on the actual processor, but with limited resources the set-up is not so efficient. The alternative is to execute on host, producing code for another processor. Usually, a simulator allows for imitation of the microprocessor (on the host) for program testing. The resources of the large host assure faster operation and ease in usage. Whichever approach is taken, the need for thorough testing cannot be repeated too often.

Also of great importance is maintenance. Among users, maintenance now absorbs between seventy percent and eighty percent of available programming resources. Among manufacturers, the range is no better as maintenance activities are still manual.

Figure 10-7 illustrates the fact that the rate of maintenance increases in order of magnitude according to two factors: the age of the program and its size. Not only should we strive to make small-size programs, but also to convert them, as much as possible, to firmware (solid-state software).

Testing is a subject to which great attention should be given. Cross-computer programs make feasible testing of object code when the microcomputer is not available or cannot handle the job; they provide diagnostics and indicate stack overflow. They also permit modification and display of simulated memory and CPU registers; breakpoints may be set; programs can be traced. (The latter is the work of the debugger.)

Whatever approach is chosen, there is a need for final debugging. The debugging faculty is a resident program (monitor) which allows display or printout of RAM, ROM, and CPU registers. It permits modification of the RAM memory, starting the program from a specific memory location; will break or stop at the specific memory location reached; and can assure optimal features:

- program load and store (disc or cassette)
- I/O configuration
- hardware and software interrupt
- single-step operation.

This software tool essentially operates on machine or object code, and is directly addressable by the programmers whose work it assists, simplifies and accelerates.

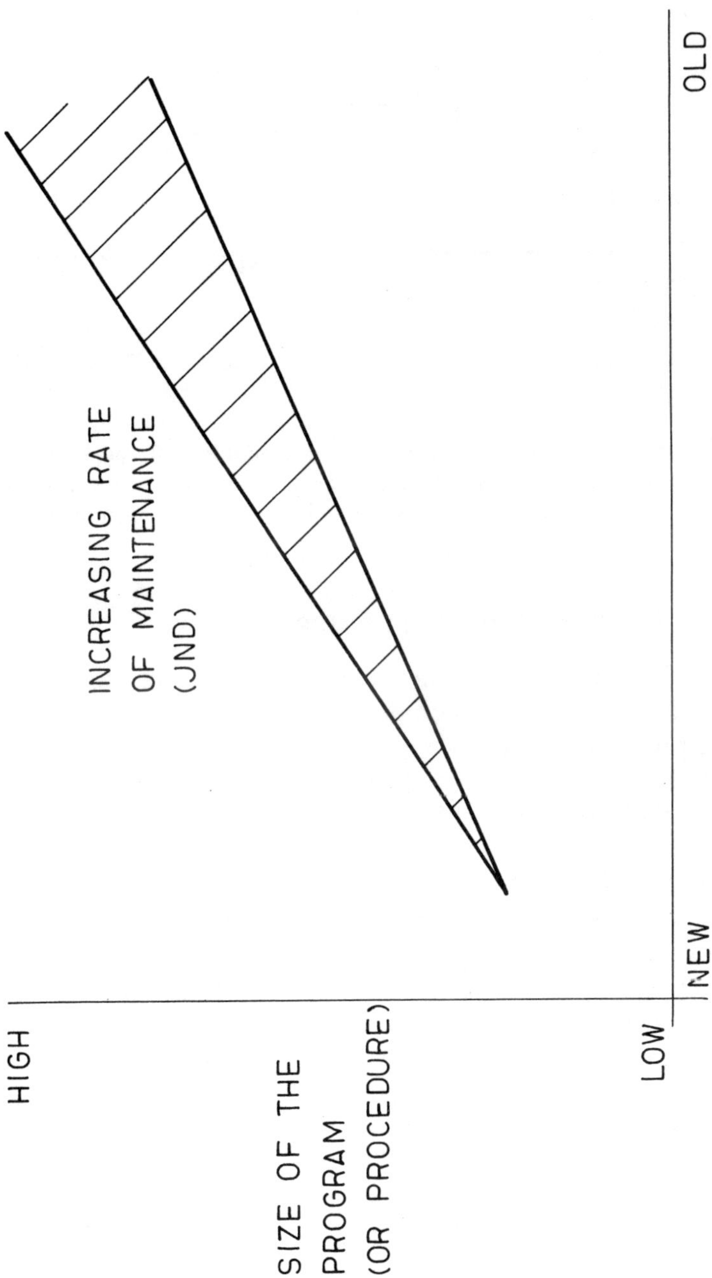

FIGURE 10–7 The rate of software maintenance increases as a function of programming and size. The scale is the order of magnitude.

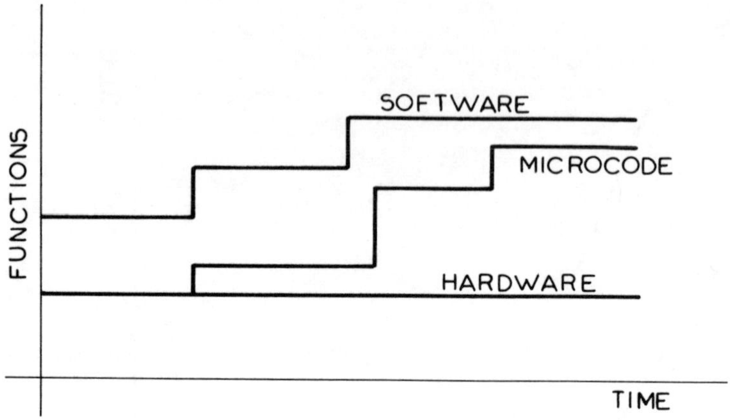

FIGURE 10–8 **Developing user requirements and technological capabilities to support them will ensure that the position microcode occupies between hardware and software will grow as a function of time.**

THE NEXT FRONTIER IN MICROCODE

Increasingly sophisticated programming faculties in basic and applications software in association with microcomputers will most likely have a large impact on data processing, databasing, and datacomm. Today's popular microcomputers have DP origins. The Datapoint 2200 is the grandfather of most of them, its instruction set being equivalent to a primitive microprocessor, the Intel 8008, though the 2200 executes instructions ten times faster than the 8008.

Since Datapoint CPUs have made good inroads into data processing and word processing (WP) applications, this should be enough of an indicator for future microcomputer possibilities. We can divide now-available microcomputers into two broad classes: those which have followed the Datapoint 2200 lead and are well-suited to DP applications, and those designed specifically for digital logic usage.

The principal differences between these two classes may be summarized as follows. Instruction sets of DP-oriented microcomputers are adequate for DP applications; digital logic-oriented microprocessors, on the other hand, tend to have rather primitive instruction sets (for DP and WP purposes) with many key capabilities absent. DP-oriented microcomputers can easily be expanded with various support devices to handle peripherals (videos, disc units, and printers) while digital logic-oriented microcomputers have I/O capabilities that are better suited to creating and processing logical signals.

The main difference between typical microcomputers of these two classes lies in the design of the VLSI devices that constitute the microprocessors; DP-oriented designs are more likely to substitute the lower end of the minicomputer range, but as they increase in capabilities they will be challenged in their former field by nanocomputers. Novel approaches (along with new structures) will evolve in end usage as nanocomputers step in. The latter will work with interpreters rather than compilers, be dedicated to elementary jobs, and form a hierarchical structure of interrelated components.

Simultaneously, parts of the OS (eventually much of it) will be written in firmware, thus speeding up the system and altering end usage concepts. A system hierarchy will develop most likely as outlined in Table 10-1. Given these premises, whichever the lower class may be, it will eventually merge into the immediately higher one, while a still lower class will fill the gap left by this movement.

TABLE 1

A SYSTEM HIERARCHY

	MIPS	*Central Memory (MByte)*	*External Memory (GByte)*	*Possible Price*
Giga	10–50 (eventually 50)	64–256	20–50 (eventually Trillion Bytes)	2–8 $M
Maxi	2–10	5–64	3–20	0.4–2 $M
Midi	1–2	2–5	0.5–3	100–400 $M
			(MByte)	
Mini	0.5–1	0.5–2	150–500	10–100 $K
Micro	0.1–0.5	0.12–0.5	5–150	1–10 $K
Nano	up to 0.1	0.12	up to 5 MByte	1 $K

By 1990, at the top end of the power scale, most processors will be array processors with a vastly expanded relational database capability and encapsulated databases also relationally oriented. At the bottom end of the computer power scale, nanocomputers will eventually be manufactured on 512 KB (or 1 MB) chips and include several capabilities of processors and central memories. Nanocomputers will have a number of standard faculties which are new under present practice, such as:

- functional languages, and
- data flow computer structures.

Picocomputers will eventually evolve based on outgrowths from Josephson technology, and though under current conditions this solution needs too much cooling, a pre-Josephson device (by IBM) seems to be a breakthrough. (Picoprocessors may be available between 1985 and 1987).

The next frontier in microcode will be determined by the range of equipment available for day-to-day operations: from computing to word processing and many supporting fields. In this sense, it is appropriate to distinguish ten main product and service categories:

1. *Mainframes*—General purpose computers, which include central memory and exclude peripherals and terminals, but include maintenance (local or remote) provided for a fee.
2. *Minicomputers and microcomputers*—All end user and OEM minis and micros and their native memories, exclusive of detachable peripherals and terminals. These include maintenance, as above.
3. *Peripherals and terminals*—In this class are all units shipped as parts of complete systems or shipped separately, including data entry equipment and add-on memory, but not equipment without functional connections to DP systems, standalone cash registers and POS being examples.
4. *Office automation devices*—Diverse equipment such as word processors, intelligent and other copiers, facsimile, Videotex, and point-of-origin equipment such as POS. Office automation will be a major battleground in the future, with emphasis on communications capabilities, electronic document distribution, executive support, and database access.

5. *Local communications*–The PBX are the basic reference along with modems. However, this class is much broader and includes stations, voice store and forward, high capacity bus units (for local networks) but excluding the knowhow and software which constitute a separate class. Local networks will be one of the hot subjects in the 1980s.

6. *Long-Haul Communications*–Here, key ingredients are Value Added Networks (VAN) and the services which they provide. Contrary to local networks, architectural software is included since VAN carriers will increasingly offer bundled services for voice, text, data and image. Satellites, optical fibers, wave guides, microwave, millimeter wave links and switching capabilities enter this class.

7. *Robotics*–Microprocessor-based machinery which makes feasible unmanned factory production through the automation of diverse production processes: from handling, painting, casting, forging, assembling, palletizing, transporting, to voice recognition systems.

8. *Software and Firmware*–Software products and all types of usage: OS, DBMS, transactional systems, applications packages (AP) along with their maintenance and customer assistance for implementation provided for a fee. The firmware line will be a direct extension of this class, overlapping in part but largely complementary. The trend we already underlined in this chapter will directly affect the microcomputer's own development costs, as Figure 10-9 demonstrates.

9. *Media and Supplies*–Discpacks and magnetic tapes are the media; supplies are of all sorts: carbon ribbons, paper and incidental forms and even electronic and electrical devices become consummable.

10. *Expertise*–This is the area with the greatest potential for the future. It includes training (at all organizational levels), consulting and, in general, knowledge-intense services. This will be the real frontier of development in the late 1980s and early 1990s.

Business opportunities in hardware, software and firmware developments will largely depend on growth perspectives of the microcom-

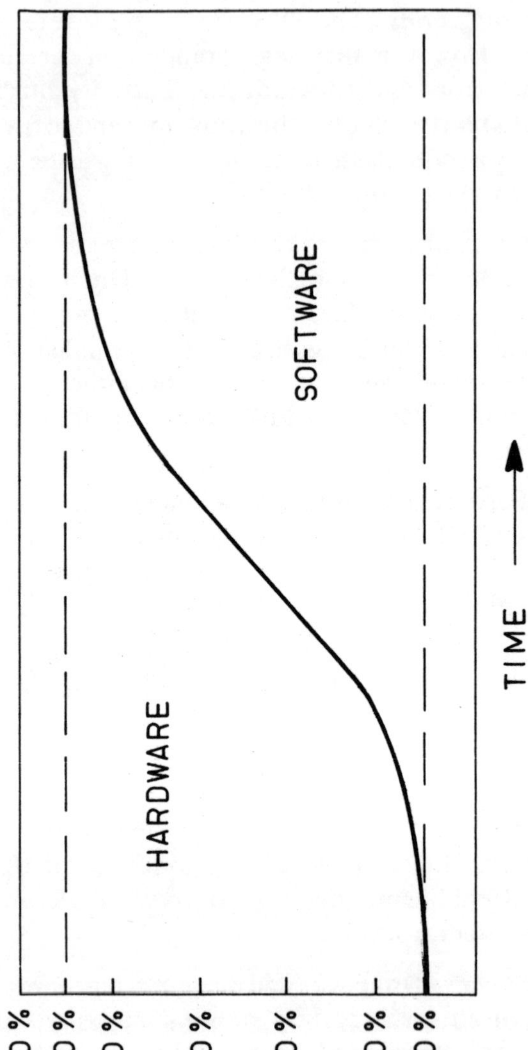

FIGURE 10–9 The development cost of a minicomputer is increasingly debited on the software side. Solid-state software may be the best way to bend this curve.

puter market. All forecasts point to the fact that such growth will not abate. In 1981, unit shipments should surpass the 500,000 mark and, by 1985, two million microcomputer systems will probably be shipped in the United States alone; international growth may reach double that figure. How fast the market will grow is an issue open to debate. Surely, however, growth will be influenced by applications perspectives.

Let us remember what the minicomputer did to traditional mainframe sales during the 1970s. By encouraging distributed information systems, the minicomputer off-loaded the processing that would normally have been done in a central fashion by large machines, and also took the play away from established mainframes, such as IBM. In the early 1980s, microcomputers may do the same thing to minicomputers through an approach which can best be described as a microcomputer on every desk and in every home. By the mid-1980s, however, microcomputers themselves will be challenged by nanocomputers which will take over an increasing range of functions including firmware requirements.

Characteristically, the nanocomputer will be channeled not necessarily by the manufacturing firm but, rather, by leading merchandisers who must become as much pricing as product innovators. This will be a significant twist in software and firmware: merchandisers will determine the price at which they wish to sell a product and then ask manufacturers to design and fabricate at that level. In turn, this will commit all firms to reduce their hardware, software, and firmware prices.

With the increased competition in terms of product cost and functionality—and with the trend toward disposable products—the difficult decision will no more be which source of supply to favor, but what criteria to use in making the choice.

PART THREE

Broadening the Applications Horizon

11 Computer-Aided Design

INTRODUCTION

THERE ARE several ways to evaluate computer-aided methods as tools for improving efficiency. One view is that of system investment capital payback. Another is that of easing the effect of personnel shortages from engineering design to teaching. A third is looking at microprocessor-assited approaches as an integral part of the overall conversion to a more efficient workplace.

There is a strong relationship between robotics, CAD/CAM, and other forms of flexible automation. It is amazing to realize how far CAD/CAM and robotics have come in such a short period of time—from an industry that was barely credible to one that is receiving serious attention.

Companies which experienced the benefits of CAD comment that payback prospects are even better than originally forecast. This means additional savings for customers, and profits for the firm. In one case, designers and drafters using seven CAD workstations online to a data processing system were 475 percent more productive than their counterparts working at conventional drawing boards.

Engineering and scientific applications are not total solutions nor should they be looked at as distinct from other phases of computer-based applications. As Figure 11-1 shows, they form a continuum from the nuclear engineering number cruncher to the polyvalent workstation, from CAD for technical studies to the interactive business environment there exists a remarkable continuity which often escapes attention.

An important advantage of CAD is a big improvement in the quality of drawings: The engineering database assures that every drawing and symbol stored in memory is reproduced exactly the same way every time. Another advantage is the elimination of tedious, repetitive design and drafting procedures. CAD has allowed contractors to grow faster, magnifying the skills of their engineers and draftsmen to meet expanding needs. They bid more confidently because they meet better deadlines

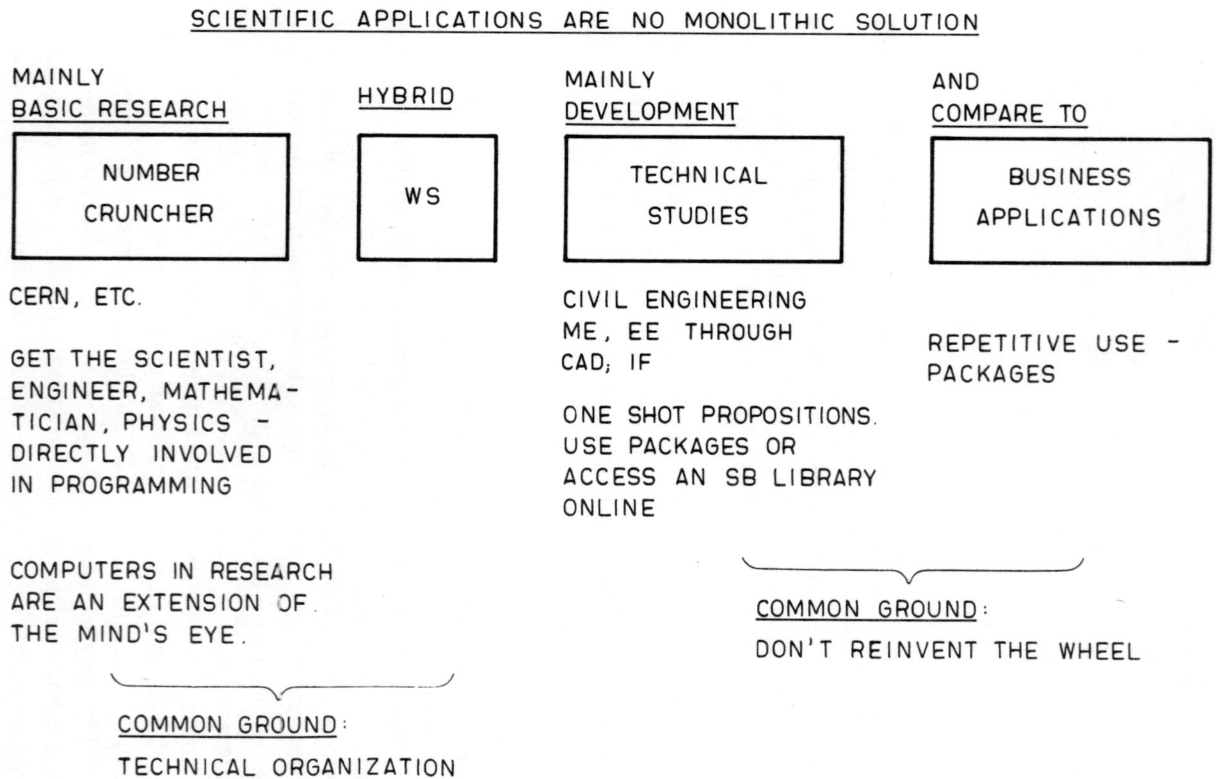

FIGURE 11–1 Scientific applications form a continuum from the nuclear engineering number cruncher to the polyvalent workstation CAD for technical studies and the interactive business environment—from bill of materials to procurement.

without running into bottlenecks on design and drafting tables. However, investment calls for new hardware, software, and facilities modification, and expenses for training and staffing during implementation.

It is nearsighted, though, to limit the concept of CAD to engineering work alone. Microprocessor-assisted approaches can help in practically every field of human endeavor, one of the best being that of computer aided instruction (CAI). In fact, CAD and CAI have many generic similarities. In the one as in the other, we amplify our brainpower through computerized support.

COMPUTER-ASSISTED APPROACHES

Knowledge has ever been a tradeable commodity, but there is a difference with knowledge of the present. We have reached the point where the more we share it, the more we have—and knowledge which is not shared decays. This is the essence of education, experience, and lifelong learning, and here is one of the major contributions computer-aided approaches can bring to our civilization.

Computer-aided instruction is not just another computer-based application; given the reasons we have explained, its potential can shake up our educational system. With microprocessors, the cost of the contact hour in CAI is steadily dropping, currently standing below that of a manned instruction process. Also, children love CAI: It is difficult to keep them away from computers. They are far more interested in learning than ever before, while schools experience improved attendance levels. Computer illiteracy among educators and administrators is still an obstacle, but one that many vendors are confronting directly; for example, the latest Apple promotion effort includes a computer literacy training package with the first microcomputer purchased by a school.

One approach to easing the entry of computers into the classroom is the work of organizations such as MECC (Minnesota Educational Computer Consortium), created in 1973 as a statewide computer service organization to plan, coordinate, and deliver all computer services to its members. Such members are the public school systems of Minnesota, the University of Minnesota, the state university system, the state community colleges, and the State Department of Education. MECC has a timesharing system that services over 2,000 terminals, linking ninety percent of all Minnesota schools. At any given time, about 350 terminals are active.

Timesharing services are purchased by MECC members, and consultants are available at no cost to assist in workshops, conversion, and the development of *courseware*. MECC also offers a library of over 950 microcomputer programs for elementary through college levels. Software supports have also been instrumental in promoting the hardware behind them. (I have started with CAI because I consider it the twin brother of CAD.)

Table 11-1 presents a list of the major manufacturers of CAD/CAM equipment. Not all companies are directly comparable in terms of their product lines, but this is too young an industry sector to settle down at this point. To this list can be added some manufacturers of graphics systems: Hewlett-Packard, Strongberg Carlson, Tektronix, Sanders, Ramstek, Digital Equipment, IBM, and CDC. Several established computing firms are expending a significant effort to provide the end user with a host of software capabilities. This is sensible: The International Data Report forsees 15,000 CAD/CAM systems in operation by 1984, more than 600 percent up from January, 1980, figures.

It is quite likely that CAD within manufacturing will be one of the most dynamic development sectors in this decade; only the personal computers market will exceed its growth rate. The key reason is the CAD/CAM capability to improve productivity and, therefore, competitiveness. To appreciate the effort behind CAD approaches, we should look at this field from a broader perspective.

TABLE 11–1

CAD / CAM PRODUCERS IN THE U.S. MARKET

CAD / CAM Manufacturer	*Share of market % (in $)*
Computervision	30
Applicon	16
Calma–GE	14
Auto–Trol	10
M+S	10
Gerber	4
Lockheed/IBM	4
Others	12

CAD AND CAM

There are two general ways of looking at CAD and computer graphics. The one is that of searching for a solution to satisfy technical requirements. In this more limited viewpoint, engineering management is essentially concerned with acquiring a personal impression of the equipment's performance and of its possible impact on technical productivity. In the case of a given industrial company, for example, the first interest in a CAD solution came as an outgrowth of the desire to extend PERT capabilities.

However, there is an alternative and much broader approach of looking at this subject: This is the drive to answer the needs of both management and technical information in an interactive manner, with a presentation based largely on graphics.

The two approaches have this in common: both require a significant effort to properly establish the facts. However, the basic advantage of an interactive computer graphics system is that it allows the dynamic generation, verification and combination of complex three-dimensional objects using two-dimensional input and displays. Here is where the list of relative advantages can start.

Computer graphics have a long history, as shown in Figure 11-2. In the beginning was an engineering use of the computer; this led to developments just prior to and during the Second World War. Fire control and radar-related systems have been an outgrowth of this. In the mid-1950s, the capabilities available through a numerical control of machine tools became evident. Then, at the end of that same decade came the Semiautomatic Air to Ground Equipment (SAGE) system for air defense. Analog X-Y plotters, CRT, microfilm plotters, and timesharing capabilities were developed in the early 1960s. At about the same time, the pioneering work of Sutherland gave birth to the ancestor of today's CAD systems, while GM Laboratories have actively worked on DAC-I (design augmented by computers).

Computers and CRT displays can be used to perform design, engineering, and manufacturing functions. Most phases and practically all areas of engineering design can be conceived, tested, and proved by CAD techniques. The same can be said of fabrication; computer-aided manufacturing (CAM) is a fast-growing domain which logically follows CAD technology and integrates into it a number of well-established computer supported faculties from inventory management to the numerical control of machine tools. This leads to *robotics*.

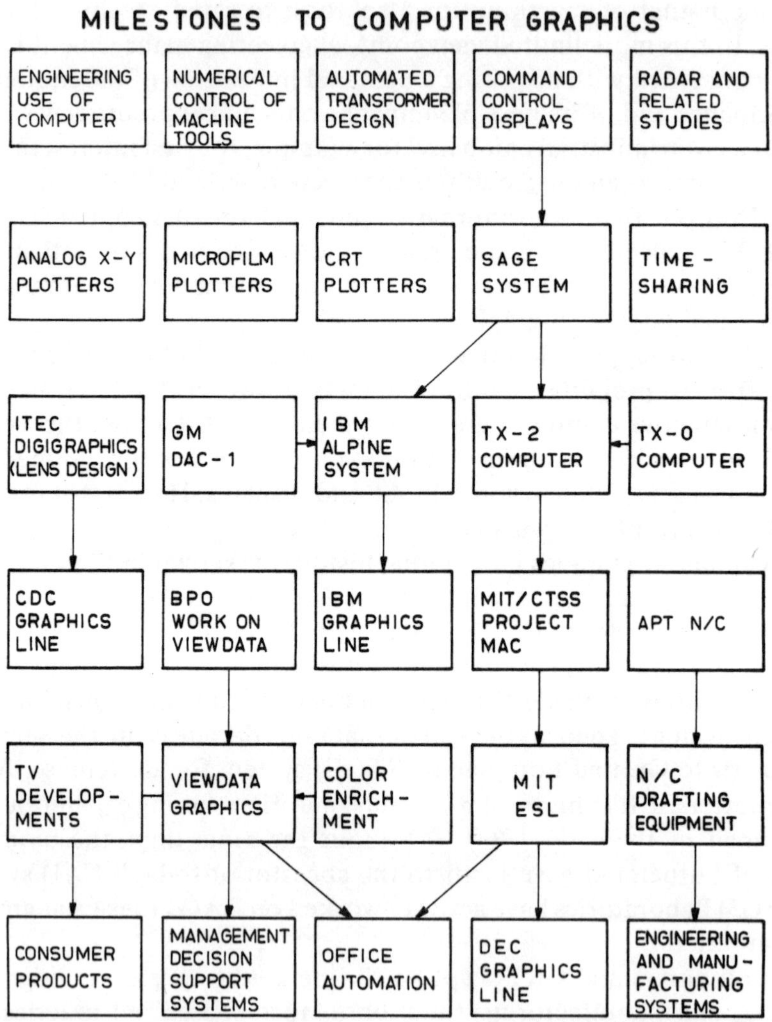

FIGURE 11-2 **Computer graphics have a long history. This figure summarizes milestones for nearly thirty years of concentrated effort.**

An example of online possibilities is weight reduction studies in the car industry. Weight reduction design is hard to accomplish because the emphasis has to be on the substitution of materials (light metals, plastics), a wider implementation of electronics in a basically mechanical product, and new power sources. Computer-based video consoles have been, however, successfully used to evaluate the structural characteristics of designs in a vehicle structural analysis program (VSAP). With VSAP, engineers can "assemble" mathematical models of components in a car and then "road test" the car on a simulated drive route.

The thorough evaluation of structural characteristics, road testing, or any other task performed by computer necessitates significant software support. This is divided into two parts:

- the basic software, or operating system (OS), and
- the applications programs.

Formerly, applications programs have been written by users; the former were written by the manufacturer. But CAD and Office Automation are two precise areas where applications packages are becoming generally accepted (a very positive trend) and tend to integrate into the OS environment (Figure 11-3). With software, design changes can be made with minimal risk and can also be effected on the physical product in the same way since they have already been proven by the online system. Much trial and error is taken out of the design process in this manner. CAD/CAM accelerate the logical progression of design by:

- identifying the problem
- correcting the design
- rendering the model
- analyzing the result.

From there it is relatively easy to determine the correct tooling to build the designed product, and this process has the additional advantage of gaining the accuracy of a single reference engineering database.

The engineering database is the other support upon which a CAD/CAM system rests and flourishes. When properly kept, it is easily updateable, consistent, accessible on demand, fast in terms of being manipulated,

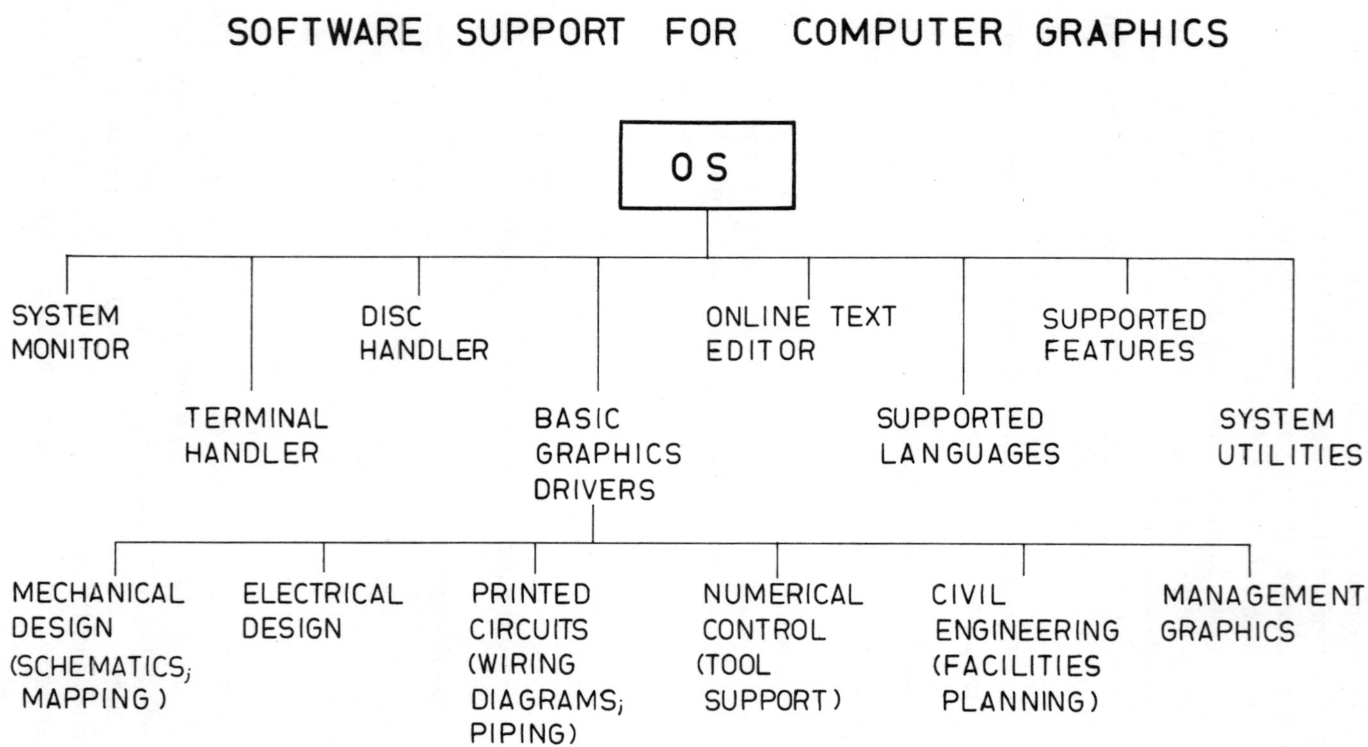

FIGURE 11–3 **The OS endowment for computer graphics is typically much broader than that which characterized batch systems for nearly twenty years. Not only basic housekeeping activities must be supported but also a good deal of applications functions.**

and includes all elements which are necessary to a variety of specialists. This—along with interactive online capabilities supported by computers—permit the integration of an entity with distant departments and a variety of skills.

We have been speaking of memory capacity as a fundamental ingredient of intelligence, and that is the goal of the engineering database. The computer's calculating power offers a fast means for experimentation and simulation. Together, they produce computer modeling from drawings, in-memory crash testing, and all sorts of prototype evaluations. Afterward come the databasing and computer-supported capabilities of manufacturing.

Typically, new machine designs include computer control related to feeds and speeds of cutting tools, improvements in their dynamic stability, feedbacks for precision machining, and design tool ruggedness. The lessons learned from earlier applications can find a wide market throughout industry.

Remember that productivity will not increase as a matter of course. We must restudy our machines, turn them inside out, eliminate all unnecessary parts, introduce computing and memory devices, and fully integrate the machine into the process to which it is designed to contribute.

Finally, CAD/CAM can play a key role in solving a problem which haunted design engineers for decades—the radical redesign of main products. The incorporation of microprocessor-based functions has brought significant interest on the issue of redesign and the associated subject of sustaining engineering costs. The problem is support on the manufacturing floor after engineering releases the specifications.

Sustaining engineering costs is presently approached in three ways:

1. Continue with a "shadow" research/development/engineering team composed of persons who developed the product. This can be effective, but is uneconomical.

2. Set up a separate department to sustain engineering. However, since the members of this department will be unfamiliar with the product, they will have technical problems. Besides, this sort of work will not motivate top engineers.

3. Once a project is completed, assign its members to other projects, but keep, say, ten percent of their time for sustained engineering. This looks like an effective solution, but may result in delaying

new projects because of the absence of some key personnel from the team. CAD/CAM can keep these men "on the team" by giving them instantaneous interactive access to the engineering database, while their main job may be a totally different assignment.

Equipment with online capabilities and a fully updated database will act as the catalyst, but the foundations should rest on a sound methodology. The best answer is in the establishment of a formal discipline known to everybody, observed and appreciated by all:

- Design specifications must be closed prior to manufacturing.
- Manufacturing engineering must be done while the product is being designed.
- Interactivity between design and manufacturing departments can be effectively supported throughout the life of the product through CAD/CAM.

The chosen methodology depends on prevailing conditions, frequency of support requests, and the amount of involvement required. An information system integrating CAD/CAM capabilities can also provide a solid ground for chargebacks (usually, but not always, to the authority requiring sustained engineering support). Cost charges against budgets and a system of demerits can help reduce the amount of sustained engineering, but it is necessary to keep track of all requests and document chargebacks with valid data.

CAD EQUIPMENT

Faculties which have been described show that available interactive devices can be used to provide a fast and simple way of utilizing three-dimensional data representing objects with sufficient complexity so as to be meaningful in a design environment. To meet such an objective, the hardware components must include:

- a picture processor capable of performing functions such as transforming, clipping, and viewpoint mapping;
- a picture memory;

- a picture generator;
- a character generator;
- a display unit;
- supporting gear (tablet, control dials, joystick, function switches, and an alphanumeric keyboard).

In the Evans and Sutherland equipment, for instance, the picture controller is a PDP 11/34 computer with a forty-eight kilowords memory. An interprocessor buffer provides high speed block transfers in both directions between the PDP 11 and the central graphics processor (Figure 11-4).

The application software covers the generation and manipulation of volumes representing sites and objects meaningful in a design context. A site can be represented by either a three-dimensional contour map, mesh, or grid network. Pen and tablet are used with an input program that employs an inking technique which draws a line to the pen position of the current update cycle from the previous position. The user places the desired contour map on the table and traces each contour, starting

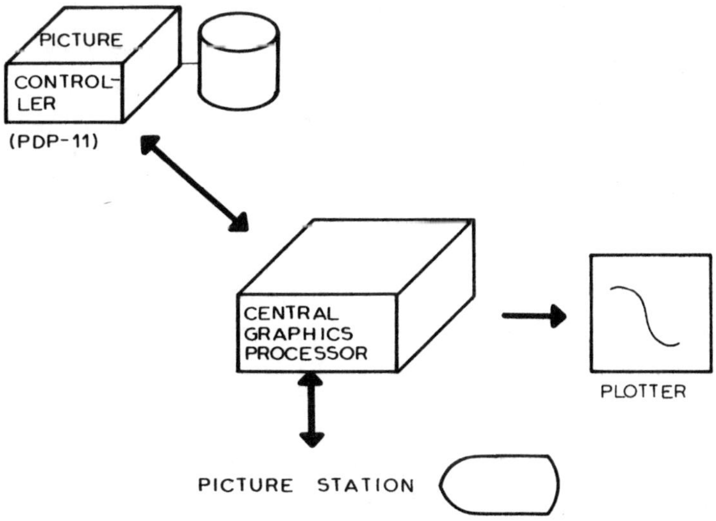

FIGURE 11–4 Main components of computer graphics equipment: picture controller, central graphics processor, picture station and plotter.

and stopping the inking process with a down/up pen motion, thereby determining the x and y coordinates.

Contour height is entered either via the alphanumeric keyboard or the control dials; the value is displayed on the screen and remains in effect until a new value is input. Each user-defined contour resides in an independent segment of the picture memory, so that although all contours are displayed, only the segment receiving the input data is active and requires updating at each cycle. This simplifies the storage and editing of data.

The multipicture system can support several users simultaneously, each interacting with pictures of two-dimensional or three-dimensional objects. Up to four central graphics processors may connect to the picture controller and up to four picture stations may connect to each processor.

The picture controller can execute several graphics and non-graphics programs concurrently. Each graphics program consists of a database describing the objects to be viewed as well as instructions for displaying a picture of the database on a picture station and interpreting that picture station's interactive devices to produce database or picture modifications.

The central graphics processor is composed of specialized graphics hardware units that create a picture of a database. The picture memory stores transformed lines and points for continuous refreshing. A picture may be segmented in this memory. The picture processor performs two-dimensional or three-dimensional rotations, translations, changes in scale, clipping, perspective computation, and viewpoint mapping on lines and points in the database. The job of the picture generator is to read the contents of the picture memory, generating lines and characters in specified intensities, and reading input from the directing output to the proper picture station. It also prespecifies what inputs it considers significant.

The picture controller also reads the contents of picture memory and directs data to the line generator, which looks up character definitions and puts them in proper size and orientation.

The picture station consists of a picture display and one or more devices for interacting with the picture. The picture display is a refresh random stroke display where lines, points, and characters comprising the picture appear. A variety of interactive devices perform picture modifications, including light pens, data tablets, alphanumeric keyboards, joysticks, function switches, lighted function buttons, and control dials.

The multipicture system graphics software package consists of a driver and library subroutines (in Fortran) providing access to the hardware's features which remain transparent to the user. A drum plotter is attached to the machine and the quality of the work is commentable.

The machine works interactively. The processor performs as above until an interrupt comes, then it gets partial value and puts in buffer. The system hangs-on until response is completed—but in the meantime it can go on with other experimentation.

The results are presented to the user in three-dimensional format, and as the design engineer running the installation was to comment, the difference between a two-dimensional and a three-dimensional approach is that:

- In a two-dimensional approach you can go from a plan to a building through a good deal of manual work.
- In a three-dimensional approach you go from a full three-dimensional building to a two-dimensional plan, by taking distinct views and cuts all being done automatically.

A number of operations can be performed after the site has been generated:

- individual contours can be identified, deleted or altered;
- new contours can be added;
- height and scale parameters can be re-entered.

The segmented-buffer mode and file structure maintain the integrity of the site as element components are edited. The initial hand-drawn site is usually in a rough form due to the low precision of the tablet and the difficulty in hand-tracing smooth contours. An interactive program employing a family of subprograms for curve-fitting is available to produce smooth contours and nets.

An architectural example made through the graph plotter is shown in Figure 11-5. It comes from the study of a monastery, Santa Maria di Torello, whose input required one hour of work. The computer can produce a complete components list for mechanical and civil engineering, and this can have significant interest to any design and construction firm.

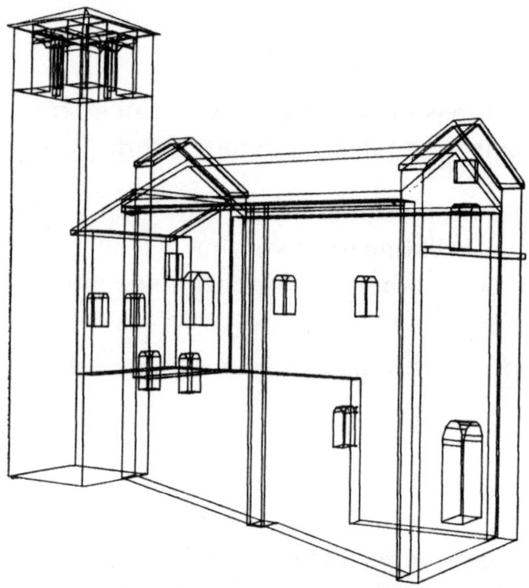

FIGURE 11–5 An architectural example of CAD design. The study of the monastery Santa Maria di Torello in the Swiss-Italian area of Ticino.

DESIGN EFFICIENCY

As time passes, good design engineers will be increasingly difficult to find and have larger salaries than today. Therefore, whatever contributes to engineering productivity should be brought to the foreground and should attract a good part of our attention. Computer-based design equipment should be of primary interest to any firm involved in design work. Management should display an interest in the productivity of its engineers—and this should be a basic criterion in evaluating a CAD/CAM acquisition.

Remote and batch programs, and even classical timesharing, are not substantial aids to engineering productivity as they contribute little more than what has been offered engineering calculation for more than thirty years. The point is that we should not be satisfied with marginal improvements, and match programs or a new timesharing service may be no improvement at all.

Furthermore, engineering programs necessarily run on a mainframe since a mini is not a number cruncher and lacks the power to process batch-type engineering calculations, supposing the software was available. We have to assure that improvements are fundamental—not marginal—and that they relate directly to engineering productivity; hence, to tangible results.

These are some reasons why the best solution lies in the use of CAD/CAM equipment. Figure 11-6 exemplifies the all-encompassing aspect of this discipline.

While in the early 1960s the ancestors of CAD/CAM were at the exclusive use of some organizations (mainly universities, the military, and companies such as Boeing and General Motors), by the late 1970s the usage of CAD/CAM had been generalized. Just the same, while early engineering applications of the CAD/CAM system have centered on design-related computations and drafting, the new environment is more imaginative.

Manufacturing companies apply the system in plan layouts and the preparation of fabrication processes, including numerical control of machine tools, bills of materials, and testing. Typically, this work is done through workstations providing the user with a visual display capability, a graphics tablet, functional and alphanumeric keyboard, and a hardcopy device which supports graphical output (text and data).

Figure 11-7 presents a system view. The following chapter will describe a structured approach to methodology and gives specific appli-

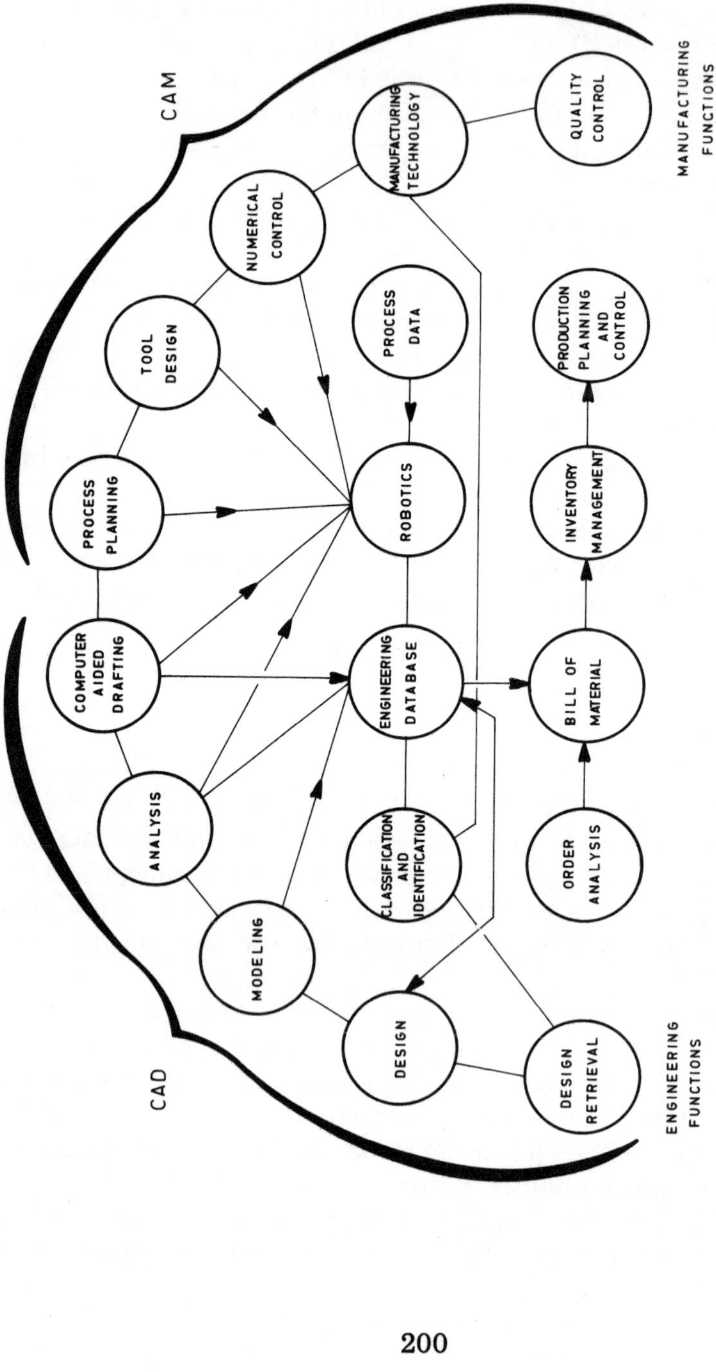

FIGURE 11–6 The all-encompassing aspect of the CAD/CAM discipline covering both engineering functions and their manufacturing counterparts and identifying the polyvalent role of the engineering database and the contribution of different disciplines to robotics.

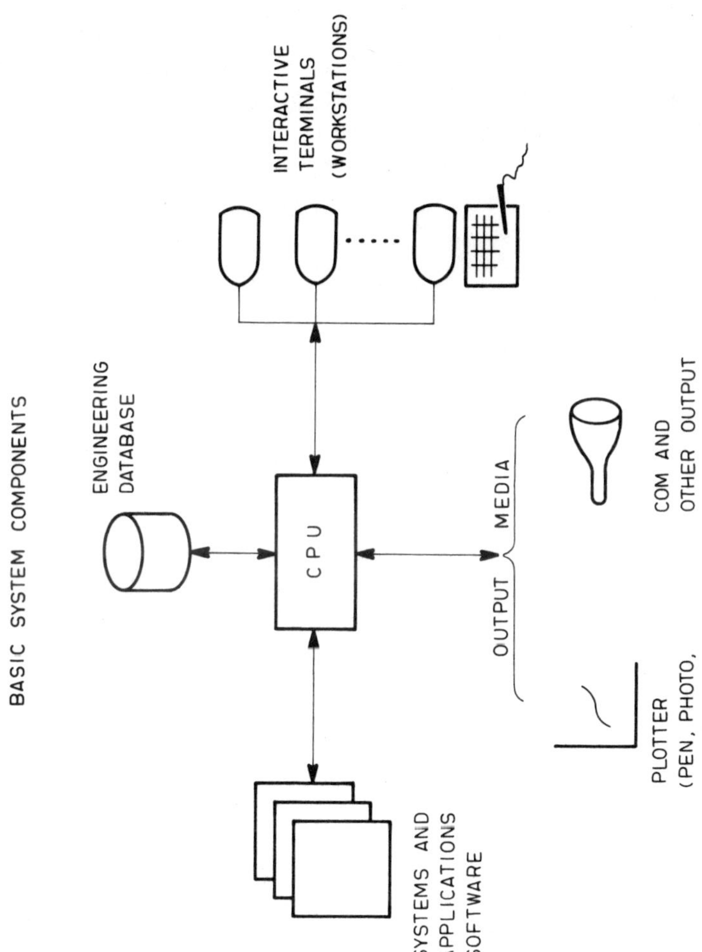

FIGURE 11–7 A systems view of a CAD facility able to support a multiplicity of workstations and applications software modules.

cations examples. In years to come, the best results in terms of design efficiency will be presented by those firms who put organization and methodology ahead of hardware—and also are keen in training their people.

We cannot and should not lose any time. While the overriding demand is for improvements in the productivity of our engineers and scientists, and much of the gear necessary for the future of our profession is already available, the methodology is present. With this situation, return on investment is minimal and the results leave much to be wanted. In a new field like CAD/CAM, we should start with the fundamentals.

12 A CAD Methodology

INTRODUCTION

A CAD system may have one or more workstations, different types of storage media and a variety of printer/plotter solutions (computer output to microfilm being an example of an upcoming faculty). Technological configurations are changing; one of the new developments is exemplified by the Architecture Machine Laboratory of MIT which is experimenting with videodiscs with still capabilities that can access 50,000 35mm slides. This is the beginning of read/write videodisc systems which can be expected to emerge in the 1980s.

The impact of new technologies on engineering design can be significant. Random access faculties to high capacity videodiscs on the one hand replace film-based microforms and, on the other hand, they merge microprocessor power with microforms and computer output to microfilm (COM) into new computer graphics systems. Such solutions are expected to take hold by the end of this decade, and we must be ready for them as they will have a competitive impact.

In configurations available today, a CAD/CAM system is basically composed of background equipment which includes computer units (central memory and disc storage) and foreground devices (design terminals, or workstations). Through them, the user interacts with the system, monitoring his work constantly through a graphics display and other supports. In a full-blown configuration, the main component units are:

- CPU (central processing unit)
- graphics display(s)
- light pen and other graphics-oriented input media such as data tablet, track ball, joystick, and so on
- alphanumeric display and A/N keyboard

- functional keyboard
- flatbed plotter and/or drum plotter for engineering and data presentation
- large and/or small surface digitizer
- electrostatic printer and/or other media such as COM and, eventually, optical discs
- different, more classical hardcopy output devices, such as a line printer
- one or more disc drives
- one or more tape drives
- a system console and, for some systems, a punch tape input/output or a card reader.

The user rarely needs to adopt the maximum number of units; he should choose only those applicable to his work. There is no unique CAD/CAM configuration: as is to be expected, the system is modular and the component units should be composed in the best way to provide needed requirements. That is why the search for a CAD/CAM system should start with the prerequisites for the end-use viewpoint. These will define the basic structure to which can be added desirable but not mandatory components.

Still, prior to equipment selection, it is wise to study other systems and, on the basis of joint work between users and specialists, plan the methodology. The CAD equipment must support the user's activities, and without the close collaboration of users, the specialists will not know what the problems are, only that they are confronted with some requirements. First of all, though, the problem must be clearly defined.

GETTING INTERACTIVE

Without doubt, the most challenging part in developing a valid methodology for a CAD/CAM system is that of projecting the database. Input makes sense only in the case of updating its content, and any output will derive its source in the engineering database. Therefore, while in the past we developed (or acquired) various applied programs for engineering calculations, we should now design and project systems which will use graphics processing capabilities. This is the most efficient answer to the requirements of modern technology.

Today there exist sophisticated computer systems dedicated to design purposes and able to provide material assistance in three dimensions:

- cost
- quality
- planning control.

Computerized design techniques allow for unprecedentedly high standards of quality and enhance production rationalization.

We have spoken of the importance of the engineering database. An engineering design database is presently supported by microforms (35 mm and 8mm film), COM, and magnetic disc storage; tomorrow it will use optical discs. The great challenge for any user (and prospective user) is not the availability of media which are relatively easy to be found, but the procedural studies regarding their employment and the structural prerequisites to assure that we derive a profit from them.

To appreciate the importance of the emerging databasing capabilities, we should look back at the beginning of the line of usage which characterized the computer-based solutions of an interactive character. The design terminal of a typical CAD/CAM system puts an electronic pen in the hands of the designer. In doing so, he can work on a touch-sensitive drawing tablet with software-supported commands such as zoom and line insertion which automate many routine tasks and improve the use of his time.

The engineer can create, modify, and refine his design interactively, viewing his work on a graphics display. With his electronic pen he can flip, rotate, magnify, move, stretch, copy and, in general, manipulate his design project in its entirety, or any part of it.

- Through an alphanumeric keyboard he can type his X, Y, Z coordinates, enter text for drawing annotation, and initiate graphics and processing commands.
- By means of either the electronic pen or the keyboard, he can ask the system to automatically retrieve any drawing he needs for reference or display.

- He can call standard design figures in his library, and insert them as requirements dictate.
- He can specify to the system at what locations on the drawing such symbols should be automatically placed, and he can assemble component parts into an emerging specification.

These are typically some of the tasks engineering departments are requesting from their management. In the past, the latter found no valid answer as the aging (in terms of its market introduction) timesharing service was not originally projected to handle such requirements. There is a great difference between the mainframe-oriented solutions of the 1960s and the microprocessor-based services of the 1980s.

With a CAD/CAM system, designs in process and those completed are stored in the database and are available on request. The online library capabilities help eliminate manual archival filing, cancel the need for redrafting commonly-used components, subassemblies and assemblies, and make instantly available to the engineer graphic displays in softcopies (video view) and hardcopies (printed forms). From functional specifications to fabrication (Figure 12-1) the designer can work on available graphs to:

- produce three-dimensional versions at any desired angle
- generate top, bottom, side and front views of three-dimensional parts
- rotate the part
- change the scale
- add text, and generally prepare documentation
- produce a bill of materials
- create mirror images.

CAD/CAM equipment is instrumental in helping to make components lists for the purchasing department, preparing materials for the production floor, producing quality control specifications, and sets-up numerical control tapes for machine tools. Software support ensures that the system is user-friendly and that the designer can accomplish computer-supported tasks without knowing a great deal about computers and programming. All the designer needs to know is how to communicate

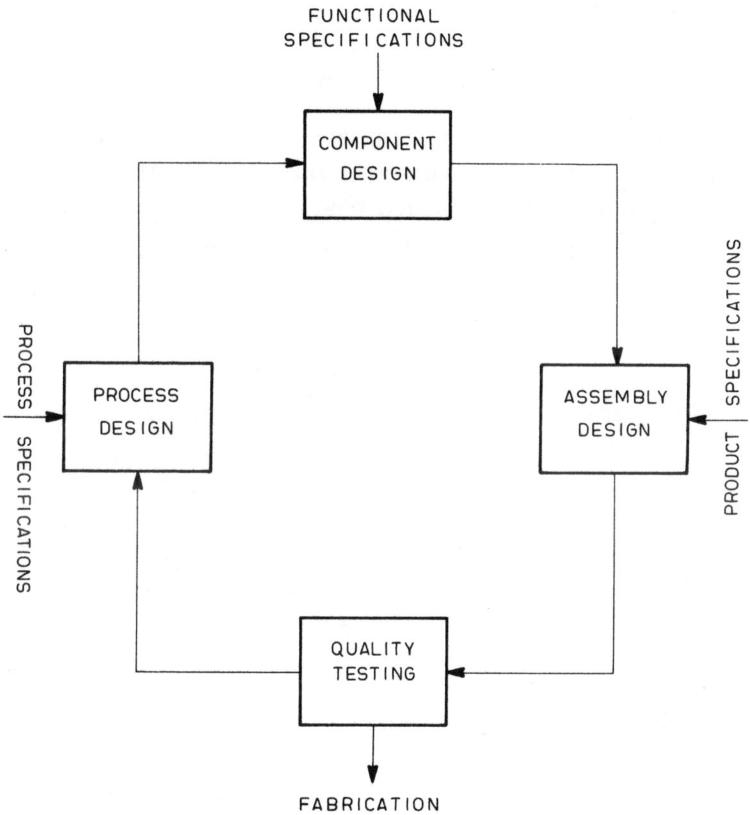

FIGURE 12–1 **This flow chart identifies the interactivity which exists between component design, assembly design, quality testing, and process design and established specifications.**

with the database to retrieve and, eventually, restore designs in process, handle standard parts, manipulate symbols and numbers, produce text and, in general, exercise the required design and drafting practices. We will return to the important issue of software support following a discussion on the different types of graphics terminals, so as to cover first the part of the interactive system which is nearer to the human component.

DISPLAY METHODS

Cathode-ray tube (CRT) display terminals are the oldest in use. Technologically, they require analog drives incompatible with digital circuits. Yet, in a way similar to that which characterized the life cycle of the punched card, though many people predict the demise of the CRT, the latter is life resistent mainly because it is still a cost/effective solution to visual display requirements.

Technologically, the answer to these requirements can take one of different forms which can be generalized under the heading *display methods*. One such form is the *raster scan* (digital television, scan graphics) which is used with home television sets; the electron beam moves on a left-to-right, top-down fixed pattern producing a single horizontal line in about sixty-seven msec. As raster systems become more common, the use of color becomes generalized and the same will characterize the hard-copy area, with the relatively low cost units which are now emerging. Along with color, technology now makes available brighter images that change faster, and a new man-machine communications capability where the designer affects the image by simply touching the large screen surface rather than using the electronic pen.

Color developments are important as color itself is a message carrier. Most present-day CAD/CAM systems are monochromatic CRTs with the color determined by color selection in the design phase. It is, therefore, significant that raster refresh systems can be used in a color mask tube thus making color pictures available to the user.

In earlier times, raster scan (digital television systems) required that the host computer define each point on the screen and store the points on a bit map, but microprocessors have relieved the host computer of scan conversion (map formatting). However, one of the disadvantages of digital television is the relatively poor resolution of the image as compared to stroke writing and storage tube, two other display methods.

1. *Stroke writing* supports a drafting capability which moves in an X, Y direction (visually projected).
2. *Refreshing* is the process of rewriting the image so that it appears steady. Refresh systems may use long persistence phosphors (ten to thirty frames per second) or short persistence phosphors (thirty to sixty frames per second), depending on the application.

The latter method illustrates an issue related to human engineering. The eye remembers a picture for about seventy msec., and if the image is not presented some 2.5 times that rate the result is a perception of flickering. Hence, rapidly changing data call for short persistence phosphors while devices provided for more static information should use longer persistence phosphors. The criteria for selecting the proper device are:

- picture quality (resolution per lines)
- data content
- dynamic characteristics
- operation without flicker
- selective erase
- color capability
- hardcopy attachment
- display life (in hours)
- equipment cost.

While different online hardcopy plotters can be used with CAD/CAM, whether for a quick look into the processed design or for more detailed drafting capability, the video unit is by far the main pillar of the interactive-capability CAD terminal. The terminal must also have an interface to the host computer (Figure 12-2), assure the digital description of a drawing (through central database access or local storage), be able to generate a steady image on the display, include a number of logical supports to translate computer instructions into operations functions and routine commands, and drive a variety of input devices for communicating with the computer.

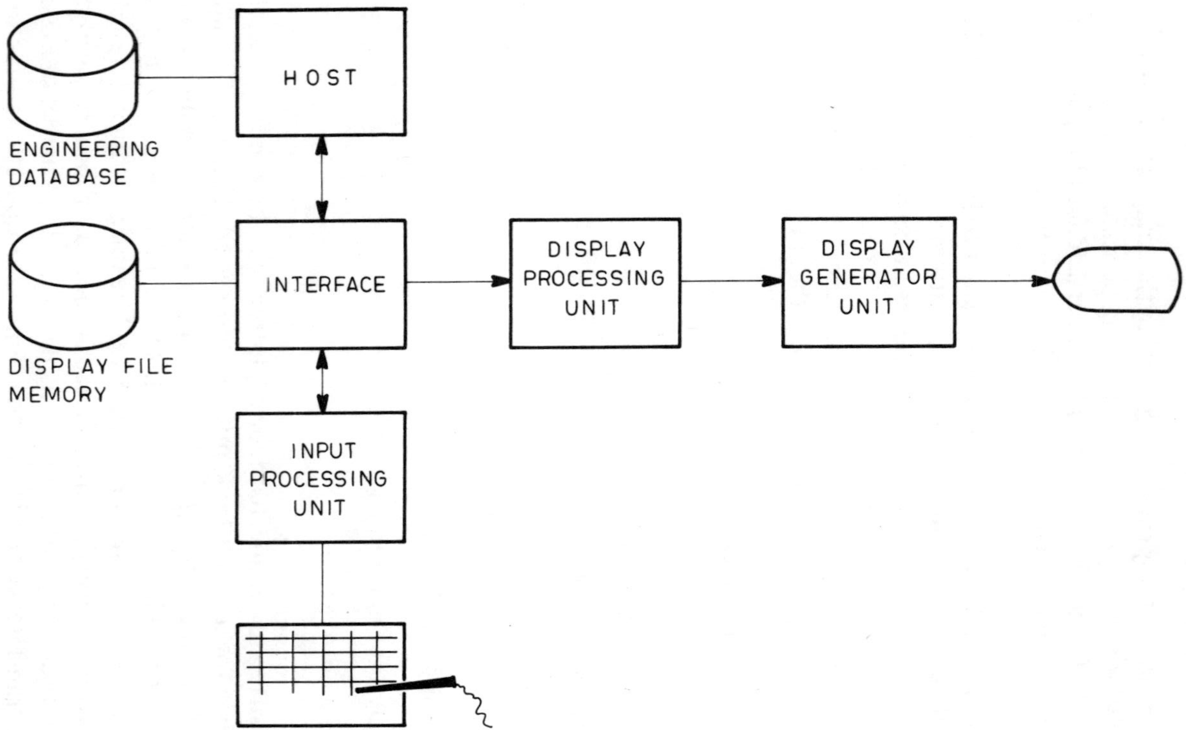

FIGURE 12-2 Interactive CAD/CAM terminals must have an interface to the host and the engineering database, must be supported by a display file memory, and must incorporate logical supports and drivers.

If interactivity is a prerequisite, an equally fundamental requirement is the development and support of the engineering database. Without it, an interactive display will be meaningless. As any other database, this should be an intregrated, organized collection of all information elements which describe the company's products and its manufacturing processes, including:

- engineering analysis
- parts definitions
- all drawings
- a variety of comments
- a variety of assemblies
- planning processes
- tool design
- numerical control information
- bills of materials
- related documentation.

One of the most important features of the engineering database is that once its information elements have been created, they are never lost and can be steadily updated. The stored geometry generated by the engineering designs can be used to produce drawings and process plans, project new tooling, generate tool paths for NC equipment, program robotic machines, outline tests, and direct automatic inspection equipment.

In other words, once a preliminary design has been created through interactive terminals and software support, by updating and then manipulating the elements in the database, all types of analyses can be applied to this design—stress, heat, wear and tear, and probably malfunctioning—to guarantee its viability.

A complex three-dimensional geometry can be divided through interactive approaches into smaller elements which are easier to manipulate without losing contact of the total perspective. These elements can be individually numbered, with connectivity being ascertained through computer-run routines. Computer-based approaches will subsequently be used in engineering design, employing as input the results of each preceding phase so as to project tooling, materials, and processing requirements.

Significantly, the same information developed through interactive terminals for design purposes is used to program the robotics gear—from parts manufacturing to final assembly and numerically-controlled equipment. CAD/CAM capabilities can easily be extended to handle the servomechanisms behind the robotics units whether the latter are used to drill, weld, paint, transport or assemble components. The robots themselves will use digital processing of visual images from television cameras to determine the orientation of parts on a conveyer, grasp and lift them, place them in an assembly, and so on.

The conversion of raw materials into finished goods requires a large amount of text and data. CAD/CAM offers just that—a computer-supported information capability which can be of significant help, not only in the various design programs of an enterprise but also, as stated, in improving the productivity of designers and in contributing to a steadier and more controllable product quality. We will return to the productivity issue in a subsequent section.

SOFTWARE SUPPORT

As with all computer-based systems, applications software is a crucial issue in equipment purchases; CAD software should be brought into the picture at an early stage of evaluation to assure that the end user will be supported with reasonably good libraries. This is a priority issue, as technology has advanced from raw graphics (line, arc, formatted digital output) to a significantly greater sophistication in design along the lines we have described.

First and foremost, the system must have good information retrieval capabilities; it must be able to handle part libraries, specification files, and text libraries. It must also be supported by design packages, preferably parametric, so that user-defined requirements are met by the available software, if not in their totality at least to a major extent. As an example, with applications software, a mechanical engineering manufacturer has found the following to be the most important components:

- instrumentation diagrams
- wire lists
- loop diagrams and equipment layout

- panel fabrication and wiring
- equipment grounding
- device mounting details
- structural layout
- various orthographic projections
- bill of materials.

Each of these applications areas calls for different support programs. For instance, orthographic and isometric studies need software capable of handling weights and line fonts. CAD/CAM software should provide automatic dimensioning (with the choice of units), the development of coordinates, flexibility for illustrative purposes (such as unscaled isometrics), and so on. Programs must also support hidden-line removable faculties and have the capability to move existing lines and equipment, eventually changing their size.

A company working on network establishment, with particular interest in three-dimensional models, identified as most important the ability to distinguish:

- starting and ending points in pipelining and cabling;
- the measurement of lengths in scale drawings;
- the associating of specific equipment with given lines; and
- the ability to separate pieces of equipment and to determine the directional flow of lines.

Equally important was found to be the orientation of components in a three-dimensional space to correspond to pipe routes, relational hookings needed for network establishment, a functional discrimination between different groups of graphical entities, and the separation of a single model into logical layers, flagging related graphical entities with textual descriptions. Figure 12-3 presents the overall systems interactivity between the supporting software and the designer's capability in terms of projection, feedback and optimization.

In fact, in a systems view of CAD/CAM, it is most helpful if software provides for the extraction of all graphs and data entered during the creation of a project or of a single drawing and its specifications. One

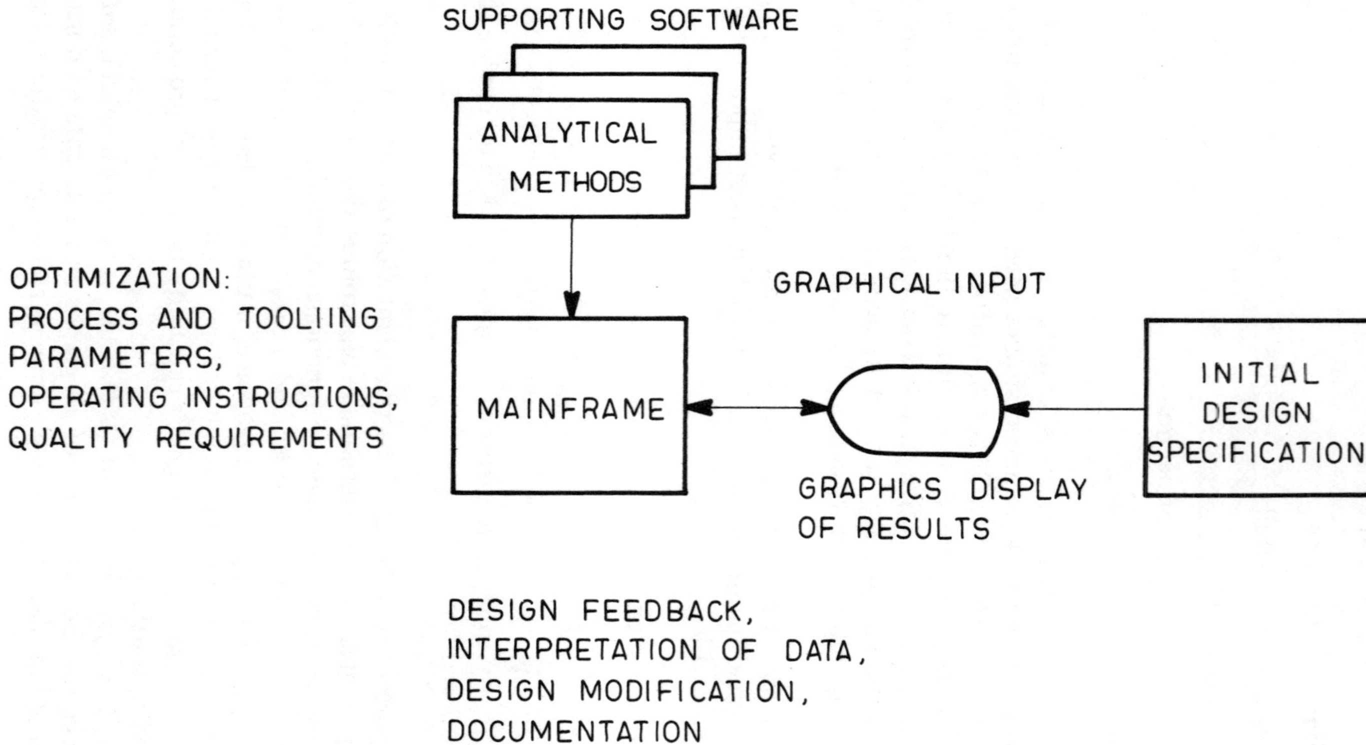

FIGURE 12–3 The overall system interactivity between software supporting analytical methods and the enhanced designers' capability in terms of projection, feedback, and optimization.

of the applications most frequently demanded is the manipulation of user-defined formats for relating data extracted from one drawing to another, or to an external file. Such an application is a prerequisite to the online generation of materials reports and cost estimates.

Graphical systems have a particular need for text processing and, therefore, the CAD unit should include a good text editor to merge, sort, and tally text lines, and copy, delete, rename or append text files. These requirements are part and parcel of a valid CAD system whose software should provide flexible techniques for:

- entity identification, insertion, and copying
- entity translation, rotation, mirroring and rescaling
- controllable display and plotting faculties, including user-definable line fonts and text parameters
- the handling of multiple redefinable views
- a goodly number of documentation approaches
- a number of faculties which should be processed online, such as the generation of the bill of materials.

As an example of software support for CAD/CAM (and results which can be obtained), let us consider one application which I followed through from design to manufacturing engineering. This is shown schematically in Figures 12-4 and 12-5.

Sixteen steps are outlined in Figure 12-4, with five feedback loops. Each iteration means corrections and, therefore, a time-consuming and error-prone upkeep of designs and documentation. Such feedbacks can best be handled by workstations and computer-based solutions, with the engineering database upkept through interactive approaches.

Figure 12-5 presents a computer-supported approach which is a streamlined solution able to eliminate manual interventions and improve the designers' productivity. Given the interconnection of the design activities, the impact of a computer-supported facility in study and projection is more pronounced; the available software is better and the database is more complete. Elements already stored in the database serve as input to the design and analysis programs which assure that the solution to be adopted fulfills the desired functions and performs according to specifications.

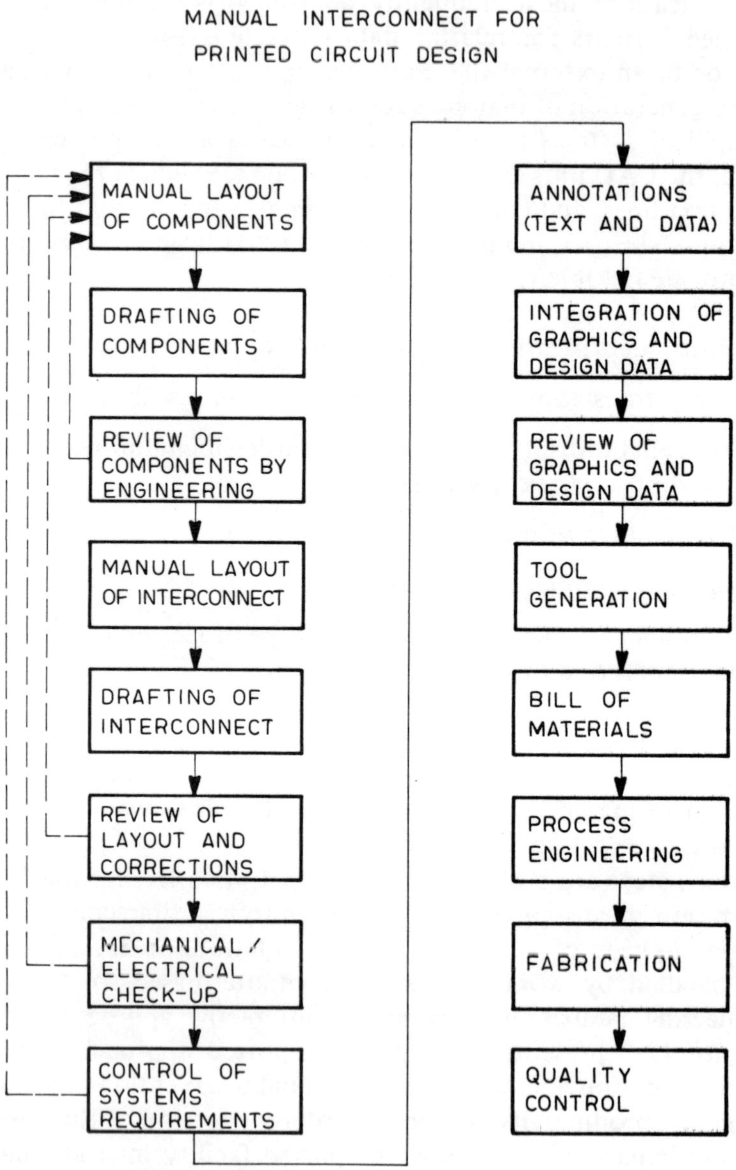

FIGURE 12–4 A manual interconnect operation for printed circuit design. The number of feedback loops shown makes it impossible to effectively handle devices of great complexity.

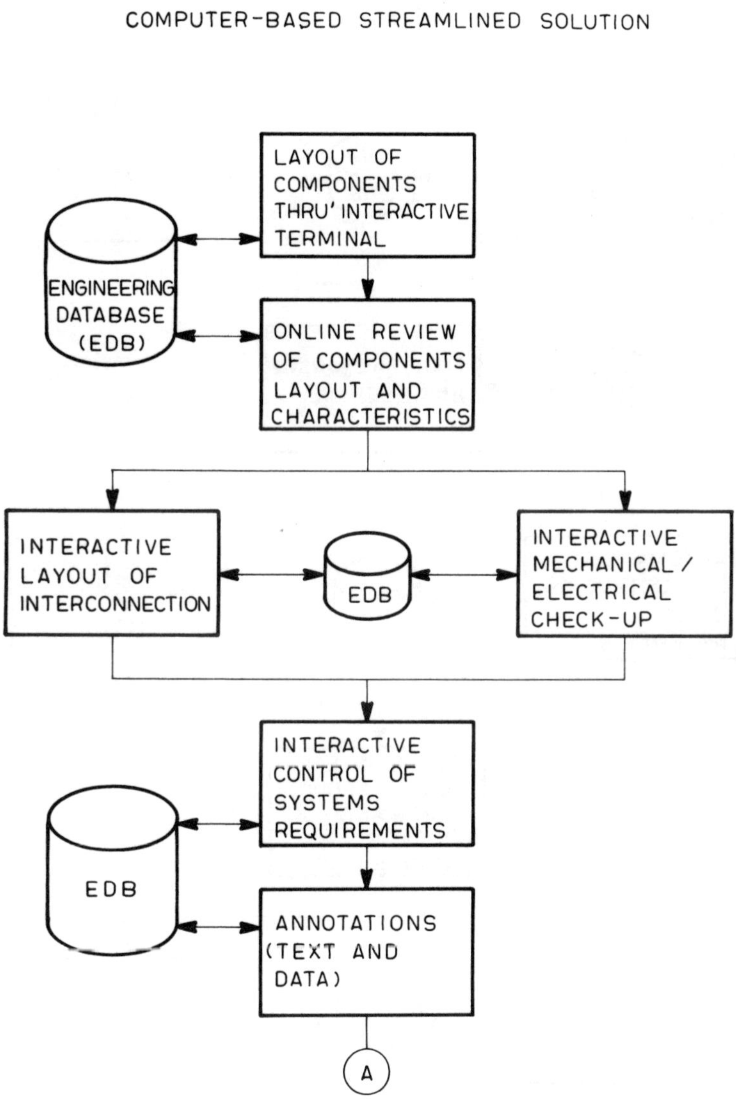

FIGURE 12-5 **Computer-supported approach to printed circuit design. CAD helps eliminate manual interventions, makes feasible experimentation and improves the designers' productivity.**

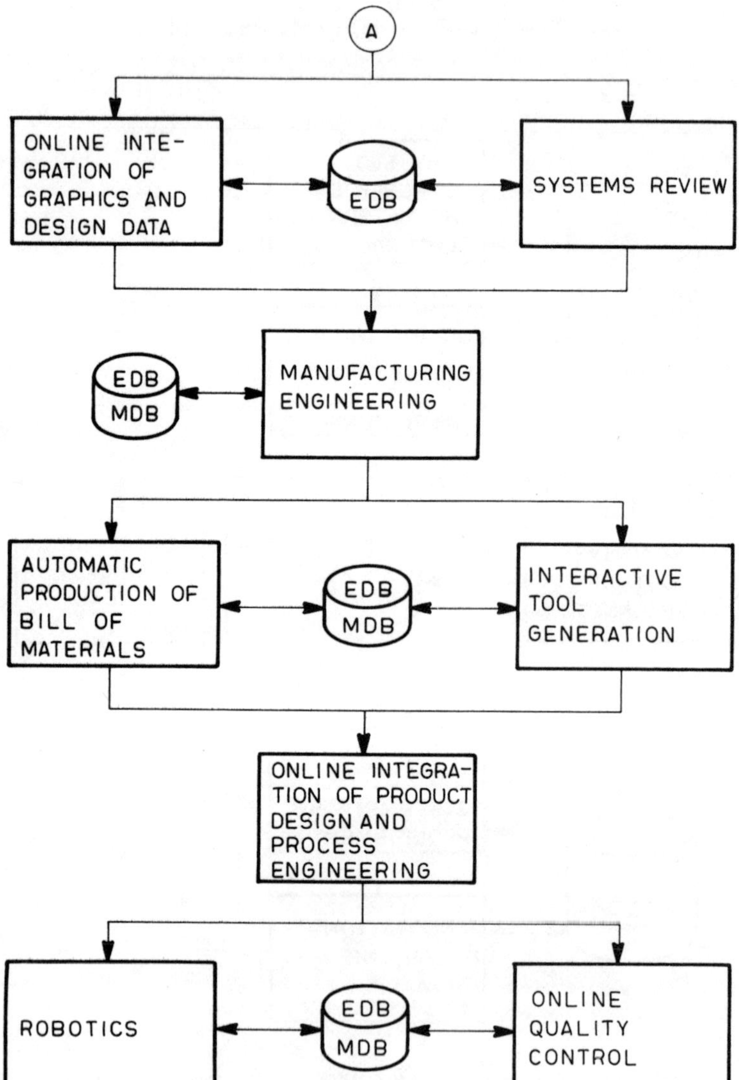

FIGURE 12–5 **Computer-supported approach to printed circuit design. CAD helps eliminate manual interventions, makes feasible experimentation and improves the designers' productivity. (Continued.)**

Experimentation is another basic advantage. Through computer-intense approaches and interactive terminals, a designer can perform both physical and logical simulation. With the former, he will verify performance specifications; with the latter, he will assure that the logic of the design is that which is intended. If either analysis produces errors or deviations, corrective action can be taken online. A similar procedure is valid in manufacturing engineering; it helps achieve necessary precision by combining different variables which are present as the result of previous processing steps.

Furthermore, online capabilities can preserve the physical and logical functions of the design, optimize the area that it will occupy, and observe all process-related constraints. CAD/CAM is of great assistance in assuring that the consecutive phases align with one another and with what has already been done, precisely sizing and locating the regions of particular attention, and producing without delays (due to lack of coordination or incomplete documentation) the design drawings.

Eventually, CAD/CAM software will change to plug-in firmware, starting with basic software modules and proceeding toward the applications environment. This firmware will be offered by hardware manufacturers as well as by independent software suppliers, while users of EPROM equipment may be designing it by themselves. As applications develop, terminals will emerge containing this firmware, and will be able to effectively handle customized input elements specifically oriented to the design needs of the user.

EFFECTS ON PRODUCTIVITY

The final justification for any equipment expenditure should be financial. This section is, therefore, devoted to the effect of a CAD/CAM solution on the most valuable (and expensive) resource of an engineering company —the designers' time. Let us recall some fundamentals:

- The aim is to improve productivity by performing a range of functions through interactive terminals serving as the designers' "scratch pad."
- This aim is served through a computer-supported database containing a valuable amount of text and data which can be used repetitively and can be retrieved at will.

- Man-information interactivity is enhanced through microprocessor-based terminals with graphics and text capabilities communicating with the engineering database.

It is the ability of CAD/CAM to manipulate online engineering drawings, text and data, which provides the designer with the most valuable support. This very issue is behind the changed perspective in CAD/CAM usage and its widening range of applications in modern industry.

Ten years ago, CAD/CAM was almost exclusively reserved to electronics, aerospace and automobile designers. Probably less than 200 workstations were in operation. However, since productivity gains became evident, and it has been estimated that certain applications of computers and advanced machine-tool technology can increase the effectiveness of a designer by better than 300 percent, the interest in CAD has boomed. New approaches also focused on manufacturing with a resulting reduction in capital and labor costs and a significant improvement in competitive standing.

It is, therefore, of no surprise that by 1980 some 12,000 CAD/CAM workstations were in place, a sixtyfold increase since 1970. Significantly from last year's 12,000 workstations, several worked on a two- and three-shift basis. At the same time, the number of users has grown from a few hundred in 1980 to an estimated 25,000 last year in the United States alone.

As users look at it, CAD/CAM provides an effective means to harness computer power, increase productivity, improve product quality, shorten product turnaround times, control costs, improve documentation and decrease product liability. The effects on productivity can be appreciated better if we keep in mind that CAD can be used in a broad range of applications including design proper, layout and mapping, plant engineering, piping, wiring, numerical control and tool design. CAD can work on a two-dimensional and three-dimensional basis, automate drafting, provide a testbed for simulation, help minimize errors and rejects, and stimulate the interest of engineers and designers. Based on these considerations, Table 12-1 outlines some typical potential savings in specialized manpower that users have outlined.

These are direct results of interactive user processes which store, retrieve, manipulate and display information, allowing the user to communicate with the database and, therefore, combining human judgement

TABLE 12–1

TYPICAL POTENTIAL SAVINGS WITH CAD/CAM

Design–Related Tasks	*Stated Productivity Ratio*
* Inspection and Control	10 : 1
* Corrections and Update	10 : 1
* Engineering Change Orders	10 : 1
* Parts Lists, Bills of Materials	5 : 1
* Circuit Routing (PCB)	5 : 1
* Component Packaging and Placement (PCB)	5 : 1
* Manufacturing Drawings (all types)	5 : 1
* Assembly Drawings	4 : 1
* Wiring Diagrams	4 : 1
* Sheet Metal Drawings (Mechanical Engineering)	4 : 1
* Detailed Mechanical Drawings	3 : 1
* Piping and Instrumentation Diagrams	3 : 1
* NC Tape Preparation	3 : 1
* Tool Design	2 : 1
* Structural Steel Studies	2 : 1

with microprocessor-supported capabilities. Through his display, the user can ask for help at any point of the design process, include human imagination to the computer's solutions, and integrate product design with manufacturing engineering capabilities. Graphics allow him to see an instantaneous picture of what he is creating at every step in the process, and take action accordingly. With interactive graphics, the designer talks to the computer in the same language he would instruct another designer but in more precise, structured terms. Also, he can take corrective action regarding not only the electronic parts, but also the most classical mechanical areas, such as sandcasting and diecasting.

Some of the most classical engineering activities are now fully revamped and made more effective by generating computer-supported casting drawings on graphics terminals, which is done automatically from a computerized finished part drawing stored in the common database. It is quite important to underline this last reference, as CAD is often thought as suited only for more modern engineering design such as that of the PCB. While its suitability in this last reference is not questioned, excellent results have been obtained through CAD/CAM applications in the older engineering disciplines which are being revamped.

The designer's productivity can be highly improved if we take particular care in preparing the workplace (including layout and illumination) and in reducing the noise level. A CAD/CAM user suggested that high-noise components should be stored separately (Figure 12-6); that communication between designers operating on the same computer-aided system should be made through the engineering database and not orally; that the designer's sessions should be tagged by the machine; and that expertise should be applied to the manner in which engineers and scientists interact with microprocessor-supported units.

It is advisable that a study on a CAD/CAM application cover all issues which concern engineering work for the foreseeable future. At stake is *product quality* which can be divided into functional and physical characteristics:

- Physical attributes go bottom-up from the component parts to the assembly, as end quality has much to do with tolerances.
- Functional attributes work top-down and are highly related to cost/effectiveness, project span, serviceability and maintainability.

Both in functional and physical areas of product quality, CAD/CAM permits the tuning of product parameters in realtime—input trials can be processed in seconds, at the graphics console, and the output viewed on the display or on hardcopy.

A quick assessment of each parameter and the immediate visualization of the effects of changes both significantly affect the lead time of a project and improve a product's competitiveness and marketability. This, too, has its effect on productivity. Man/machine communication at the console of a workstation eliminates the repeated manual handling of input/output graphics, text, and data, performs optimization activities, and permits the designer to respond quickly to special situations.

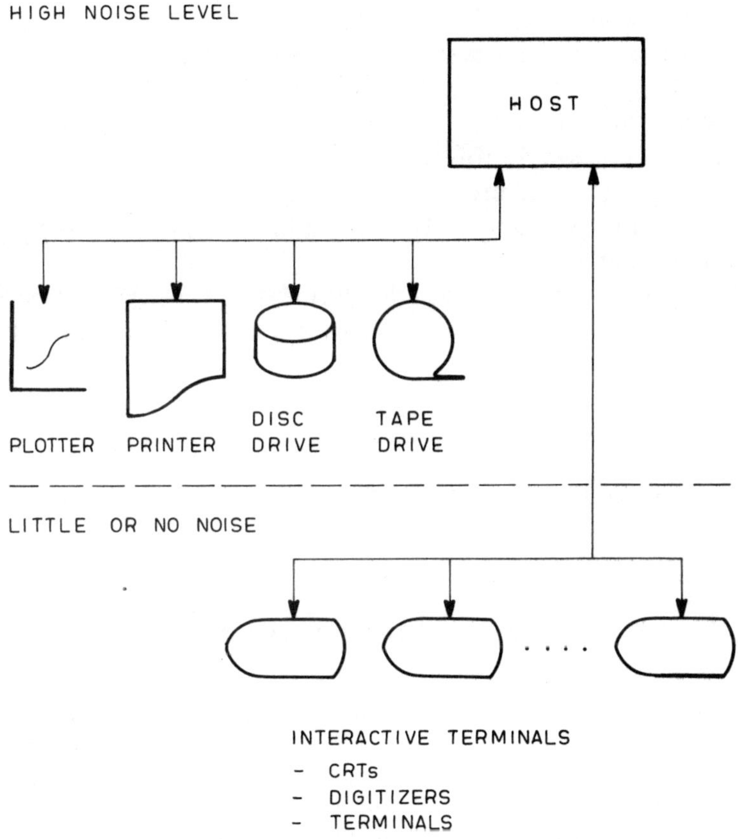

FIGURE 12–6 **It is advisable that high-noise components be stored separately, and that communications between designers operating on the same CAD system be made not orally but through the engineering database.**

COST JUSTIFICATION

Evidently, the benefits to be obtained from CAD/CAM must be evaluated against the cost of the investment. In estimating the cost of a CAD system, we will be well advised to include not only the hardware components and software routines needed to run the applications, but also the extra costs such as training, systems services, maintenance, and the changeover from the current methodology. On the credit side are the designer's productivity, the automation of routine activities, online retrieval, consistent updating, a valid project documentation, reduction in errors and lead times, and a better product/project quality. Each of these benefits require procedural and organizational studies so as to lead to a favorable and lasting outcome.

The expected benefits should define the type of system we are seeking. Among the basic characteristics a CAD/CAM solution should possess is:

- ease of maintenance
- the availability of features which make it inexpensive to operate in terms of human interfaces
- short response times
- standardized rules of regulations concerning database management
- effective communication among workstations using the same database
- management's ability to exercise efficient control over its usage and the faculties which it supports.

The way a CAD/CAM system may appeal to the end user is most important as there are bound to be some social and professional fallouts; job content will visibly change as intelligent tablets, electronic pens and videoscreens replace the drawing board; unstructured and undefined design processes will be standardized; repetitive tasks previously done by the designer will be accomplished by the system, and so on. In turn, along with technical and operating issues, these factors identify the need for effective formal training which should help overcome resistance to change.

The cost justification will be less likely if resistance to change prevails. This is written in the understanding that, as past experience suggests, some engineers and designers distrust or even refuse to accept CAD. The need to overcome such opposition is both a professional and a social problem not necessarily related to age.

It should further be noted that at least some of the resistance is due to misconception. It is, for instance, thought that CAD/CAM can limit creativity, reduce job security or fragment available skills. In fact, the opposite is true; if properly implemented, computer-supported approaches increase the possibility of being creative, automate trivial standard tasks, and, hence, make available more time for creative thinking. They enrich the job content by requiring different skills, and by improving the job status.

At the technical side, having tentatively selected suitable CAD/CAM equipment, we should run benchmark tests to analyze its performance. For a hands-on evaluation to give any meaningful results, the benchmark environment should be identical to that which will be used in the final configuration. While realistic benchmarks may provide a good insight into equipment selection, too much abstraction and compromises are a waste of time, causing lengthy delays without appreciable results. Any evaluation should be realistically done and include a sample of real-life applications.

From equipment selection to implementation, the golden rule is that of preparation: goals must be advanced, organizational plans formulated, test data prepared, the benchmarks done, timetables established, training procedures elaborated, and installation requirements reviewed in advance and implemented.

13 Robotics

INTRODUCTION

THE IMPACT of microprocessor-supported tools will be felt both in the engineering office and in the factory. There is a continuity in this effort. Once in action, CAD can nicely link online to CAM. Here, in an attempt to boost productivity, new technologies are being developed around CAM, which include numerical control of machine tools (NC); its more advanced state, robotics; and factory data management at large.

It is no secret, for example, that General Motors has projected an installed base of robots in its facilities of about 14,000 by 1990, up from 302 through 1980. In 1981 alone, GM is adding an estimated $45 million worth of robots. At present, there are over fifty United States-based companies that are selling or have announced their intentions to sell robots.

In the background of this drive is the new concept of reindustrialization. Labor has become expensive and people do not want to perform repetitive routine work anymore. Besides, quality goes up so dramatically with robotics that the industry employing them becomes a better competitor.

The traditional labor-intense restaurant business can serve as an example. Patrons who complain that their waitress is too slow will be pleased to know that a small fast-food restaurant near Windsor, Ontario, plans to inaugurate robot waitresses. The Burgerworld International chain will open a prototype restaurant where the serving staff will consist of three $20,000 robots. Customers sitting at horseshoe-shaped counters will give their orders directly to the cook in the kitchen via intercom. When the order is ready, the cook programs each robot to serve the food. The robots can tote four trays at a time and serve nine tables in seventy-two seconds, a feat rarely matched by people. Each robot has interchangeable heads with different flashing lights and "personalities" so the cus-

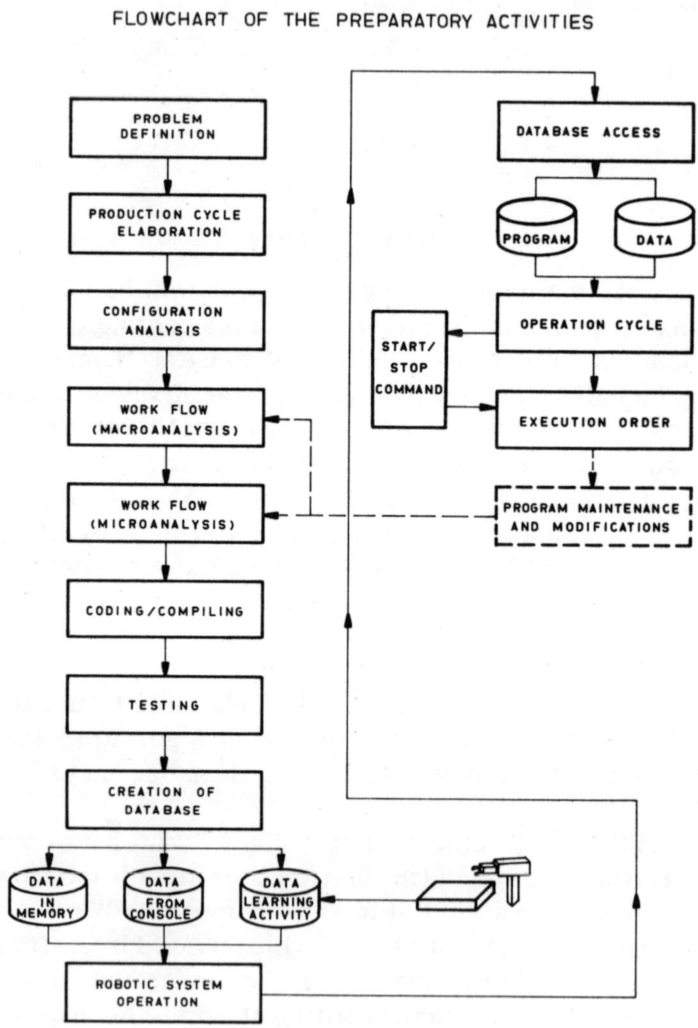
FLOWCHART OF THE PREPARATORY ACTIVITIES
PROBLEM DEFINITION
PRODUCTION CYCLE ELABORATION
CONFIGURATION ANALYSIS
WORK FLOW (MACROANALYSIS)
WORK FLOW (MICROANALYSIS)
CODING/COMPILING
TESTING
CREATION OF DATABASE
DATA IN MEMORY
DATA FROM CONSOLE
DATA LEARNING ACTIVITY
ROBOTIC SYSTEM OPERATION
DATABASE ACCESS
PROGRAM
DATA
OPERATION CYCLE
START/ STOP COMMAND
EXECUTION ORDER
PROGRAM MAINTENANCE AND MODIFICATIONS

FIGURE 13-1

tomers do not become bored with exact duplicates. They cost less than waitresses, do not call in sick, ask for raises, take coffee breaks or complain that their feet hurt.

A robot is a programmable, multifunction manipulator designed to move dishes, materials, parts, tools, or special devices through variable programmed motions in the performance of a variety of tasks. This definition does rule out the most rudimentary pick-and-place machines, but keeps emphasis on the fact that the microprocessor- or computer-controlled robot should be in complete command of all its component parts.

Figure 13-1 presents in a nutshell the preparatory activities which characterize the typical robot installation. From problem definition to configuration analysis, work flow, coding, compiling, testing, database creation, robotic system operation, and the execution cycle, there is an orderly progression of activities which closely resemble our experiences with computers. (The same is true of program maintenance.)

Robots come in many types and styles (as we will see in this chapter) with widely-varying degrees of sophistication. Their technology is in full swing, but industries who wait until sophisticated vision and tactile sensing and other fancy devices are available will miss the opportunity. The time to study robotics implementation is now.

Remember, however, that robots are often only a small part of the total cost of an installation. Along with a robot are often required expensive conveyors, parts presenting devices, and feeders. So, sometimes, a robot priced at $50,000 will represent thirty percent of the total cost.

INNOVATION IN BUSINESS PRACTICES

Robots range from high precision equipment required for fine mechanics to heavy duty; from manipulators, to transporters, welders and assembly robots. All of them are important steps toward the automated factory. It is projected that by 1990 almost half of factory assembly operations will incorporate robot technology, compared with only 5% today, according to a study by the Society of Manufacturing Engineers' Robotics Institute.

Robots are taking on a new character: that of being able to imitate humans. A Japanese company recently announced it has produced a prototype of the most human-like robot in the world: it has arms and legs and is equipped with basic intelligence functions, including perception, hearing and speaking.

Sumitomo Electric Industries said the robot follows instructions from a human voice and is capable of moving towards a group of objects, selecting the right one and carrying it to a designated place. Its manufacturer plans to use the robot for assembling electronics parts at its plant in Osaka capitalizing on the fact that the robot perceives objects with two movable eyes, made of 300,000 optical fibers which allow it to differentiate shapes and sizes through image recognition technology.

A carbon-fiber arm can grip and carry objects weighing up to 1 kg (2.2 lb). Its legs are equipped with an optical character reading device which permits the robot to follow written instructions and to detect objects in its path.

Worldwide, the trend is towards the use of new materials: high strength low alloy steels, plastics, composites, for robots—and vendors are noting that compact, lightweight, and streamlined robots with equivalent strength will become more prevalent. A number of end users refer to the growing trend away from hydraulically driven robots, with greater sensory capability being an issue which users intend to explore in greater depth in the near future.

Senior American executives now believe that innovation should be central to their business strategies. Taken together, foreign competition and the boom in microelectronics technology will define a new competitive environment, characterized by even more rapid technological change. Microelectronics technology will dramatically influence R&D efforts in most industries.

- The interactive capability of microprocessor technology will cause innovation to occur from a systems perspective.
- The expected forward integration by microprocessor-based companies into customers' industries will blur industrial distinctions.
- Three industries—electrical, leisure time, and industrial machinery—will be forced to reexamine their product development strategies.

Much is related to legislation and tax incentives. Industry executives expect a revision of tax policies to provide incentives for reinvestment, a more reasonable and consistent approach to regulation, greater funding of research, improvements in the current educational system, and relaxed antitrust laws. If this expected government contribution is fulfilled, industrial and business executives are ready to alter their own constraining factors in innovation, including corporate policies in research and planning targeted to the short term which limits risk-taking projects.

Why is a tax policy related to robotics? Because the challenge is *there*—not in technology. Computers, communications, and modern production equipment are available in greater quantities and are more developed than ever before, but industry needs incentives to use them extensively and revamp its fabrication base.

An example can be found in Japan. The government has a program which, through the use of low interest loans, encourages companies to employ advanced automation, including robotics. Companies can get loans at interest rates that are a function of their size, so smaller companies pay lower rates on loans to modernize their manufacturing capability.

Let me repeat: The reason why low cost loans and tax advantages are so important is that they provide incentives to modernize and survive in an increasingly competitive world. No industrial country can afford to miss the dramatic advances being made in manufacturing through the introduction of industrial robots.

How can the typical manufacturer look at robotics? In the introduction to this chapter I gave the definition advanced by the Robot Institute of America. In three words, a robot is a "programmable multifunctional manipulator," which means a combination of grasp, hold, place, transport, and sensing elements, and of computer-controlled machine tools.

How can we classify robots to help orient our study and make a choice? Four levels can be distinguished as specified by the Japanese Industrial Robot Association (JIRA):

1. Manipulators that perform fixed preset sequences.
2. Playbacks that repeat fixed instructions.
3. NC robots that execute operations by numerically loaded information.
4. Intelligent robots that function through their own recognition capabilities.

Since the beginning, R&D has concentrated on the most vital component of a robot: its arm and the manipulation capacity it expresses.

The robot's arm is an essentially mechanical part and is characterized by *degrees of freedom*. These express any elementary displacement of the arm.

Six degrees of freedom can be distinguished:

1. Rotation of the arm around its principal axis
2. Up and down the axis
3. Advance or retreat of the arm

The 4th, 5th, and 6th degrees of freedom express rotations around the arm's fist, to which is added the manipulating capability: A robot must be able to take and hold things.

Let's notice that not all robots need six degrees of freedom, however, to accomplish their mission, robots must move with great precision. This is a function of design and in its fundamentals rests on the motor and its servomechanisms.

THE PROGRAMMABLE MACHINE

The major difference between other automatic machines and robots is that the latter:

- are polyvalent, and
- can be reprogrammed and reset in real enough time.

At the current state of the art, the programming of the robot is assured by humans; the execution by a microprocessor. For any and every robot, programming must take care of all of the degrees of freedom which it supports. This can become a complex mission: One of the challenges with robotics is to establish a language which is easy:

- for men to manipulate,
- for robots to understand—and
- it permits the latter to react quickly.

A robot can perform a number of tasks, but basically it has specific abilities. Its key advantage is its ability to adapt to different tasks. When we install a robot, it becomes the nerve center. It turns devices on, checks to see they are operating properly, assures that parts are inspected, and does essentially what a human must do in running the same operation.

We can easily contrast an assembly shop of the Industrial Revolution with a fully automated assembly line of today served by robotics. The mass of operators has disappeared, and with them the supervisors. Mechanical devices for power transmission have been replaced by electrical and electronic ones, and the "brain" behind the machine is the microprocessor.

Accuracy is very important both in the program mode and in subsequent execution. Speed is vital in the execution mode. A third basic demand is reliability. Many robotics manufacturers typically cite a mean time between failure (MTBF) of 500 hours, but some installations have reached a 2,000-hour MTBF. At least one manufacturer claims his machines have been operating for more than 90,000 hours, which translates into about 45 man-years. Applications-wise, though, it is too early yet to speak of sound statistical documentation.

Design requirements in reliability (for an integrated process control system) include functional partitioning or isolation of modular subsystems, new computer-oriented procedures for essential control functions, and environmental protection. Software must be ready to analyze input data, evaluate sampled data errors and generate the feedback control. Reliability considerations also demand a backup control system.

In terms of basic technology, there are essentially two classes of robots: servo- and non-servocontrolled.

- A servocontrolled robot can generally be programmed to stop at any point within its radius of motion, both accelerating and decelerating.
- With a non-servocontrolled robot, the tool center can stop only at the fixed end points of each axis.

Many motions can be made in sequence with a non-servo device, but only to the end points, and without provision for either acceleration or deceleration.

The majority of industrial robots installed in the United States today are low- to medium-technology devices, such as the pick-and-place manipulator. The simplest pick-and-place manipulators usually offer only two or three degrees of freedom. Medium-technology robots are designed for purposes such as spray painting.

A major application of larger robots is in spot welding, this by the dominant user industry—automotive. Similar applications are arc welding, assembly, machine loading, press loading, and materials handling. Another large application is die casting. The degrees of freedom current technology permits with robots are shown in Figure 13-2; they closely emulate that of the human manipulator.

Even lower- to medium-technology robots can perform better than human operators. Difficult, monotonous or dangerous work left aside, we still cannot expect someone to work at the speed and consistency at which a robot can work, and there are plenty of functions already served by more than 3,200 robots currently in use in United States factories. The Robot Institute of America predicts that sales of robot equipment will grow from about $70 million in 1980 to $255 million in 1985.

A view of current statistics is given in Table 13-1.

TABLE 13–1

ESTIMATED POPULATION OF INSTALLED ROBOTS

Country	*Number*	*%*
Japan	7,500	59.0
U.S.	3,200	25.0
Europe	2,050	16.0
Total	12,750	100.0

The European installations are approximately divided:

West Germany	1,000	7.8%
Sweden	400	3.2
France	200	1.5
England	200	1.5
Italy	100	0.8
Switzerland	50	0.4
Netherlands	50	0.4
Denmark	50	0.4

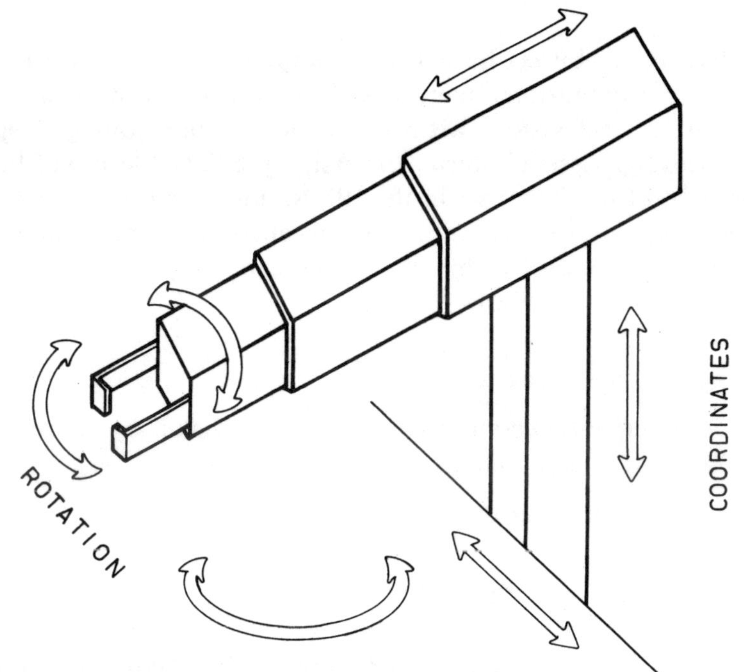

FIGURE 13-2

RESEARCH ON ROBOTICS

Robotics research is currently concentrating on enhancing two developments:

- sensory capabilities, and
- offline programming.

Sensory capabilties have three components: force, with application in fitting operations; tactile, with application in both positioning and orienting; and vision, with application in positioning, inspection and monitoring. Case Western University predicts there will be much development of tactile senses in the 1980s, similar to the course of action followed in the last decade. Such sensory capabilities would allow a robot to work with unoriented objects. Tactile capability (sensation) will be important if we want robots:

- not to damage parts
- complement current two-dimensional vision by increasing the range of sensation, and
- to thread parts correctly.

Primary programming methods are:

- *lead through*: the operator controls the robot through desired positions and locations by means of a remote teach box;
- *walk through*: the robot is physically manipulated through desired motions;
- *plug-in*: the robot operates via a prerecorded program without manual intervention.

Online programming involves:

- taking the robot arm,
- putting it into "program mode,"

- following a sequence of elementary tasks the robot needs to perform, and
- storing on a support medium: floppy, disc, tape, cassette, or bubble memory.

Speed is not relevant in the programming mode though it is in the execute mode.

Current technology provides point-to-point and continuous path. With the former, a robot can be programmed to stop at many predetermined points, but movement is not controlled between these points; point-to-point robots usually offer greater accuracy of repeatability. A continuous-path robot can follow an irregular path exactly.

An industrial robot must be a practical device, and that entails flexibility of application, reliability, availability, and ease of teaching with online or offline programming capability. Economics will evidently play a major role in terms of acceptance. If the effect of the robot generation results in a significant reduction per annum in manufacturing cost, then the cost of computer-based robots can be quickly recovered. This has been the experience in the computer industry.

Based on such expectations, General Electric, for instance, is initiating a sweeping automation plan that may eventually replace one-half its 37,000 assembly workers with robots, and the leading automobile manufacturers have already introduced robots to handle many of their subassembly routines. General Motors has announced that between 1981 and 1984 it will install between 1,000 and 1,800 industrial robots in its modernization program, mainly for body welding jobs. That is more than the entire United States automotive industry has used in the past twenty years. Should such drive accelerate, robots may eventually displace as much as seventy percent of today's factory work force. Yet, such solutions, radical as they may be, are fundamental for survival.

Of interest is a new line of robots from Unimation called Puma (programmable universal machine for assembly). Their design stemmed from a GM study which found that ninety percent of the parts that go into an automobile weigh less than five pounds. The Puma line resulted from a request for tenders for a machine about the size of a human arm that could lift five to seven pounds and do simple assembly tasks. GM is reported to be studying their use in assembly operations such as an electric motor/gearbox combination for car seats which consists of an electric armature, three gears, some springs, and retaining clips.

In Japan, one line in an automotive operation has eighty-four different types of large and small robots that place some 1,500 spot welds on a car. Adjacent to that line, which produces a car every 53 seconds, is still another line, again with eighty-four robots.

Apart from being instrumental in terms of manufacturing capability on their own merit, robots can also serve as catalysts in changing production methodologies which became obsolete over the years. The studies done to renew and revamp fabrication lines bring to light statistics on equipment utilization which have surprised many industrial engineers. One example from Cincinnati Milacron concerns a part moving through a factory. Only five percent of a part's life in a factory is spent on a machine where value is being added, and of that five percent, only three percent is spent cutting or forming that part. The rest is dead time, a good deal of which is materials handling, and that is a big area where robots come into play.

ROBOTICS AND PRODUCTIVITY

Vision is generally considered the key to the implementation of "smart" robots, as they must be able to adjust to slight changes, such as parts arriving at the workstation out of sequence and damaged components. The sense of touch can also be essential: a gripper hand with a tactile sense seems to be the answer. Robots can measure displacements during assembly, and their programming allows them to draw conclusions about trends, in case a process (whether human-based or run by another machine) must be altered.

Industrial robots are capable of twenty-four-hour operation and thereby greatly enhance capital investments. They are free of fatigue, can help reduce the number of defective products, increase the service life of tools, prevent industrial accidents and occupational diseases, and obviate problems caused by a decrease of workers willing to engage in simple, monotonous labor. Typically, applications range from press processing, casting, die-casting, forging, glass handling, furnace, arc welding, machining processing, spray painting, paletizing, transporting, tool changing, and plastic moduling, to voice recognition systems.

Quite evidently, development will not stop at that point. The next generation will involve thinking robots able to integrate sensory systems with more sophisticated computer software that will enable them to make decisions, instead of being limited to looking at parts individually. Such discretionary robots will typically:

- pull parts from a bin,
- examine each part for defects, and
- use or reject a part after analyzing any observed defects.

If analyses of long-term defect rates indicate the need for corrective action, the robot would communicate with a computer overseeing the manufacture of the part, its quality control, warehousing, and inventory handling. Exactly because of these capabilities, intelligent robots could displace between two-thirds and three-quarters of today's factory work force—and would perform the work faster and better with faultless performance and lower costs. Yet, a factory without workers does not mean that it is totally without human components.

As robotics assume tasks formerly assigned to blue collar labor, workers and employees must be transferred to better-trained jobs to assume higher functions. In this sense, robotics become an opportunity both for industrial survival and for the upgrading of skills. To remain competitive, industries estimate they must improve productivity by six percent annually, and the strategic plan for reaching such a goal calls for a wholesale installation of robots wherever technology allows. "For every dollar spent on robots, you save $3 annually," says one user, and I had a professor of banking at UCLA who used to say, "A banker will be happy to spend one dollar if he can make $2 in return."

Productivity is the crucial theme; over the last decade, United States productivity rose twenty-three percent while Japanese productivity showed an eighty-nine percent gain. The impact on the American economy showed up as inflation and the importing of more and more products, from automobiles to television sets. For better productivity and the competitive structure which follows it, robotics promise to radically affect factory routines.

One of Japan's most technologically advanced companies is bringing the workerless factory one step closer to reality. In January, 1981, Fujitsu Fanuc Limited opened a $38 million plant that uses robots and numerically controlled (NC) machine tools to turn out other robots and computerized tools. In the first year of production, the new factory employed just 100 workers to produce about 100 robots per month and a large number of NC machine tools. This is only one-fifth the number of workers that a conventional plant would need to do the same job. By 1986, Fujitsu Fanuc expects to be producing nearly four times the number of robots and NC machine tools at this plant with only 200 employees—one-fifteenth the work force of an equivalent nonautomated factory.

The fully computerized plant will operate twenty-four hours a day, with persons coming in for eight hours during the daytime to assemble the parts made by the robots and NC machines. All "cells," consisting of a robot and an NC machine tool, will be linked to an automated warehouse and to each other by copper cables embedded in the floor that will guide unmanned carts. The latter will be automatically loaded and dispatched by computer to the appropriate cells, where the robot will unload the parts. The NC machine tool will cut and shape the parts, and when finished, the robot will reload them onto the cart for return to the warehouse or to another cell for additional work.

AN INTEGRATED APPROACH

Of the various industries, automobile manufacturers are leading in the use of industrial robots, with major research efforts taking place at General Motors, Stanford, Fujitsu and Toyota. Due to automation, for the same productive output a Toyota factory has half the floor space of a typical auto plant in the United States; it also requires only a third of the capital investment and fifteen percent of the inventory. In the United States, next to each machine tool is a week's supply of parts; Toyota has only a two hour supply. Can we afford to miss the benefit of such computer-based systems? Let me give another example: The most automated plant of Nissan Motors produces seventy-two cars per man-month, but in Detroit, the still semiautomated automakers reach a maximum capacity of fourty-one cars per man-month. Who is the better fit to survive?

A different way of making this reference is that robots, though welcome and necessary, will not do the job by themselves; we must take an integrated approach. Capital investments create the need for more knowledge work and, at the same time, a capital-intense environment has to be managed for greater productivity.

One function in which the change will be dramatic is telecommunications. Communications software to interconnect computers has advanced from simple batch and interactive capabilities to sophisticated networking:

- No longer is communications limited to movement of data between computers.
- Networking software allows multiple systems to be intimately linked for complete resource sharing.
- New approaches allow the integration of text, data, image, and voice for greater efficiency.
- Communications solutions can greatly affect productivity.

It is no more an issue of allowing optimal physical placement of communications devices. Both logical and physical factors must be considered as they interact with one another. When we look for a system approach, we should buy a solution to a problem, not just hardware and software. The benefits of improved quality and timeliness of information brings better decision-making and increased productivity, and that translates surprisingly soon to greater revenues and earnings per share. However, we must take a medium- to long-range approach to the subject.

The implementation of microprocessor capabilities should cover the whole range from robotics to line balance, which requires data processing, databasing and datacomm faculties. This broader approach will eventually result in a sharply accelerated trend toward fully distributed information systems bringing computer power to each and every work place.

Let us return to the fundamentals. The phrase *distributed system* is used in current literature to denote a very varied assortment of computer types, ranging from prototypes constructed from VLSI-level modules, through homogeneous and heterogeneous combinations of micros, minis, and maxis, and through configuration schemes which include both the very tight coupling typical of multiprocessors and the broader networks of autonomous computer systems. Does "distribute" have different meanings in different circumstances? Or is there a conceptual unity underlying all these seemingly disparate ideas?

If we consider the resources of a computer system on a functional basis instead of in terms of its hardware, software, and firmware, a distributed computer architecture can be thought of as a collection of resources working in concert to achieve a given set of objectives. The essence of this definition is the right emphasis on *functions*: the important aspect of any system (or system component) is what it does, not how it does it, and this is true both of the factory and the office environment.

Recent advances in VLSI techniques and the availability of low cost processing power have led designers to examine the functional behavior of computers, with a view to dedicating processing power to particular functions and to tailoring each processing element to the purpose it is projected to achieve. Thus, we have the idea of a collection of different resources working together comparatively. This idea is valid only when we study the system and its components from their inception with a view toward integration.

The architecture of a robotic system (Figure 13-3) observes this principle: it integrates in itself computer, process control, and numerical control experiences. As we all know, the body of knowledge in these fields is significant. Hence, what still needs to develop with robotic systems is expertise in the application per se; but the components already exist.

Remember that such approaches have been adopted at many different levels of system design and construction, bringing microprocessor-supported functions to the level where they belong: the post where the work is being performed. Functionality can be implemented in a variety of fashions as the work commands, but to know what exactly is required we have to study in the most thorough manner the whole range of possibilities:

- At the lowest level, a distributed system may be a microprocessor running a dedicated functional component.
- At the next level, the distributed system may consist of an interconnection of dedicated, functional microprocessors running standalone machine tools.
- At higher levels, a distributed system may consist of multiple programmable processors interconnecting fabrication and storage equipment into a complete system.

The system which contains several calculating elements—from general purpose computers to microprocessors—has to assure that, though they may be physically separate, they are effectively communicating with one another through efficient channels and that they form a coherent aggregate. Basic economic factors are in the background of this philo-

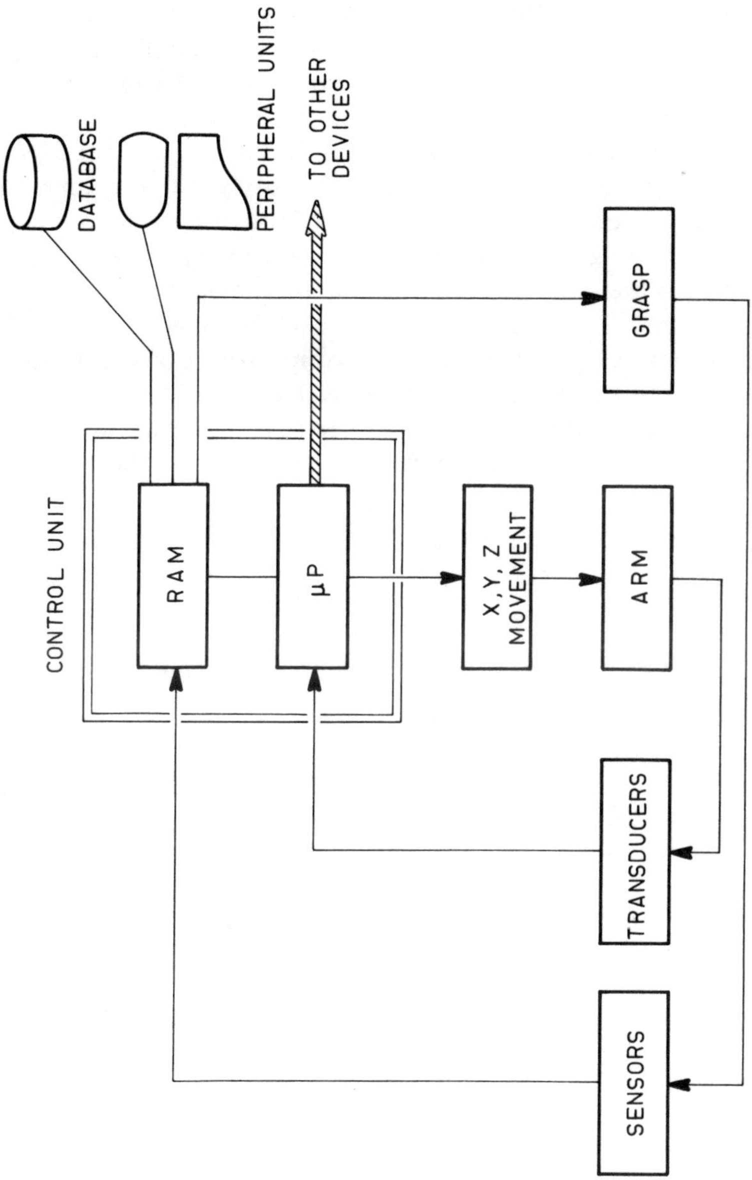

FIGURE 13-3 Architecture of a robotics system.

sophy. Whether in the factory or the office, the relative advantages of the centralized approach no longer apply, and its drawbacks have become apparent during the 1970s. As is well known, they include heavy supervisory overhead, increased complexity leading to unreliability, inefficiency in servicing non-standard workload demands, and sharply fluctuating response time due to resource sharing and overhead.

Such drawbacks were accepted in the past because of the high cost of the processing facility: the overriding necessity was to keep our expensive computer system fully utilized. Now, through microcomputers the capability of bringing computer power to the work place is documented and the result is the swing toward distributed systems employing microprocessors as the driving force.

In Part One, we mentioned that current projections indicate some 10^{18} bits and gates to be produced yearly by the mid-1980s. This statistic equals 250,000,000 bits and gates for every person in the world. Those who know how to utilize such potential power will be in dominant positions.

14 Tuning the Manufacturing Capability

INTRODUCTION

It is not enough to install robotics in order to improve productivity and competitiveness, killing two birds with one well placed stone. Nothing short of a full, detailed, often painful (in terms of tough decisions) and learned preparatory period can establish the solid grounds necessary for a robotics implementation to produce wanted results.

In 1980, the Gross National Product of the United States was $2.6 trillion. Sales of robots by United States-based companies were about $100 million, less than 0.004 of one percernt of the GNP. It is hardly the size of the robot industry that is responsible for our interest in robotics or its potential impact; the impact stems from the fact that robots, and other forms of flexible automation, can have an enormous multiplier effect throughout many industries.

In nearly all studies on productivity, two variables stand out as being of critical importance:

- capital investment, and
- technological improvements.

Technological developments are embodied in the capital base and thereby into actual production. Investments in advanced technology join the critical variables. Embodied technology is what robotics is all about, and this is just as true of the thorough reorganization the manufacturers must undergo in order to make once again the production system cost/effective.

We have the experience with computers. For nearly thirty years, companies thought (and computer manufacturers did their best to support this thinking) that the more gear they bought, the better they would be. Their problems would be solved by magic just after crossing the threshold of investment, and this escalation continued for years without the expected results. It could not be otherwise: without fine tuning of the system on which advanced machines are going to rest, the outcome will most likely range from chaos to disaster.

The need for such fine tuning has now reached the entire range of manufacturing. There was a time when new product planning garnered great attention, and manufacturing was taken almost for granted once the factory was equipped with machine tools. However, as computers, business machines, peripherals, avionics, and other advanced product firms found much to their surprise, it is almost impossible to shift painlessly from making electromechanical equipment to electronic products by maintaining the same manufacturing facilities or procedures.

For instance, when NCR decided to radically revamp its production line, management found the company was no exception to this new rule. No change in the company's history caused more disruption than the decision in the early 1970s to decentralize manufacturing and modernize the whole production structure. What NCR was intending to fabricate were cost/effective computer-based devices, machines and systems which should be produced by robotics so as to keep costs down through a low labor content, while increasing product uniformity and enhancing its reliability.

(When we speak of modern manufacturing, we mean a broad range of activities employing seemingly diverse machinery which has in common microprocessors for control purposes and data requirements. We mean robots for production proper, conveyor belts for materials transfer, efficient computer-based warehousing, computer-supported information handling to minimize stock requirements, and a sound financial and management structure to look after the factory's survival.)

Manufacturing processes have been stable for decades, but the invention of the transistor and the subsequent development of integrated circuits has changed all that, bringing into the spotlight a process of cross-fertilization: new ideas rarely come from within one specialty. Prior to the labor-saving capabilities integrated circuits have presented, much of the cost reduction effort was in replacing a given part with a cheaper one. This led to an appreciation for what affected costs and "value engineering," but did little to alter the manufacturing process as such. Now, when we speak of modern manufacturing we imply a whole new range of activities, much more efficient than ever before.

THE CHANGING ENVIRONMENT IN MANUFACTURING

A basic principle to understand is that not only products die but also machines and even factories as new production techniques are currently emerging. Computerized robots with advanced vision, touch and other sensory systems have, and will continue to have, a significant and growing impact on a broad range of industries. They provide increases in productivity and an improved product quality no company can forego if it wishes to stay in business.

By sticking to labor-intense machinery, management lives with yesterday and thereby misses tomorrow. Intelligent, microprocessor-based robots are on the way, performing tasks ranging from microelectronic assembly to heavy metal processing, testing and packaging. Still, their usage has not been widespread, as we are, to a large extent, still experimenting and learning what we can do with them.

Robots need sensory mechanisms—vision, touch, proximity—and programming techniques. Management must acquire the ability to choose the correct robot for a given application, to perform documented cost/benefit analyses, to learn how to plan and implement a pilot installation, and to estimate the future. A company must also have products designed around the new production methodologies: using robots for products designed for human operators is an unsound practice, nearly comparable to that of designing new products to be fabricated by old machines.

From design automation to micropackaging, there is a different approach to product development than those classical solutions we have practiced in the past. For example, miniaturization of components has been for years an increasingly important problem in the electronics industry. Computers and weapons systems are built with thousands of components of various types: the requirement to make things smaller is not so much to save space as it is to simplify the complicated, labor-intensive, costly, and time-consuming business of wiring the components together. Related goals are outgoing product quality, reliability and maintainability.

In the early 1970s, Texas Instruments developed the micromodule—interconnecting parts by making them all the same size and shape, stacking them vertically in little squares and then running wires up the stack.

This concept did not make the manufacture of the components themselves necessarily simpler, but it forced a thorough understanding of the design and manufacturing cost structure which, in turn, unveiled a new philosophy. A short time thereafter, this procedure led Jack Kilby to the realization that further improvements were possible through horizontal rather than vertical micropackaging structures and, from there, to the development of integrated circuits (see also the discussion in the second half of Chapter 1).

Efficient products and new manufacturing processes are born of such ideas. Even discoveries can follow a logical path: once the number of circuits on a chip got high enough, it was inevitable that somebody would combine the functions of a computer on a single chip. So, we cannot separate chip manufacturing from its design. If we project computer architecture while developing the circuits, we must also think of the whole range of manufacturing activities which will come into play, and eventually this leads to a virtual integration of engineering design with manufacturing engineering.

These few paragraphs suggest a great change in design and manufacturing technology. Not only the product to be made is being radically altered, but also the microprocessor's impact is greatly felt in the design and implementation of the production equipment, affecting traditional ways and manufacturing processes. From there, new opportunities arise for the dynamic firm. Japanese companies have shown the way by the emphasis which they put on robotics: They make feasible improvements in productivity through the automation of diversified production, and ease the transition from large to smaller factories—a new necessity as we will see in the following section. In sequence, robotics programs can be easily modified to cope with:

- model changeovers
- variations of the working and movement paths, and
- other matters requiring flexibility.

Such microprocessor-based machinery can be easily diverted to different applications, transferred to other plants, or programmed to meet substantial changes in production volume.

It is, therefore, of no surprise that companies rush to this field (largely dominated today by the Japanese) and that IBM is about to unveil a new division dedicated to the robotics line of products, starting with the establishment of an institute for manufacturing technology. Project White Cloud, IBM's internal development group for industrial robots of the sort used to assemble CRTs in Raleigh, has reportedly been reorganized as the General Robotics Division. This marks a major commitment by IBM in an emerging marketplace, and other electronics and avionics manufacturers are expected to follow.

A ROBOTICS FACTORY

A robotics factory will typically have advanced software tools for material requirements planning and online inventory management. Packages for manufacturing industries, along with the data collection and reporting systems to implement them, are available in considerable varieties to suit companies in various product lines. Getting these production systems to work, however, takes careful implementation and change in attitude on the part of production workers. Then, manufacturing automation can only be properly implemented if the organization is able to maintain an absolutely accurate inventory. This, in turn, calls not only for computer supports but also for a continuous planning, analysis, and a control cycle on manufacturing resources.

Classical programmable controllers, as we have known them for twenty years, are suitable for simple controls in processes or machines whose total behavior can be expressed in terms of yes/no decision statements. They can be used in applications characterized by long-production and high-volume activities. Yet, replacing conventional controllers with minicomputers can provide for plant automation to be implemented step by step, with system expansion governed by available resources.

When we speak of computer-supported activities, there is a basic change in reference. The justification can be found in such potential advantages as improving production control and product quality, monitoring and regulating material flow, increasing production availability, better safety improvements in maintenance, a reduction of machine and manpower idle time, monitoring personnel, and better machine life.

A good deal of proper preparation is in the integration of CAD/CAM within the mainstream of factory management, a valid approach presented in Figure 14-1. The whole range of activities from planning to controlling must be examined, and proper attention given to the training of the human resources.

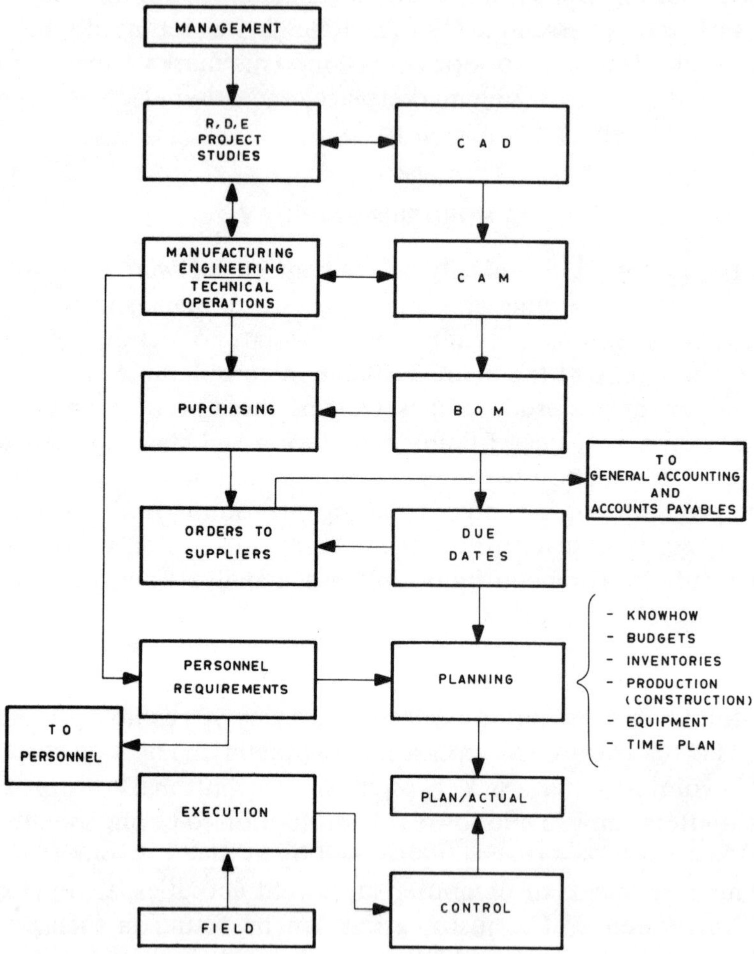

FIGURE 14–1 The integration of CAD and CAM within the mainstream of production operations. A wide range of activities from planning to controlling can be included, important among them the bill of materials and the observance of due dates.

A new emphasis on lifelong learning is in the offing as top industrial executives believe that most of their personnel is not thoroughly conversant with technological concepts, and therefore a low priority is often assigned to innovation—and to preparing for it. Yet, it is most important to understand that the automation of the fabrication process presupposes understanding and support on everybody's behalf. It also calls for flexibility: maintaining current plans up to date so that future plans can be adjusted.

Through CAM, line operating departments and the engineering function in the manufacturing organization must interface with materials control so that materials are available and work is dispatched promptly. Inventory management is itself dependent on the sales and marketing groups for sales forecasts and marketing policies. All this suggests a smoothly flowing circle of events. To maintain this, organizations must undergo a thorough revamping of their sales, inventory and production methodologies.

The management of the production floor needs a system that generates the costs of inventory and product lines and an estimate of plant-load capacity. If any problem arises, it should be immediately noted and rectified. In a major manufacturing facility dozens of departments must interact to satisfy scheduling requirements for different product programs.

Any impact in the suppliers' network or of other divisions of the company can be significant. Coordination and rapid interchange of information is essential if there is to be efficient control from changing bills of material to keeping track of capacity limitations for the manufacturing of sophisticated products at the lowest possible cost.

Factory management needs an economical way to cope with its demanding product structure while maintaining tight control over the fabrication process. Databases must be created and accessed online in realtime through transaction-oriented systems. Errors in manual entries are unacceptable, and the same is true of lagging, inaccurate shop-floor data.

While the need for computer support is unquestionable, a number of programs must be available along with modern, efficient procedures on manufacturing standards, inventory of record controls, master scheduling, procurement management, forecasting, and dynamic requirements planning. Computer assistance should enable managment to determine customer order backlog and potential inventory buildup, and also make business decisions based on people and machinery resources.

All this will give manufacturing a level of visibility it may have lacked in the past. It will be possible to control multiple stage production and inventory systems, resulting in lower inventories, lower stockouts, and better utilization of plant capacity. It will also be possible to avoid past delays and error rates which have often plagued, and sometimes destroyed, the most carefully laid plans.

As it cannot be repeated too often, though, the key is not in the machines (which are available) but in the preparation and in the procedures (which are not). We must have a complete image of what we wish our workplace to be: from the general concept (Figure 14-2) to the details. We must be ready for the implementation, but also assure the transitional period which may last five years.

Within the new applications concept, the CAM part of the CAD/CAM system should be used to store inventories, establish the bill of materials from engineering, be updateable through all transactions (such as creating and tracking purchase orders, production and moving tickets), and allow the company to change data online. This is more important today than in the 1960s, as close to seventy percent of the cost of sales is in materials, so management must control purchase variance and the delivery of those parts and make sure they are available when needed.

Capacity planning, too, is crucial. It pertains particularly to work centers which may develop bottlenecks. A manufacturing floor, for example, may have a work center that is part of a critical pass. It is vital to locate the source of the problem. A formal capacity planning system would take the material and routing file, run through them, evaluate the prevailing flow and work stoppages or delays, and come up with vital information.

This is another example on the need for a procedural understructure. Many companies do not even have routing files; they just have a stack of process sheets that are passed out as the jobs go through production. Wherever this case prevails, procedures are antiquated and simply do not lend themselves to systems-oriented management perspectives.

As cannot be too often repeated, machines cannot do the work without the proper organization.

NUMERICAL CONTROL

Robots have been in development for about twenty-five years, though in the mid-1950s, they were known as numerical control of machine

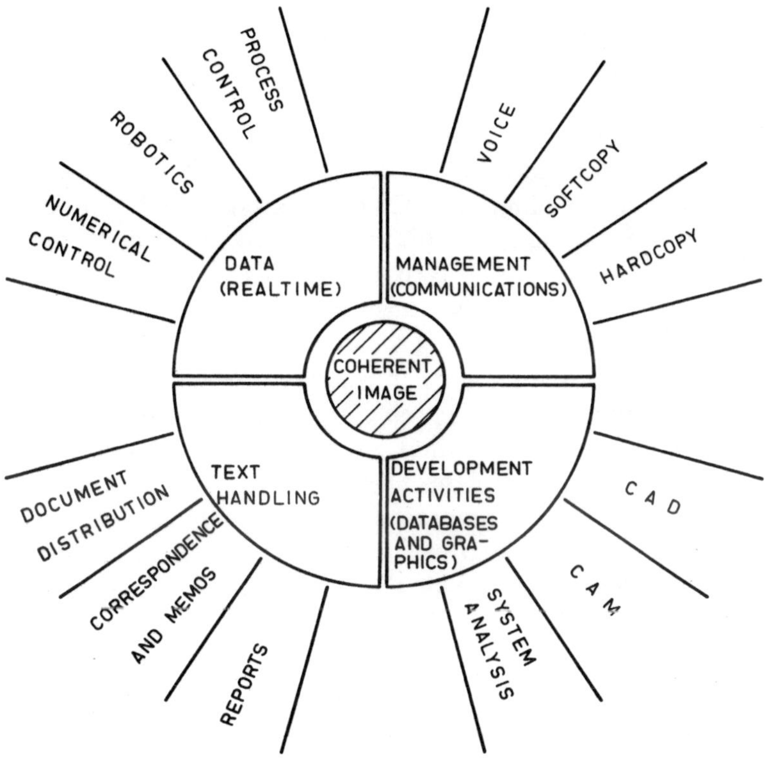

FIGURE 14–2 **A basic need is the creation of a coherent image to act as the pivot point for the integration of data and text capabilities, the computer-based assistance to development activities and the support of management communications.**

tools (NC). Granted, at that time, the NC devices were rudimentary compared to what present-day robotics mechanisms can do, but computer technology was not yet that much advanced at the time, and the microprocessor was nearly two decades away. In the mid-1950s, there was also another significant development. Let us remember that 1955 is a historic year in the way companies do business: The starting point when, for the first time, white collar workers outnumbered blue collar workers in the United States.

These are two reasons that led me to include this section in the present chapter. Looking back to the origins of an applications domain gives insight. In 1956, while in the Engineering faculty of the Catholic University of America in Washington, D.C., I published a syllabus for my course on "Factory Automation," predicting the concept would take twenty years to materialize. In fact, it took twenty-five.

There are well-known advantages in the application of NC methods in machine-tool operation. One is the elimination of retooling. In certain industries, machine requirements are such that set-up time may be longer than actual production time. A job shop schedule is an example of this type of production. The machines are set up, a small quantity of parts are made, and then the templates, jigs, and fixtures changed and a different batch of parts run off. Numerical control can reduce the time, effort and expense accrued under these conditions, enabling the machine to become a flexible unit more valuable to the product engineer. Among other advantages are:

- flexibility
- accuracy obtained as specified by the instructions (with NC, limitations are mostly inherent machine characteristics)
- independence from manual skills
- wide possibilities for a complete redesign of the machine tool which can be made to perform at rates well above those designed for operator safety.

The critical steps for the numerical control of a machine tool start with the specifications to be developed in a CAD system. The digitally coded signals would actuate the servos of the machine tool, which in turn will position and command the tool through its proper path. The whole process is streamlined.

One of the main considerations in the automation of machine tools is the nature and amount of information needed to carry out the desired operations. From the start, research workers tried to solve this problem with the use of digital information processes. For instance, the machine component used in the early MIT project of the 1950s consisted of a universal milling machine, three servomotors operating its moving parts, and instruments used to measure the relative position of these parts (Figure 14-3).

The reader adjoint to the machine tool was composed of three components: a data system, a data interpreting system, and a set of decoding servomechanisms. This data system consisted of a tape reader and six relay registers (two for each machine motion), supplied in pairs so that one could control the machine while the other received information. At the end of each command there was an immediate transfer of store information from one register to the other.

The data interpreting system sent out pulses generated by a master clock, which was also the master time reference for the system. These pulses were controlled by a set of flip-flops, and sent to the decoding servomechanisms. When the latter received the pulses they rotated one degree per pulse, thus translating the digital information to machine usable analog form.

To make certain that the digital-to-analog conversion was carried out properly, a feedback circuit consisted of the shaft connected to the synchrotransmitter, a coder, and a small two-phase induction servomotor with appropriate gearing. The coder generated a feedback signal in the form of one electrical pulse for each degree of shaft rotation. The number of these feedback pulses was then compared with the number of pulses emanating from the data interpreting system by a summing register. If the two counts agreed, the summing register rested at zero; if not, an electric voltage was generated and the two-phase servomotor rotated the shaft to grind the count to zero. The electrical commands received from the decoding servomechanisms went to the hydraulic servomechanisms which drove the lead screws, thus directing the machine. Feedback was again introduced here.

Hence, since its early conception and development in the mid-1950s, a numerical control system would provide: a system for translating information about a desired part into mathematical data which can be stored on some medium; equipment on the production floor capable of reading and following the instructions; a machine tool whose operations can be

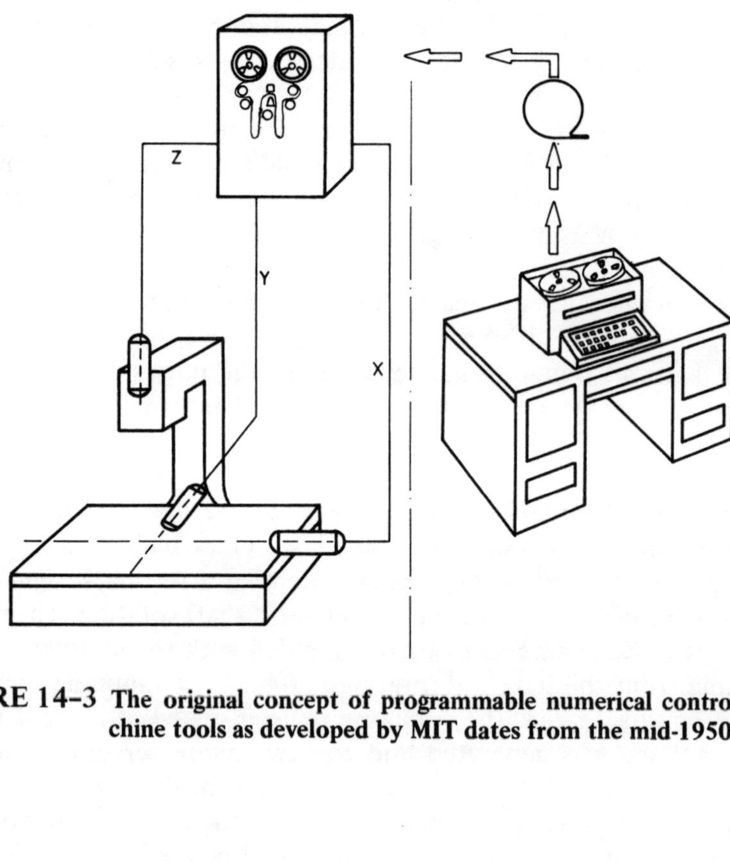

FIGURE 14–3 The original concept of programmable numerical control of machine tools as developed by MIT dates from the mid-1950s.

electrically controlled; and an independent feedback system which monitors the machine actions and introduces correction factors into the control system when required. Among the benefits are a minimum changeover time or a reduction in setup time, allowing a new part to be produced quickly; increase in productivity due to faster machining and automatic cycling; reduction in direct labor per piece; decreased amounts of material in process; decreased spoilage, since human error is reduced; and that information existing in engineering follows a more direct path in controlling the product being produced.

Generally, though not necessarily, the process begins with a production drawing of the part to be made. With pre-CAD procedures, a detailed manuscript of all machine operations required to make the part was prepared from the drawing. This described feed, speed, tooling, distance, dimensions, and so on. When NC was introduced (where there is a continuous path control as used in contouring), more steps were added. A computer calculated and recorded the tool path and cutter offset in the primary storage. From this point, the system was a servomechanism whose input is from the storage device and whose control goes to the machine tool.

Numerical controls may be classified in different groups as to their application: positioning, straight cutting and contouring being examples. Positioning is the type of operation performed in drilling and punching. This generally involves moving the table holding the work in combinations of its two horizontal axes. Overshoot may be tolerated as it will be corrected by feedback before the cut is made. Because only the end points need to be controlled, and the path between them is generally of no consequence, these controls are the simplest of the three types.

Straight-cut control might be used in turning a stepped shaft on a lathe. Control includes both path and end-point, and no overshoot is allowed because of the continuous cut. Usually more than one machine motion is required; however, coordination between position controls is not necessarily in a multiple-motion scheme.

The most complex of the three types is contouring. This involves programming and a tool path that can be generated by machine motions, and may involve simultaneous control of the two axes and feed rate, or three axes including the height of the cutting head enabling production of highly accurate three dimensional parts.

Still another classification of NC systems is known as "referencing holes." Three systems are distinguished—incremental, absolute, and delta modulation. The incremental system specifies a new position with reference to direction and distance from the former position. An error in programming at one point will cause error in all successive points. This system is relatively simple and dependable, but it does have a disadvantage of tolerance build-up. The absolute system, however, refers each point from some arbitrary base, thus eliminating tolerance build-up, but necessitating more equipment.

Delta or differential pulse code modulation (DPCM), uses a linear predictor based on the values of the preceding methods. If the coefficients of the predictor are chosen with care, it is much more effective than predictors based on either the incremental or absolute reference system. This method is also more modern and is often used with high frequency processes such as television. The predicted value of a sample is subtracted from its actual value and the resulting difference signal applied to a compressor/expander device within the transmitter.

INTO THE MAINSTREAM

Skin mills for the production of airframes were among the first to be numerically controlled. Originally, information was punched on a paper tape by the programmer. This was checked on a visual copy prepared by a Flexowriter. The paper tape was then fed into a unit which converted the digital information to time coordinated, phase modulated analog signals on magnetic tape.

For instance, Numill was a magnetic tape input control developed in 1957 by North American Aviation, Autonetics Division, for the economic production of single unit or small quantity parts. It was designed to produce templates, profile bars, and other two-dimensionally designed parts. This greatly simplified the then existing procedure in making a part. Master contour lines were put on metal loft boards by skilled loftsmen using previously developed coordinates. These master lines were duplicated on template material by an expensive printing process, each filed to shape by a template maker.

NC eliminated these steps and made preparation almost automatic. The information used by the loftsmen was coded and fed into an IBM 700 series computer, producing a magnetic tape for control of the machine tool. Computer processing was controlled by a master program which directed the operation and checked the accuracy of the calculations. Any curve was approximated by a series of straight line cuts, and the acceleration of the tool controlled to prevent overshoot.

Typically, such units combined both point and path control in their two horizontal axes of operation for speed and flexibility, in both milling and drilling operations. Movements on the horizontal axis were measured by a digital guage which sensed interference patterns generated by optical gratings. Pulses representing .0005 of an inch provided accurate control for a distance of over eight feet. Direction was sensed as "add" or "subtract." This process fairly indicates the merger of computer ideas with those of machine operations.

The reason for paying great interest to these early beginnings is that the fundamentals have not changed so much. The early steps give insight by having led us to discover new things, and in producing imaginative combinations of already existing concepts.

Computer-controlled machine tools may have done no better than the most able machinist, but they did excel in production and in quality that of average operators. The effort taught us that the optimum path would be a compromise between the key variables of the process subject to the criteria of the job, and the lesson has been learned and applied with robotics.

To recapitulate, the real gains obtained with NC have been summed up as depending upon two points. First, with no tolerance in commands given to the machine from the beginning of manufacturing, any piece can be made acceptable. Second, since essentially zero time is required at the machine to insert control commands, the latter can produce parts during a greater percentage of the time.

The first consideration has a high dollar value in complex operations; the second leads to a whole series of interrelated possibilities affecting the economics of the solution. Furthermore, NC techniques have been applied to other situations where sequencing, positioning, and calculating are performed. Some examples are ultrasonic testing requiring sequencing of test points, electronic circuit testing requiring sequencing and switching operations, and so on.

TOWARD SMALLER, MORE EFFICIENT PLANTS

Leading manufacturing companies are very much aware of the changing computer environment. U.S. Steel and GM are rumored to have sent key people to Japan to purchase robotics information. A great number of firms are engaged in in-depth studies about revamping their traditional production facilities and, as an NCR study in 1971 showed, are finding that the best way to go is toward smaller plants chartered for a limited line or group of products with fully automated fabrication capabilities.

One result of the NCR study has been that its Dayton plant work force, which at its peak numbered 14,500 (about ninety percent of its labor force in the United States), today numbers only about 850, and for many workers jobs are reduced in pay and skill—from metal workers earning as much as $8.50 an hour to electronic assemblers earning $3.70 an hour. This is not necessarily representative of the automated plant, but it does reflect some of the changes which may involve the skills and composition of the workplace.

Another basic reference taught by experience is the degree of planning which should precede the changeover, whether to full automation or a simple distribution of the fabrication activities. The decision to centralize seems to have been traumatic for NCR's manufacturing management, as the switchover involved great conceptual changes in manufacturing. Within five years, except for two men in the United States, none of the old manufacturing management remained. The problem was adaptation: all of the old hands in manufacturing management had come up vertically—none were generalists; few were college-educated; and the new manufacturing technologies were not their forte.

The company had a big centralized plant in Dayton, with copies of it all over the world. Engineering was almost totally independent of manufacturing. By today's standards, the approach to production was simplistic: the only way to reduce costs was to work the machine and men harder. There was a great vertical integration—NCR even made its own screws—but manufacturing control was rudimentary.

Complicating the move to smaller plants was the need for each to have its own engineering and development group so that product changes could be made quickly. Manufacturing engineering had followed product design in the slow pace of change: As the new management which took over in the early 1970s found out, one of NCR's cash registers retained its same design from 1921 to 1959, while in electronics product lifespan is four to five years. Not surprisingly, the change to smaller plants with their own resident engineering brought a whole new style to NCR's production.

The old policy to make everything was reversed. Purchasing, engineering, and manufacturing were restructured and the company made much greater use of the technical talent of its vendors. Thus, NCR evolved from maximum vertical integration toward a reasonable solution where the company retained only the parts it could produce competitively in terms of quality and cost.

A good deal of this change was structural. In the old mechanical fabrication plant, labor costs accounted for seventy-five percent or more of product cost; another fifteen percent was materials. In the new electronics products plants, fifty-five percent to seventy-five percent of production costs are parts and materials; labor accounts for twenty percent or less and is decreasing. These are some of the fundamental changes which helped reduce NCR's total domestic manufacturing work force from 15,750 to less than 6,000, with only fifteen percent or so retained at Dayton which used to be the central manufacturing base.

Are these radical changeovers really necessary? Is management well advised to follow a radical path? The answer is "yes," and the reason is survival. If a company does not take these measures, it will lose its leadership. Commodore, the personal computer manufacturer, held in Japan a market share in excess of fifty percent in 1979; by 1981, its market share in personal computers had slipped to under fifteen percent due to competition from the Japanese. The Japanese manufacturers are not stopping at the home market; they are rapidly entering those of Europe and the United States. It is now projected that they may gain a respectable thirty to forty percent of the American personal computer market by the mid 1980's.

Due to good production management and quality control, it seems logical that highly competitive Japanese products will be appearing in quantity in the world markets. Nobody can therefore blame the NCR or any other management for trimming its workforces, revamping, reorganizing, and otherwise cutting the fat in order to remain competitive. The keyword must now be *efficiency*.

This point is so important that it needs to be reiterated, using proper statistics. No further back than 1960, for basically accounting machine firms such as Burroughs, NCR, and Olivetti, just fifteen percent of manufacturing costs went for materials; today, with the vastly changed technology (and product lines), materials account on the average for two-thirds of production costs. The share of labor and materials in the cost of goods sold has been reversed; the criteria have changed.

The NCR case is no exception. Other business equipment companies, too, have switched from large centralized metal-working and assembly plants to smaller, dispersed production units. Due to the impact of technology, within ten years (1967 to 1977) Burroughs increased its sales per employee from $13,000 to $37,000. Yet, that still did not come close to matching IBM, which in 1977 boasted sales of $55,800 per employee. Since then, the pace has accelerated with the automation of the production floor.

Let us recapitulate the key points. On the production floor, information technology makes feasible a better coordination: a largely automatic machinery in fabrication, shorter lines making goods, non-labor intense operations, a sharp reduction of buffer stocks between manufacturing stations, better outgoing quality, and an accompanying cost control capability. In other words, robotics not only displace labor and alter classical manufacturing chores but also make feasible significant cost improvements through computer-based production planning and control—including scheduling, inventory management, quality control, and purchasing.

Careful scheduling of incoming shipments allows the manufacturing firm to cut its work-in-progress inventories. For many business systems manufacturers, this reduction has been significant: from seven months' worth to just one-half of that. Imaginative purchasing and the mass effect a major firm can have on costs and timescales can help keep under control the overall price tag of the end product. There is one field, however, in which vertical integration is nearly a "must" for a company on the fringes of technology, and this is semiconductors: memory chips and picoprocessors.

The high content of materials costs (as opposed to labor costs) of the end product is one reason why key components should receive much attention. The other is the crucial role semiconductors play in the making of technology-intense devices. It is, therefore, not surprising that one area in which some manufacturers start having their own capability is semiconductors. As IBM has done, they set up facilities to design and produce integrated circuits, leading to the development of advanced technology and proprietary products.

In-house semiconductor technology offers a company the expertise to look at how chips might be combined in new applications. For instance, one thing that struck researchers and engineers with experience in semiconductor technology and with a grasp of marketing reality is the illogical fact that people pay almost as much for scientific calculators as for minicomputers. This simple but fundamental observation is credited to be in the background of the original idea for putting extra functions on a single chip. Customers want extra functions for free, and an able designer can see simplifications that make this possible within the range of products his company is marketing.

In-house design can also see to it that cost factors are controlled. "Our production costs are lower," the management of one leading firm said. "We have reduced costs of some circuits by ninety-five percent in six years." No wonder that in order to support manufacturing, some firms have doubled their research and development expenditures since the early 1970s.

Priorities have also changed. For several firms, R&D expenditures were mainly on development projects expected to result in marketable products within a year or two. This near-term emphasis on R&D extended even to such high-technology areas as semiconductors. Management was not interested in doing basic materials research; emphasis was placed on what the company needed within two years for a steady price-performance improvement in products of some fifteen percent a year. Now, not only the more fundamental research comes back into the picture but also a major share is devoted to manufacturing engineering and the technology related to robotics.

15 A Process in Control

INTRODUCTION

A PROCESS is in control when the key factors characterising its performance fall within an allowable range of variation. No process follows a straight line in the behavior of any one of its key variables; there are always deviations, which is why in every engineering design we specify an object value and the tolerances.

In a calibrated production process, we aim to tune the expected value of the variable under control to the object value specified in the blueprints. In regard to variation, we speak of upper and lower control limits within which values of the variable in reference will be free to fluctuate.*

A fabrication process is tuned to keep the upper and lower control limits within specified tolerances. The process itself has to be monitored to assure that it remains in control. When this monitoring is done through automatic media (as it should) we speak of a *closed loop system*. Technology today provides the logical (algorithmic) and physical (computer) tools to successfully implement this concept.

The processes that can be controlled by computer fall into four major classes: closed and open loop, discrete and NC processes, continuous control processes (process control), and system or component testing. Though considerable design variations exist among them, they do include common functions:

- adaptive qualities
- data formatting and conversion
- testing of data

*See also "Statistical Processes and Reliability Engineering," D. Van Nostrand and Co., Princeton, NJ, 1960; same author.

- corrective control action
- report generation.

A closed loop system is one in which the output is measured and fedback for comparison with the input. The open loop control system has no means for comparing output with input, thus actuating corrective action.

In an NC system, control action is regulated by providing intermittent (discrete) data at some point. The mechanism must automatically interpret the position of this data. A computer can, for instance, control discrete input/output in response to sensor data or stored information. The sequencing logic is programmable to continuously monitor sense lines until some external condition occurs to interrupt the process.

System and component testing situations integrate assembly, quality control, and inspection techniques. They may involve inspection of dimensional accuracy, acceptance control, quality control histories, failure trends and so on. These systems constitute a greater sophistication of closed-loop systems by providing the ability to monitor critical process parameters, predict out-of-control conditions, signal preventive actions, and keep quality histories.

QUALITY MONITORING

In any fabrication process, whether mostly automatic or still largely manual, *quality monitoring* is essential. The concept involves a steady collection of dependable data, easy storage and retrieval, a calculating capability for testing against standards, and the interpolation and extrapolation of values. The quality database must contain time dependable figures (current week, last week, quarter average), machine defects, operator defects; workstations out of goal or control, and trends. All this should point to corrective action by management.

Automated inspection systems should combine assembly, quality control, and inspection techniques including inspection of dimensional accuracy, acceptance and process control inspection and computer recording of quality control and failures—in short, a quality history. Equally important is to predict out-of-control conditions and signal preventive action.

The computer-assisted system should provide control coverage, collect inspected data, perform data analysis, determine acceptance or rejection of controlled parts, and maintain a database on inspected and tested parts. Failures and causes of failures should be properly identified, test sequences established, and the aggregate lead to total manufacturing control. Figure 15-1 gives a layered approach to an online quality control systems architecture.

Online quality control and test systems assure improved efficiency by testing each item produced, rather than sampling goods for test purposes. This guarantees higher quality products with a greater degree of safety to the consumer. Through computer controlled manufacturing, a decrease in production cost can be economically combined with product variety, while at the same time minimizing in-process inventory and controlling production to meet delivery dates. Furthermore, a properly designed quality control system should extend both to the supplier's premises and to customer installations. This, too, is an example of the care the factory takes in assuring quality.

To gain insight on how these matters are being expedited, management should visit the factory floor and offices to examine manufacturing and quality assurance methodologies. The latter should cover the reception tests, rework procedures and quality standards. (Even the garbage bin is a quality indicator.)

As an example, Table 15-1 presents the analysis of process defects and component failures for two computer systems in the end phase of manufacturing:

"A" is the identification of a new CPU

"B" is that of a reworked processor.

Failure statistics are interesting. The higher failure rate is (as expected) with manual processes. For instance, for the new CPU the missing wire on background is eight out of 2,000, or

$$\frac{8}{2{,}000} = 4 \times 10^{-3}$$

which for the automatic dry joint is one out of 320,000, or

$$\frac{1}{320{,}000} = 3 \times 10^{-6}$$

So, there are three orders of magnitude of difference in favor of the automatic process.

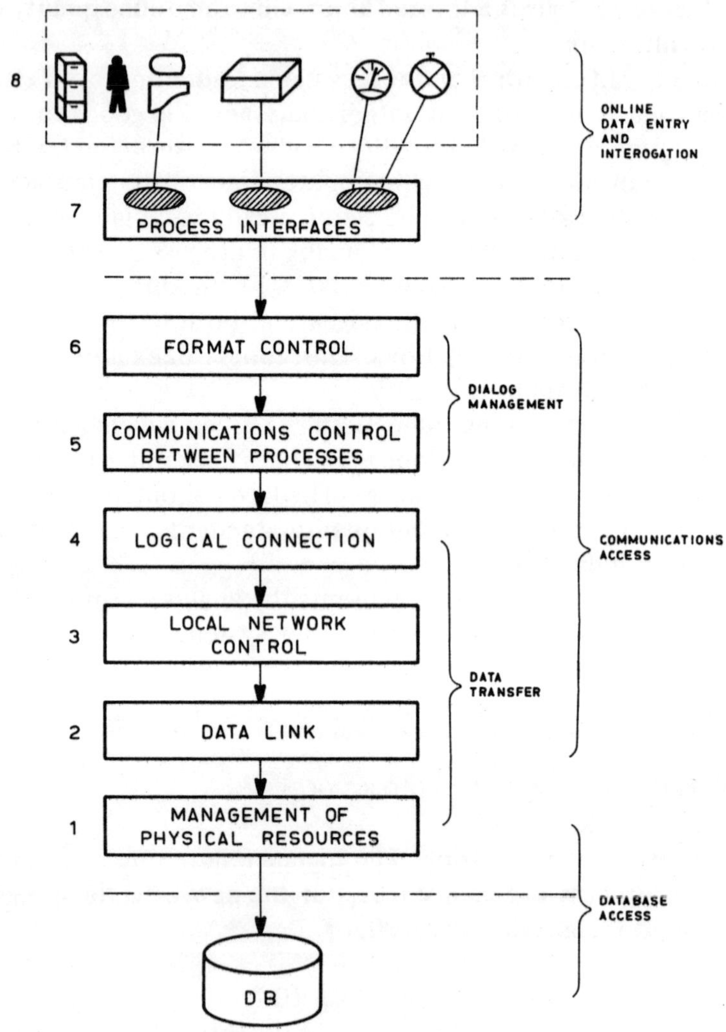

FIGURE 15–1 **A layered approach to control system architecture. Processes can be controlled through sensors or manual input, and should all progress toward a common database in a timely and accurate manner.**

TABLE 15–1

ANALYSIS OF PROCESS DEFECTS AND COMPONENT FAILURES DURING UNIT TEST AND SYSTEM CONFIGURATION TEST

1. UNIT TEST DEFECT TYPE	*"A" New CPU*	*"B" Reconditioned*
Mission wire on Backpanel	8	9
Debris	1	2
Broken Wire	–	1
Solder Bridge	1	–
Niched Solder Joint	1	3
Dry Joint on wired wrap board	1	–
Bent Pins touching on Backpanel	1	–
Bent Pins touching on Board	1	–
Defective Wire wrap	–	1
IC Fail	3	1
2. CONFIGURATION TEST DEFECT TYPE		
Debris	1	–
Broken Wire on Backpanel	2	–
Niched Wire on Port Board	–	1

Figure 15-2 gives a sample of ten days from the daily statistics at the plant, and shows that the missing eight or nine manually set wires are, in fact, better than the average performance. Such statistics are valuable in informing management, both for corrective action and for decision-making on new investments.

Table 15-2 identifies the test times necessary for quality assurance (unit and system configuration level) for two different pieces of equipment made on the same line. These statistics, on two CPU and the complete system configurations, are compared to the average test time required by factory procedures. The length of time devoted to tests depends upon the number of "bugs" which have been discovered (Figure 15-3).

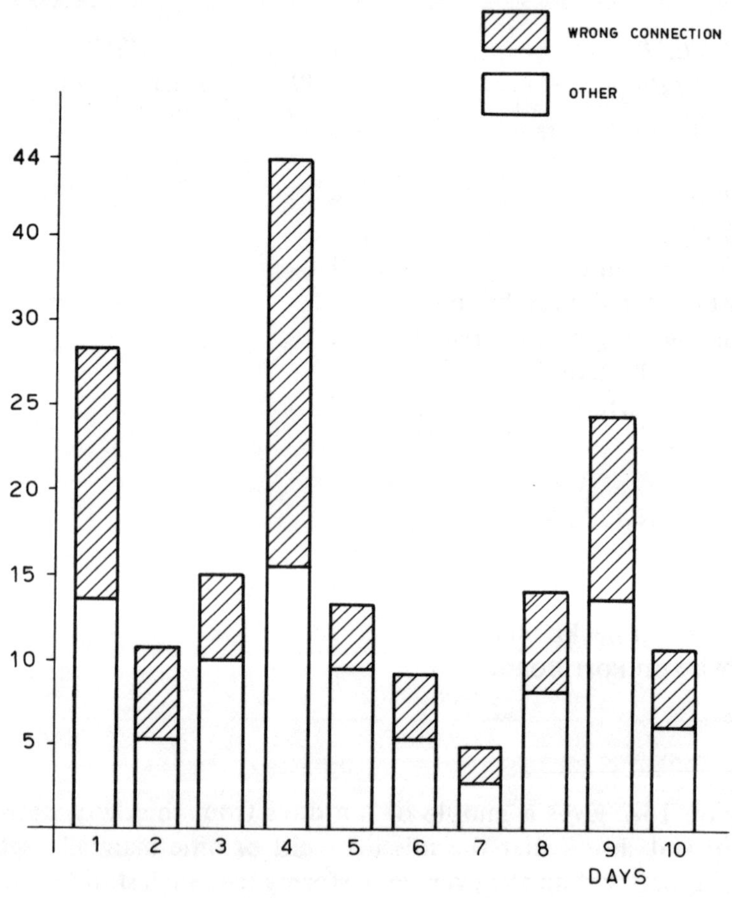

FIGURE 15–2 A ten-day sample from daily statistics of a computer-manufacturing plant identifying a missing wire on the background panel.

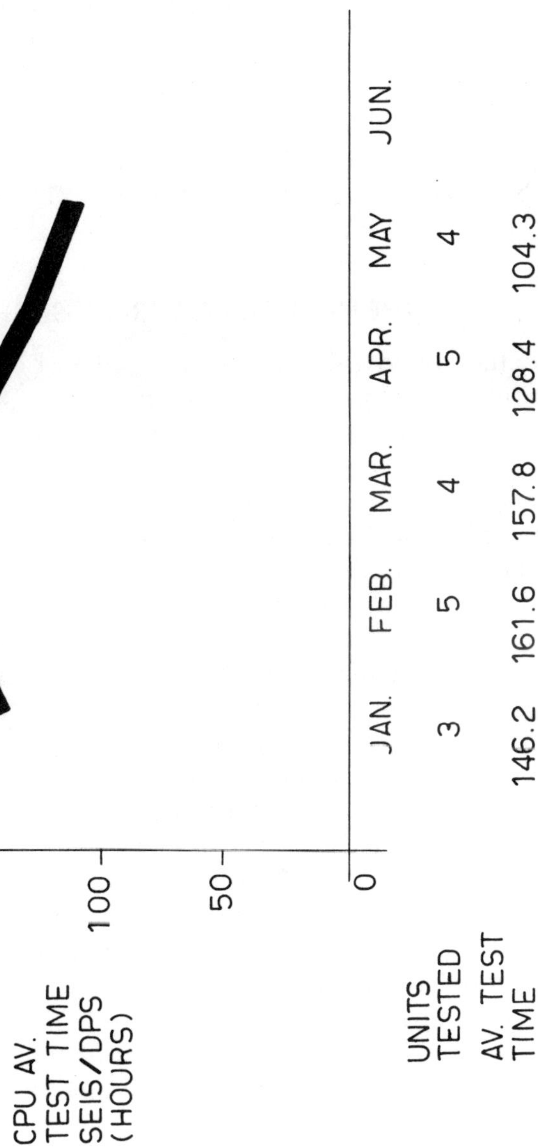

FIGURE 15–3 The length of time devoted to tests is a function of bugs which have been discovered. This graph provides some statistics.

TABLE 15–2

TEST TIMES FOR QUALITY ASSURANCE

	Type of Tests	
	Unit	*System*
"A", new	121.6 hrs.	143.9 hrs
"B", reconditioned	96.4 hrs.	116.3 hrs

THE MAINTENANCE PROCESSOR

In the introduction to this chapter, we spoke of a process in control, and then defined the closed and open loop systems. Of course, a complex computer system resembles a process: whether we manufacture goods or data is a characteristic relating to the goal of the process itself; but the fundamental principles are basically similar. We will, therefore, now examine the present application of the *maintenance processor*.

The newest announcements in computer hardware (IBM's 4300 Series; the HIS System 8) feature a dedicated processor for diagnostics and maintenance purposes. The principle is simple: Availing the possibility for remote maintenance through a dedicated mini, we make it feasible for the field engineer to exercise the machine through online diagnostics *as if* he was there. Quality statistics is the other objective.

As we know from other systems, the advantages to be obtained from the maintenance processor will depend on what it is used for, how, and how much. The dedicated maintenance processor should permit quality histories not available today. Such a facility, though, may go unused if people are not properly trained to take advantage of it. This is also true of the online tests which, apart of expertise, require special software (for instance, for loopbacks), and the same is true of any factory computer dedicated to quality control assurance.

System-wise, the fact remains that the maintenance processor is a massive change to product performance and quality. The benefits will be that much greater if we stress training in maintenance terms. The incorporation of the maintenance processor and the fact that computers tend to be more reliable as they have fewer boards and joints, smaller number of wire joints, and less debris should provide more reliable equipment.

The value of the dedicated quality control and maintenance minicomputer to:

- the user
- the maintenance engineer
- the factory engineer
- the designer

is exemplified by the results which each party can obtain. For every unit (and, in some cases, major sub-unit) of his system, the user must be familiar with or prepared for:

- Power-on (start/stop)
- Runtime (statistics, accounting, turnaround, I/O, communications, database accesses)
- Unusual events (downtime, diagnostic logs, available supplies, actual repair, H/W or S/W reasons, recovery, database deadlocks).

The maintenance engineer needs:

- Failure diagnostics (symptoms tracing, media, jobs)
- Exact configuration (H/W revision; S/W: release, significant hints)
- Diagnostics results; fault location (part, action, follow-up); experimental possibilities.

The factory engineer needs:

- Correlation of quality control action with field results (MTBSI, MTOSI)
- Product mix; environmental conditions; job mix
- Cause of the failure (system, environment, operations).

The Designer needs information reaching down the fundamental component level, and must be able to integrate the foregoing quality records into one coherent and comprehensive picture. Reliability is a major goal, but also the balancing-out of design feature including the choice of materials, costs, lead times and overall effectiveness of the end product.

Such considerations become more critical as systems operate increasingly online, within less controlled environments and in direct contact to the end user. Here, again, factory experience can be a valuable reference when we wish to obtain the best results.

(Projecting on the future of maintenance processor implementation for local and remote networks, some lessons may be learned from the automated unit test operation (AUTO) designed and implemented as a basic component of the factory floor information and control system to support test activities for central processors, system control units, input/output multiplexers and other central system mainframe components.)

A LAYERED APPROACH

Let us now see how the same principles can be applied on the factory line. On several occasions, we have underlined that the assurance of product quality is no monolithic standard. It is a steady, uninterrupted process which guarantees that specifications are observed by judging the factory's capability in observing established tolerances and other quality standards (such as product life requirements).

In the particular case of the example we will be following, the quality assurance project has included technical needs for the development and implementation of a distributed test system for mainframe components (in a network fashion) able to utilize a microprocessor-controlled maintenance panel. The overall task involves:

- Level 1–database
- Level 2–transaction processing routines
- Level 3–communications
- Level 4–software control
- Level 5–operations.

Two basic components constitute this system to enable unit testing capabilities. A test driver utilizes a microprogrammed peripheral computer to communicate with the operator and control the execution of the various control and data switches available on the maintenance panel of a central processor.

The support of the test system calls for a detailed understanding of the method to generate and modify the subject tests. The method is fairly complex and requires highly trained and capable individuals. In general, it involves:

- loading of required test data
- online documentation
- error logging
- history file update and reporting
- known error list maintenance
- test cycle time logging, and
- management reporting.

The test control capability of the system enables management to better investigate and develop methods to improve the test process for system units. As this capability matures, additional items can be incorporated to extend the faculties to the test environment. Test execution time, errors encountered during a test, error log and solution cross reference, labor vouchering, and system statistics logging are examples of such capabilities.

When an error occurs, the test module writes the current test identifier to the disc and reports the error. The report of the failure contains the following information:

- date and time of day
- application identification
- test identification
- subtest dump of should be/was data
- identification of failing signal
- indication of most probable failing component

- application revision level
- test software revision level
- any other pertinent data in regard to the failure.

This information is displayed and generates an error transaction for logging of this error. A routine will scan the history file of failures and report any information held in this file. This history file is composed of previous failures and the solutions used to fix the failure at the same place in the automatic test.

The operator may now call on the module to aid in isolation of the failure and speed correction of the failure. The solution to the failure should be entered into the system by the operator. The entry of information will be structured so that as much control over the information content placed into the system defining a solution will be standard. Misuse of the solution reporting system will place illogical information into the system, which must be edited and updated by the associated test specialists.

If an entry into the history file represents a recurring error, the information will be made available to the quality control specialists as a potential process-related problem that may be preventable. The impact on fault location is self-evident.

This procedure identifies to a certain extent the background necessary for a valid quality assurance methodology. However, even if the methodology is sound, it is just as true that no chain is ever better than the weakest of its links—and the weakest link is man.

Machines can augment the capabilities of people—if such capabilities exist in the first place—but they cannot substitute for good personnel. It is the top-most job of management to give its people the clear and unambiguous message that they should convert themselves to the new technology, to outline why it is necessary to be open-minded, and to be productive and action-oriented. There should be no widespread confusion between technological progress and (ill-advised) resistance to it.

Productivity and performance goals should be dominant. In this manner, everyone will profit. Automation or not, the job is done by people—and the more skilled, open-minded and willing to adapt to changing conditions our people are, the better it will be for everyone and for the company as a whole.

CONVERTING A PRODUCTION RESOURCE

The evaluation and review of the inspection process for reconditioned computer equipment reveals attention to detail. In the robotics factory, this procedure should be applied to both computers to be installed and the overhaul of the robots themselves. It will constitute a major effort to keep the process in control.

Since this work costs money, a question may be posed on the financial incentives for reconstructing equipment as opposed to purchasing newly fabricated units. In the specific case of the reconditioned CPU which we will consider, the cost for auditing, stripping and production was about equal to building a new CPU, but other implications—taxes, lead time, scrappage, component useability (fifty-one of eighty-one boards were still useable)—suggested reconditioning.

Timetables are also important. Because of the time-lag in getting components and other supplies, it took (at the time of this study) about forty weeks to collect the needed components for building a new machine (Figure 15-4). Correspondingly, the reconditioning job was done in ten weeks. Even with plenty of supplies, a new computer has twenty-eight weeks lead time, while with major shortage it can exceed one year.

Let us now follow the case study. The CPU of a computer is designed to fulfill specific objectives in terms of the processing capacity which it supports and the options which it offers. Reconditioning it can affect either or both of these issues—and in so doing requires a change in the backpanel(s) which act(s) as the signal cord of the machine.

For any meaningful change in variables which enter the capacity equation, the manufacturing plant has to intervene—particularly so when background functions are involved because of changed board interconnections. If the work is properly done in the factory, reconditioning will evidently affect quality assurance and reliability characteristics. Thus, establishing thorough inspections will assure that equipment has undergone the promised interventions.

Let us recapitulate the objectives. In a CPU conversion, the intent is to:

- add options.
- give the CPU the functionality of a currently built processor, and
- assure a valid outgoing quality level.

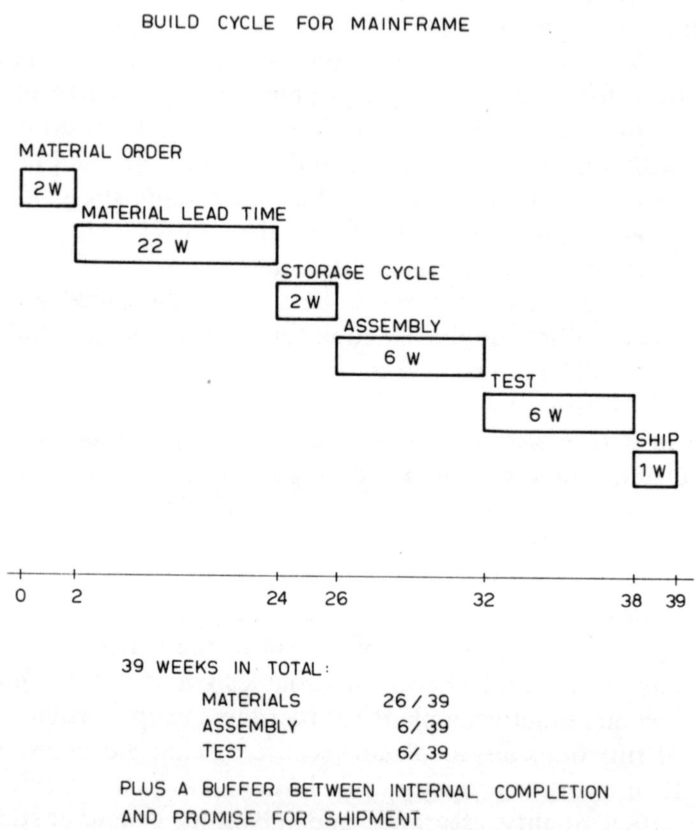

FIGURE 15–4 A typical time-lag in 1980 for getting components and other supplies, thus influencing construction time for the mainframe.

The same methods, systems, tests and test equipment have to be used as with the building of a new CPU. Therefore, one has to be sure of the methodology which is used. The conversion process involves these phases:

incoming audit/inspection,

definition of missing functional parts, if any, and

stripping the system to defined levels.

Such phases parallel to a certain degree those we find in new machine construction (Figure 15-5). In both cases, quality assurance is a preoccupation of the drafting board, procurement, receiving, assembling and test functions.

When the prerequisite work has been correctly performed, then begins the individual checkout of the units. In the particular case which we are following, of eighty-one boards contained in the CPU, thirty were replaced by totally new ones. Precisely:

- twenty basic boards had to be changed;
- ten boards were optional, but were still changed;
- a tenth backpanel was added;
- the maintenance panel was modified;
- the backpanel wiring was completely redone.

The backpanel approach is to rework individual modules (adds, deletes). Five side modules were roasted and rewired; a sixth was added.

Each individual board was tested, and audit reports were established. Any damage which was traced, was repaired—as indicated by the methodology. Each component was evaluated individually, at the following levels:

1. Backpanels.
   - Semi-automatic wiring tests
   - Check of wires and tracing
   - Card cage assembly review
   - Backpanel assembly evaluation.

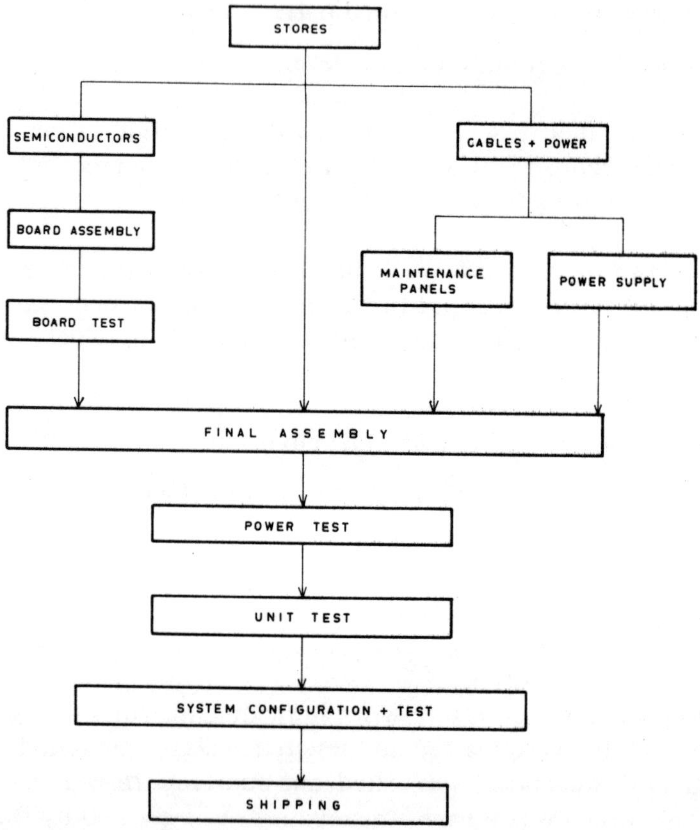

FIGURE 15-5 Sequential phases followed in machine construction.

2. Boards. Generally, the amount of evaluation depends on model changes. The change of boards is quite significant as it means tests of 250 hours. The cycle breaks down into debug, configuration, and confidence, each level being properly traced and logged.
3. Channels. Both speed and number depends on customer requirements and on the stated system capabilities.
4. Harness Assembly (Cable Wiring)
5. Maintenance Panel Test
6. Final Assembly
7. Unit Test
8. Final System Test

If new boards are integrated in the machine, then wiring, connector boarding, and soldering are also affected. Comparative calibration *and* absolute tests to reduce the problem of variation between calibration periods as steady calibration of the test equipment are a must. Furthermore, board revisions are subject to tracking of control results.

Quality engineering considerations thus involve computer process evaluataion, process description(s), control procedures and documents, quality standards, inspection methods, data collection, test equipment control, and a quality monitoring system. Figure 15-6 details the steps which are followed from the incoming and storage of the recycled CPU to the final tests and shipment.

The computer-based quality monitoring system collects inspection and test results from each inspection area and produces weekly reports by work area containing:

defect distribution,

operator feedback, and

management action reports.

Such a computer-based system must see to it that management's corrective action is monitored to assure follow-up. A major issue is that of costs. The cost issue finds its justification in the extent of the rework.

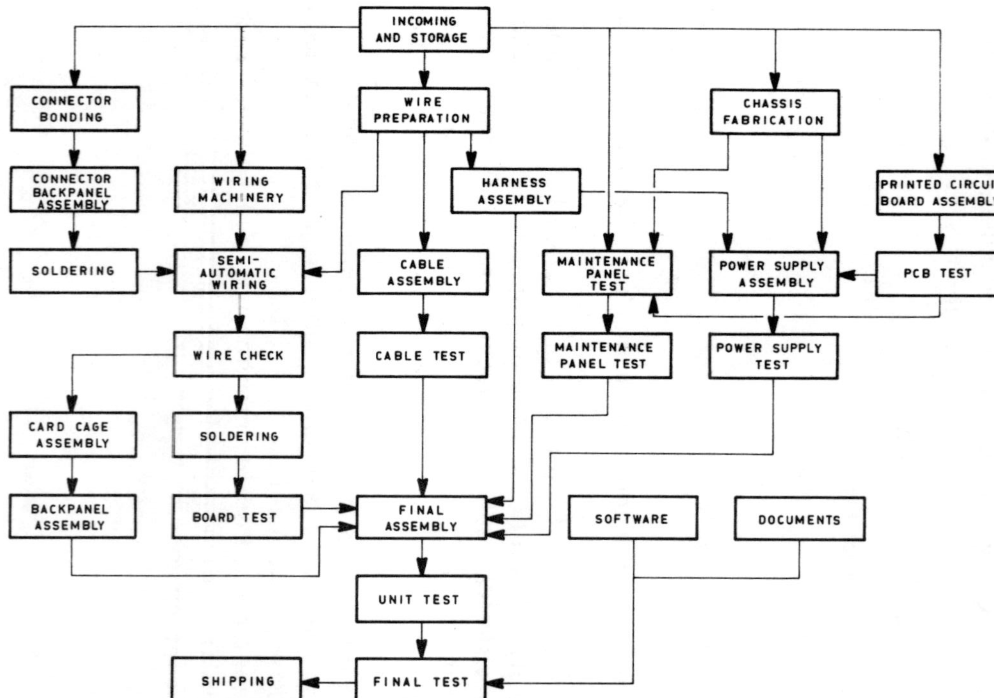

FIGURE 15–6 A flow chart of steps followed from the incoming and storage of recycled CPU to the final tests and shipment.

Of the technical milestones identified in Figure 15-6, the following were necessary to implement on the CPU under reconditioning:

1. Connector bonding, backpanel assembly, soldering
2. Gardner Denver Wiring, semi-automatic wiring, wire check
3. Card cage assembly, backpanel assembly
4. Board test
5. Harness assembly
6. Maintenance panel assembly and test
7. Final assembly
8. Unit test and final test.

Each level of inspection and rework imposes its own prerequisites and technical procedures. At the wire wrap process, every board is traceable through all operations via a route sheet; a preventive maintenance

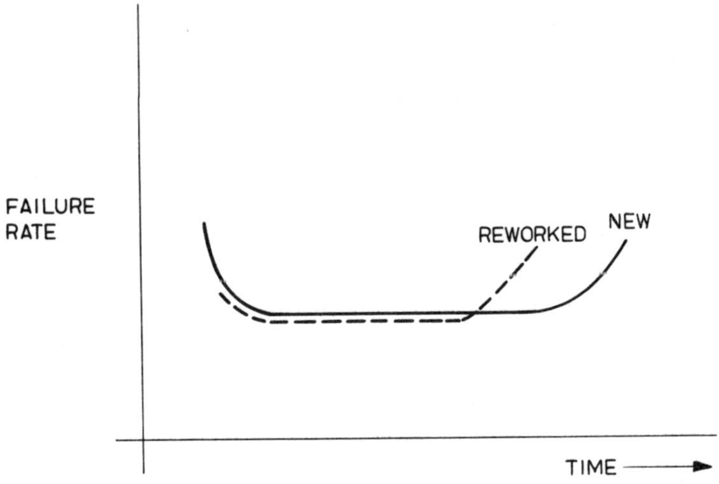

FIGURE 15–7 **Any system, natural or man-made, demonstrates a higher failure rate in its initial days (baby failures) and by the end of its life cycle (wear-out failures). A reworked system, however, tends to have a slightly different reliability curve.**

schedule is in place on all machines; rework and re-qualification is controlled by the standards room (inspection); the automatic wiring ring-out tester gives a high level of confidence on wired assemblies; and wrap quality is controlled by 100 percent inspection and fast feedback to the technicians.

In the solder area, the fluids used in preclean, preserve, solder, and cleaning processes must be sampled monthly and assayed by external analysis, and an action report issued. A close monitoring of results of the wave soldering operation is maintained by first-off inspection before batch operation and then by inspection straight from the machine. An ultrasonic bonding process is controlled by ensuring regular change of components and by close inspection and push-out testing.

At cables and harnesses, the major inspection effort is put in at early stages. The tools used are subject to a strict calibration schedule with "comparative" and "absolute" techniques. Material deviations are authorized only by the manager and are issued only by specific cable type. Assemblies receive 100 percent ring-out where possible on an automatic tester.

REMOVING FUNCTIONAL DEFECTS

The prime function of the board test is to detect and remove functional defects introduced by the manufacturing process. Such is the case with debris (which may be conductive), with defective solder joints, and early life component failures (see Figure 15-7).

All system boards are tested on a standard MQX board tester. Each board undergoes test evaluations in high and low nominal voltage margins. All system memory boards are tested on a memory test system, and defects are input on a weekly basis to the quality monitoring system.

In the assembly areas, most operations are man-dependent and receive detailed in-process and final inspections. The organization aims to minimize disturbances in test areas. The power, maintenance panels and major units receive power-up functional tests. There is a revision control and tracking of board revisions attained by change control logs.

The prime function of unit tests is to remove early life failures (Figure 15-8) and components which fail to function correctly under *marginal* conditions of

voltage, and

timing.

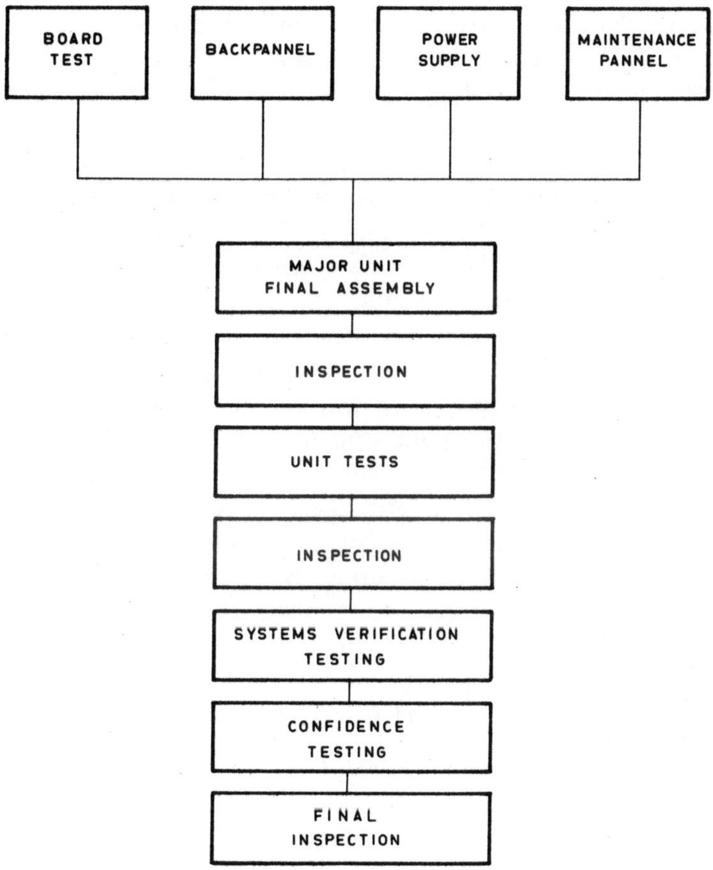
BOARD TEST
BACKPANNEL
POWER SUPPLY
MAINTENANCE PANNEL
MAJOR UNIT FINAL ASSEMBLY
INSPECTION
UNIT TESTS
INSPECTION
SYSTEMS VERIFICATION TESTING
CONFIDENCE TESTING
FINAL INSPECTION

FIGURE 15-8

This inspection also fleshes out effects introduced by the manufacturing process.

All major units must be tested. Both standard tests and diagnostic procedures are followed for the CPU memory, I/O and other major units. The objective is to remove all detected defects. The CPU must run ten error-free hours running automatic margins and during vibration. This is an example of defect goals implementation.

As stated in a preceeding section, the time scheduled for testing is a function of product quality. A "good" CPU would take about twenty-five hours under test. With failures, it may take 140 or even 250 hours. The quality of the man that works on the machine can also influence the results.

Table 15-3 presents the monthly average and the last quarter average for system tests and for selected unit tests, as implemented by the factory in reference. During testing, voltage and timing margins can be activated dynamically. We made reference to the fact that voltage variation is ±5 percent of nominal; critical CPU timing standards are also tested and observed. Control, operations and unit tests are closely monitored.

Units and system control documentation include test planning instructions, test logs; "sign off" summary sheets, repair reports; quality control instructions, and technical memos. Inspection methods reflect sound planning by quality engineering. Both equipment-supported and visual inspection was observed, with routine feedback loops to ensure process correction in the minimum time.

TABLE 15–3

AVERAGE UNIT TEST TIMES

Model	*Monthly Average*	*Last Quarter Average*
System	121.6 hrs	154.9 hrs
DP Master	–	170.1 hrs
DP Slave	86.9 hrs	142.4 hrs
U.R.	11.8 hrs	18.9 hrs
I/O	13.5 hrs	9.8 hrs
Storage Controller	45.0 hrs	21.4 hrs
Front End	42.2 hrs	33.0 hrs
Disc Units	–	12.0 hrs

Sampling inspection takes place where process capability has been well-proven and recovery of defect batches is demonstrable. At the pre-shipping level is made a full customer configuration check—a clearance of all repair reports, including an accumulation check, and spot checks on packing. Acceptance criteria are followed: documentation, assembly, interconnection processes, fabrication, finishes, safety, and packing.

The test strategy can be seen divided largely into four levels:

Level 1—Basic subassembly (defects identification)

Level 2—Board functionality

Level 3—Unit functionality

Level 4—System functionality and stress test.

The computer-based quality monitor system collects inspection and test results from each inspection station on the shop floor and test areas and then produces weekly reports by workstation containing:

- summary quality performance results
- comparison against goals
- operator feedback information
- machine process feedback
- defect distribution
- trend calculation
- quality performance evaluation.

The quality review follows the feedback sheets, in a daily fashion by factory engineers; it involves a report summary, reviewed weekly with senior management, and includes the monitoring of management's corrective action, as has already been underlined.

PRODUCT ASSURANCE

The restructuring and quality inspection processes which have been outlined have provided a reasonably good level of confidence. *Product assurance*, as a functional department, provides controls on appropriate test documentation, test planning, and the technical liaison with field engineering. The same organization handles both hardware and software issues and qualifies successive releases, prior to expediting to the field.

A computer-based information system is tuned to detect even a small number of failures. This is not only good practice but also a necessity given the new technologies a modern factory puts in action.

During testing, voltage and timing margins are activated dynamically. Each major unit has a mode register which can be accessed by a master mode program. The following margins can be activated in any required sequence:

- Voltage + 5V varied ±5 percent of nominal
- Voltage ± 12V varied ±5 percent of nominal
- Critical CPU timing
- Signals are varied ±10ns within the following control units:
  - operations unit (OU)
  - control unit (CU)
  - decimal unit (DU).

Other test functions can be attached from the mode register. Inspections after unit tests particularly look for workmanship standards. Inspections after confidence standards have been set look after the strict observance of client order(s). Figure 15-9 identifies the major parts of a computer system test process.

After completion of the standard hardware tests (unit tests, system tests), the central memory (CM) and a limited number of peripherals are attached to the CPU. With this basic system configuration will be run the software test:

basic software,

selected applications (mainly utility programs).

The factory attached particular interest on this subject as experience has demonstrated that basic software tests done on small-system system configurations sometimes flesh out defects which are invisible with large configurations. (For instance, allocation of disc space.)

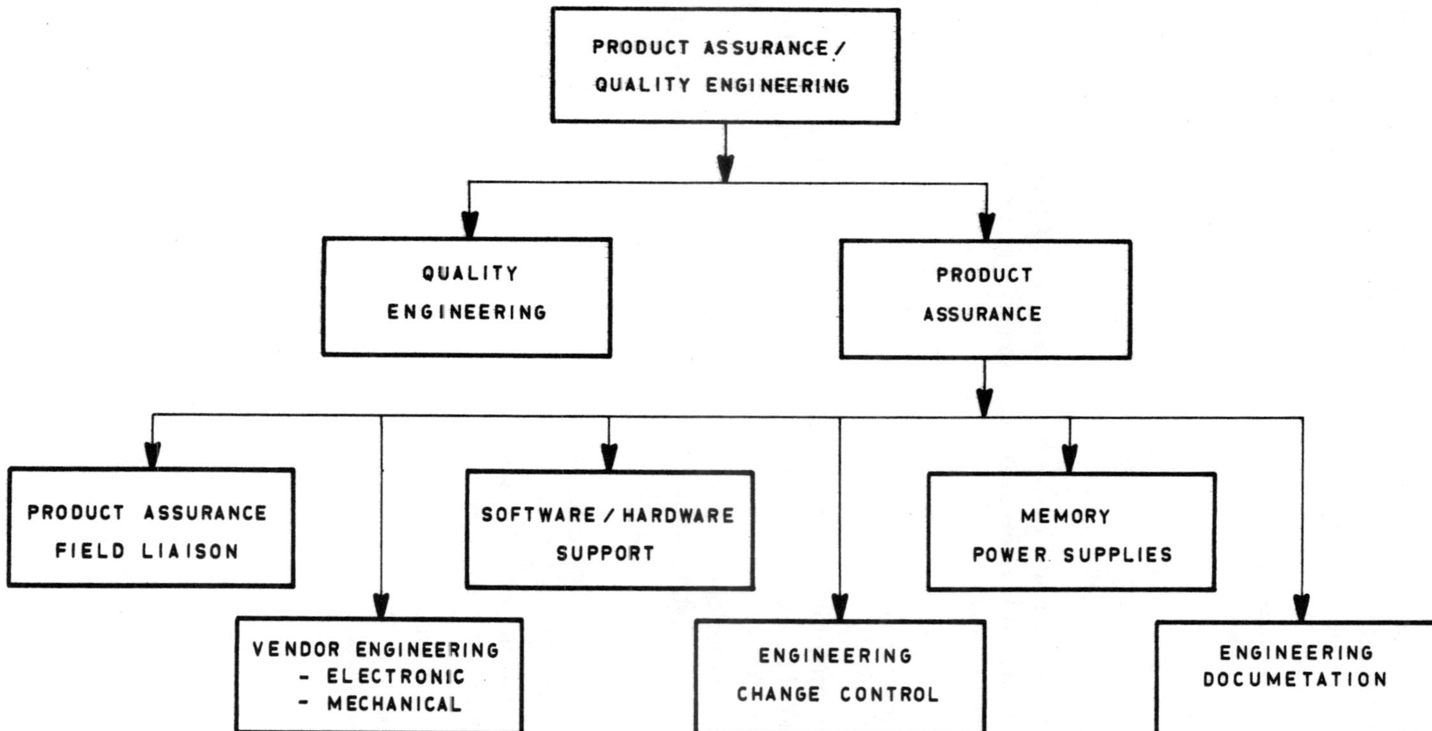

FIGURE 15-9 A computer system test process. Robotics require quite similar steps.

Another subject concerns organization and structure. Correctly, factory management placed the whole range of product assurance and quality engineering—both for hardware and for software—under the same department head. Upon him depends the product assurance/engineering function as demonstrated in Figure 15-9.

Among the product assurance and engineering functions we distinguish:

Engineering change control, including the technical authority for the control and implementation of all large system change orders.

Documentation services, a records (input/output) organization of all technical documentation relating to the manufacture and test of large systems.

System confidence testing, which specifies procedures and criteria all systems must meet for acceptance.

This lays the groundwork for failure modes or conditions to be identified and resolved. The purpose of system verification and confidence testing is to establish that the system will operate in a manner similar to that which will be experienced in the customer environment.

Tests aim to establish system reliability via burn-in—and a number of test phases are time dependent to ensure adequate burn-in hours.

Software/hardware support provides detailed analyses of all system dumps as they relate to the hardware and operating system, and interfaces the machine components assembled at the factory to the operating system software.

Vendor engineering aims to establish and enforce guidelines in regard to technical vendor approval, technical assistance (internal/external), and accept/reject criteria for the inspection of the goods.

Vendor engineering procedures are vigorous. As an example, incoming inspection procedures for integrated circuits involve:

- Ten pieces per incoming batch to be tested for marking, marking permanency, dimensions, solderability, lead formation, gross leak, and thermal intermittents.

- One percent of all batches are tested at 25°C and 75°C for D.C. and dynamic parameters on acceptance; a 100 percent test is performed at 25°C.
- Memories (MOS 16K) are subjected to 100 percent tests for D.C. and dynamic parameters and 100 percent burn-in at 125°C for sixteen hours. The same is true of bipolar memories.
- PROMS are subjected to D.C. parameter tests (25°C and 75°C) then programmed; burn-in (sixteen hours); and a 100 percent electrical screen is applied at 100°C.

The product assurance/field liaison has the goal to provide product assurance support, to control all appropriate test documentation, to assure a technical liaison with field engineering and a similar liaison with prime source. This enables the feeding of resolutions in both directions to all problems of a technical nature which affect the factory and/or the field. Regular meetings (once per month) are held to serve this objective and, as well, field seminars aimed at the solution of interface problems to the factory—and, as well, to monitoring and controlling effective resolutions.

A field installation reporting scheme serves these aims by providing an agreed position between manufacturing and field engineering. The directives imply that installation reports for all new installations will be returned to the factory for evaluation. Such reports must contain information on site readiness, system completeness, physical damage reports, time needed for installation, and details of all functional failures.

The factory responds to field engineering via the field liaison engineer on what corrective actions are required, and agree on implementation. The factory also carries out a minimum of four installation audits per year. They are performed by experienced engineers who remain on site until the audit has been successfully run. The purpose is to review in detail:

- system completeness
- physical condition of system
- site readiness and suitability
- functional defects

- installation time
- effectiveness.

Each audit produces a detailed report which culminates in an action plan to implement problem resolution. Quality assurance is responsible for ensuring satisfactory resolution to all problems.

To monitor these activities and provide a unified record, a quality analysis and action report is produced by quality line engineering. It contains:

Performance charts for each area: detailing the implementation date of any major procedural changes or special actions.

Revised objectives: with approximate guides to the savings to be achieved.

Action proposals: to reach the stated objectives.

Possible alterations: to report formats or the reported information.

Significant statistics: deduced from the quality control reports through engineering knowledge.

Quality and inspection activities enable management to deploy their resources in the most profitable areas. As a development from the quality analysis and action report, line quality supervision and management can produce a further analysis of quality department performance. A performance index is based on improvements achieved in product quality and quality costs. A performance chart can be displayed as a graphical illustration of quality effectiveness.

The following list is offered as a suggested checklist of important aspects of the quality system:

1. *Implementation*:
   (a) Procedures and documentation clear and easily accessible
   (b) System operation understood
   (c) Defect categories
   (d) Materials available
   (e) Support and maintenance
   (f) Degree of detail required

2. *Operation and Maintenance*:
   (a) Documentation maintenance procedure
   (b) Checks on materials supply
   (c) Audit procedures
   (d) Control cycle
   (e) Needed accuracy
   (f) Mandatory levels of confidence

3. *Reports*:
   (a) Most useful report type
   (b) Most useful statistics
   (c) Best distribution
   (d) Information accuracy
   (e) Misleading information
   (f) What can be deduced
   (g) Best display

4. *Application*:
   (a) Input costs
   (b) Inspection time savings
   (c) Over/under inspection
   (d) Reduced scrap
   (e) Reduced rework
   (f) Investigation costs
   (g) Advisable action.

No order of importance is implied and the list should be kept fluidly dynamic. As examples of quality reports, the following reports identify the number of defects per unit, the percent accepted and the percent rejected. A comparative table on defects as percent of the total population inspected indicates within the examined time period an acceptable rate of two per thousand.

The following definitions have been used:

Total Units: total number of units inspected

Percent Inspected: refering to the percent of units in inspected samples

Percent Rejected: the percent of units inspected that were rejected

D.P.U.: defects per unit: $\frac{\text{Total Defects}}{\text{Total units Inspected}}$

D.P.U.R.: defects per unit rejected

Total Defects: Total units rejected

Totals of each of these measurements for the whole 'product' are also given in the quality reports which accompany this text.

In conclusion let me once again repeat that whether or not we wish to be competitive is indicative of the interest we put on *quality*. When we speak of computers, communications, online databases and robotics, diagnostics leading to corrective action is a critical issue. It is also an art in full evolution.

Quality is a major factor in being and staying competitive. Market forecasts and product evolution are the beginning phases of a process aimed to assure that management attention is focused on product strategy. The selection of a product line is a crucial decision, and we all know that products and markets are two highly interrelated matters. They are necessary, but they are not enough.

In a fiercely competitive market, survival obliges us to position ourselves against the forces of this decade. This means being cost/effective, caring for productivity, assuring quality, and using the best technology can offer. Microprocessors are at our disposition, CAD/CAM has developed to a stage that we can consider it a worthy and reliable partner, and robotics promise to revamp our machine tools and revolutionize our factories.

This book should be read in a spirit of open-mindedness. Its goal is to focus the manager's attention on the tools at his disposal, and to document what is said through examples and not to give opinionated advice. In any event, it has not been written in a didactic sense. What Bernard Shaw said—

"Don't gamble,
don't lend,
don't marry,
and never take anybody's advice."

—is enough to have prevented me from adopting such an orientation. Advice should be given only after a careful study of the specific case, not as a matter of generality.

The only general statement to be derived from this book is that for many enterprises the industrial environment in which they exist is comparable to a layer of thin ice. In skating over thin ice, our safety is in our speed. It would be wise if engineers and managers take this fact into account for the years ahead.

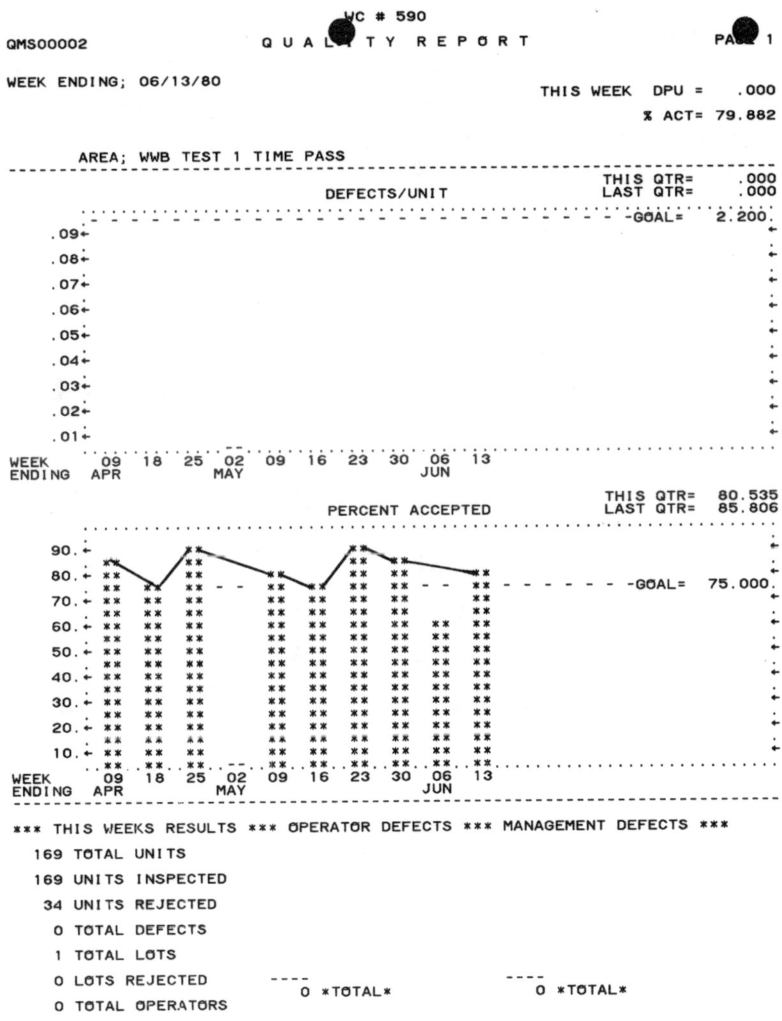

WC # 593

QMS00002 Q U A L I T Y R E P O R T PAGE 1

WEEK ENDING; 06/13/80

THIS WEEK DPD = .000

% ACT=100.000

AREA; MOS B/TEST 2ND PASS

DEFECTS/DEFECTIVE

THIS QTR= .923
LAST QTR= 1.394

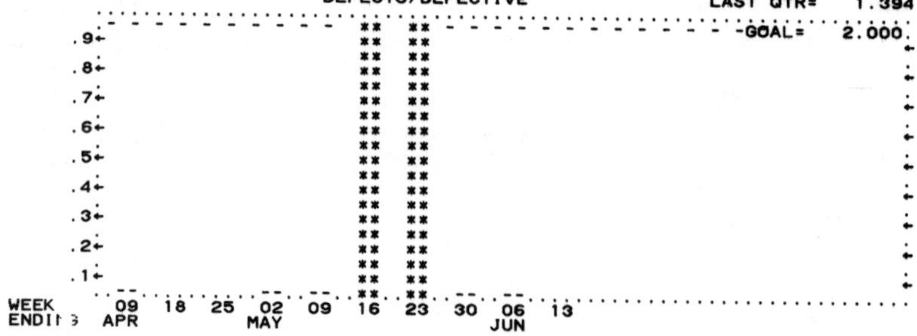

PERCENT ACCEPTED

THIS QTR= 67.500
LAST QTR= 62.500

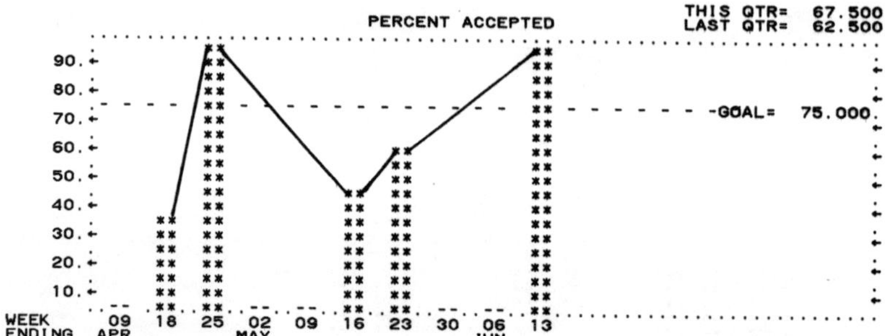

*** THIS WEEKS RESULTS *** OPERATOR DEFECTS *** MANAGEMENT DEFECTS ***

9 TOTAL UNITS
9 UNITS INSPECTED
0 UNITS REJECTED
0 TOTAL DEFECTS
1 TOTAL LOTS
0 LOTS REJECTED ---- ----
0 TOTAL OPERATORS 0 *TOTAL* 0 *TOTAL*

WC # 593

A PROCESS IN CONTROL

WC # 682

QMS00002 Q U A L I T Y R E P O R T PAGE 1

WEEK ENDING; 06/13/80

THIS WEEK %-U-R= .000

% ACT= .000

AREA; NCO GOODS IN MECH

THIS QTR= 4.000
LAST QTR= 2.434

PERCENT UNITS REJECTED

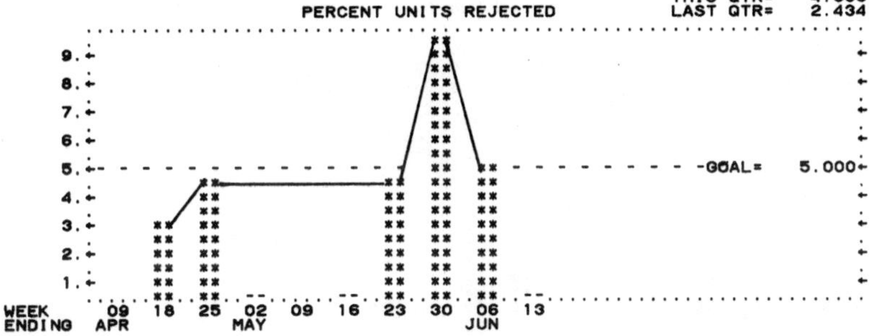

THIS QTR= 96.000
LAST QTR= 97.566

PERCENT ACCEPTED

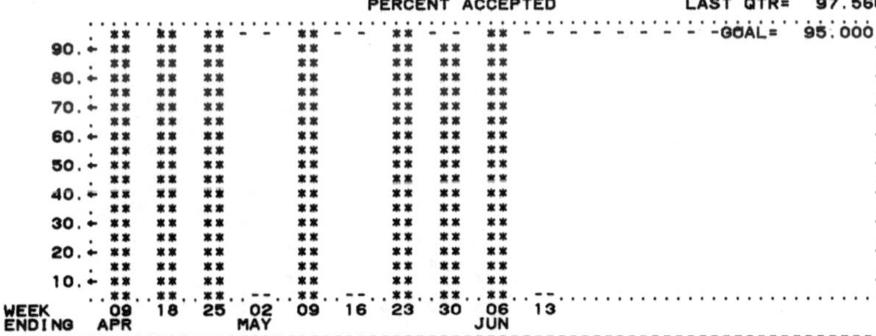

*** THIS WEEKS RESULTS *** OPERATOR DEFECTS *** MANAGEMENT DEFECTS ***

0 TOTAL UNITS
0 UNITS INSPECTED
0 UNITS REJECTED
0 TOTAL DEFECTS
0 TOTAL LOTS
0 LOTS REJECTED ---- 0 *TOTAL* ---- 0 *TOTAL*
0 TOTAL OPERATORS

WC # 682

WC # 507

QMS00002 — QUALITY REPORT — PAGE 1

WEEK ENDING; 06/27/80

THIS WEEK %-U-R= 27.083

DPU = ,562

AREA; HARNESS BOARD FINAL

PERCENT UNITS REJECTED — THIS QTR= 11.955 LAST QTR= 15.258

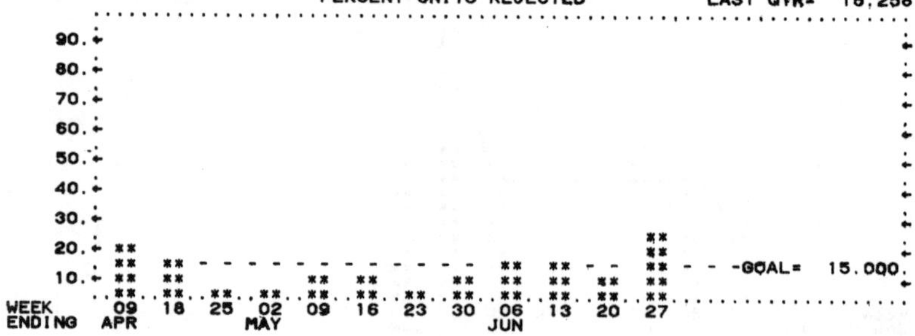

DEFECTS/UNIT — THIS QTR= .235 LAST QTR= .519

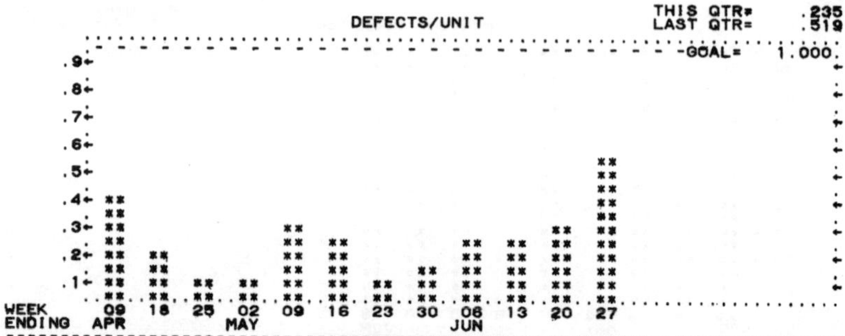

*** THIS WEEKS RESULTS ***	OPERATOR DEFECTS ***	MANAGEMENT DEFECTS ***
48 TOTAL UNITS	8 WRONG LOCATION	
48 UNITS INSPECTED	8 MISSING	
13 UNITS REJECTED	3 PIN SEAT/MATING	
27 TOTAL DEFECTS	2 MARKING	
15 TOTAL LOTS	2 DAMAGE	
0 LOTS REJECTED	----	----
0 TOTAL OPERATORS	27 *TOTAL*	0 *TOTAL*

WC # 507

Appendix

GLOSSARY

ALU	Arithmetic and Logical Unit
ATE	Automatic Test Equipment
BCD	Binary Coded Decimal
BPW	Bits Per Word
CAD	Computer-Aided Design
CAI	Computer-Aided Instruction
CAM	Computer-Aided Manufacturing
CM	Central Memory
CMOS	Complementary Metal Oxide Semiconductor
COM	Computer Output to Microfilm
CPU	Central Processing Unit
DCM	Data Communications Multiplexer
DIS	Distributed Information Systems
DMA	Direct Memory Access
DTL	Diode Transitor Logic
ECL	Emitter Coupled Logic
EPROM	Erasable Programmable Read Only Memory
GB	Giga (10^9) Bytes
HMOS	High Speed Metal Oxide Semiconductor
IC	Integrated Circuit
ICE	In-Circuit Emulation
KB	Kilo (10^3) Bits
KBPS	Kilo (10^3) Bits per Second
LIFO	Last In/First Out
LSI	Large Scale Integration
MB	Mega (10^6) Bytes
MBPS	Mega (10^6) Bits per Second
MIPS	Millions of Instructions per Second
MOS	Metal Oxyde Semiconductor

MPM	Micro Program Memory
MSI	Medium Scale Integration
MTBF	Mean Time Between Failure
MTBUI	Mean Time Between Unit Interruption
NC	Numerical Control (of Machine Tools)
NMOS	Higher speed arsenic based MOS
OA	Office Automation
OS	Operating System
PBX	Private Branch Exchange
PCB	Printed Circuit Board
PERT	Program Evaluation and Review Technique
PDT	Programmed Data Transfers
PMOS	P-junction MOS, with lesser speed than NMOS
PROM	Programmable Read Only Memory
Puma	Programmable Universal Machine for Assembly
RAM	Random Access Memory
REPROM	Reprogrammable Read Only Memory
ROM	Read Only Memory
RTL	Resistor Transistor Logic
RWM	Read and Write Memory
SAGE	Semiautomatic Air to Ground Equipment
SOS	Silicon-on-Sapphire
SSI	Small Scale Integration
TTL	Transistor Transistor Logic
VAN	Value Added Network
VHSI	Very High Speed Integration
VLSI	Very Large Scale Integration
VS	Virtual Storage
WP	Word Processing

COMPONENTS OF A TECHNICALLY ORIENTED PROGRAM

THE INTRODUCTION has properly underlined that this text is written for managers, and aims to give them an appreciation of microcomputer technology and what can be done with it.

A text written for technical people should complement the approach which I have taken with the following specific subjects:

1. *Microcomputer Architecture*
   - CPU
   - Registers
   - RAM, ROM, Addressing
   - I/O Structure
   - Bus Structure
2. *Programmed Logic*
   - Basic Approach
   - Instruction Set
   - Stored Programs
   - Documentation
3. *Microcomputer Programming*
   - Addressing Modes
   - Fundamental Programming Techniques
   - Flow Charts
   - Looping and Interation
   - Writing a Program
   - Running a Program
   - Debugging
   - Testing
4. *Structuring a Software System*
   - Partitioning a Problem
   - One-shot Design vs. Reusability
   - Optimization-Time vs. Space
   - Addressing Modes
   - Additional Features
   - Troubleshooting
   - Software Examples

5. *Software Support*
   - Assemblers
   - Compilers
   - Subroutines and Subroutine Nesting
   - Multiprecision Arithmetic
   - I/O Software
   - Masking, Shifting, and Decisions
   - Tables, Table Indexing, Branch Tables
   - Entry and Execution of Programs

6. *DB/DC*
   - Database Access
   - Database Protection
   - File Organization
   - Message Organization
   - Communications Requirements
   - Peripheral Devices
   - Modem on a Chip

7. *Documentation*
   - Obtaining Documentation
   - Writing Documentation
   - The User's, Operator's, and Programmer's Manual
   - Using Documentation
   - Where to Find Unbiased Information on Processors

8. *Fundamentals of Interfacing*
   - Input/Output Ports
   - Dedicated I/O
   - I/O Operations
   - Bus-Oriented I/O
   - Memory-Mapped I/O
   - Direct Memory Access
   - Interrupts
   - Programming I/O
   - Buffering
   - Sensors
   - Basic Control Methods (On-off, Proportional)
   - Analog to Digital and Digital to Analog Conversion

9. *Peripherals*
    - Video
    - Printers
    - Disc
    - Audio Tape
    - Bubble Memory
    - I/O Requirements
    - Line Control

10. *Overview of Microprocessors*
    - Intel 8080, 8085
    - Zilog Z80
    - Motorola 6800 and 6802
    - Fairchild F8
    - Synertek 6502
    - Texas Instruments 9900

11. *Introduction to, for instance, Intel 8048 Control Computer*
    - Storage Capacity and Allocation
    - I/O Ports
    - Timers
    - System Operation
    - Programming
    - Movement of Data
    - Arithmetic and Decisions
    - Subroutines and the Address Stack
    - I/O and Systems Procedures
    - Bit Manipulation
    - Relationship of Performance to Program Size

12. *Other Single Chip Microcomputers*
    - Mostek 3870
    - Fairchild 3859
    - Texas Instruments 9940
    - Trends in Single Chip Systems
    - Single Board Computer Systems
    - Support Boards (Memory and I/O)

13. *Development Systems*
    - PROMT–Intel
    - EXORciser–Motorola
    - System 65–Rockwell

14. *Applications*
    - Data Acquisition
    - Process Control
    - Instrumentation
    - Machine Control
    - POS Terminals
    - Peripheral Control
    - Automotive
    - Appliances Control
    - Other Consumer Products
    - Environmental Control

15. *De Facto Bus Standards*
    - S-100–Pertec
    - Multibus–Intel
    - 9900 Bus–Texas Instruments
    - Microbus–National

Index